Best Trees
for Your Garden

ALLEN PATERSON

SPECIAL PHOTOGRAPHY BY STEVEN WOOSTER

Best Trees
for Your Garden

ALLEN PATERSON

FIREFLY BOOKS

A FIREFLY BOOK

Published by Firefly Books Ltd., 2003

First printing

Publisher Cataloging-in-Publication Data (U.S.)
(Library of Congress Standards)

Paterson, Allen.
    Best trees for your garden / Allen Paterson ; special photography
by Steven Wooster. – 1st ed.
[208] p. ; col. photos. :   cm.
Includes bibliographical references and index.
Summary: How to choose trees and use them effectively as part of a
successful garden design.
ISBN 1-55297-770-6
ISBN 1-55297-769-2 (pbk.)
1. Ornamental trees. I. Title.
635.977 21   SB435.P4851 2003

National Library of Canada Cataloguing in Publication Data

Paterson, Allen
    The best trees for your garden / Allen Paterson.

ISBN 1-55297-770-6 (bound).—ISBN 1-55297-769-2 (pbk.)
    1. Ornamental trees. 2. Landscape gardening. I. Title.
SB435.P37 2003   635.9'77   C2003-900396-5

Published in the United States in 2003 by
Firefly Books (U.S.) Inc.
P.O. Box 1338, Ellicott Station
Buffalo, New York 14205

Published in Canada in 2003 by
Firefly Books Ltd.
3680 Victoria Park Avenue
Toronto, Ontario, M2H 3K1

Printed in Singapore

PHOTOGRAPHIC ACKNOWLEDGEMENTS
a = above b = below l = left r = right

Photographs copyright © Steven Wooster, except for those
listed below

Allen Paterson 6, 8, 10–11, 26–27, 28, 30, 31, 35, 41, 42, 55, 59,
62, 63, 70, 83, 86, 88, 93, 94, 95, 97, 99, 103, 107, 111, 114,
118, 121l, 122, 124, 126, 127, 129r, 130, 131, 136, 138, 139,
142, 143, 144, 145, 152, 157, 158, 160, 161l, 162, 164, 165, 167,
174, 176, 179r, 182, 183, 184, 187, 188, 189, 190

© Fa. C. Esveld 166, 171

John Glover 116, 128, 135

Jacqui Hurst © FLL 133

PREVIOUS PAGES: Grown for its elegance of habit and distinctive,
almost circular leaves, which provide a spectacular autumn display,
the katsura (Cercidiphyllum japonica) is a good choice for medium-
sized gardens. The wispy spring flowers are easily overlooked.

contents

introduction

This book was just about finished when the cousins with whom I was staying took me on a Sunday walk through a number of Cambridge college gardens. It was the perfect, evocative Cambridge May morning—sun on the old stone, dappled shade along the Backs and, leaning over the wall of Trinity Hall's Fellows' Garden, we watched all those beautiful young people punting, with varying degrees of success, on the river below. To the left, the fine bridge of Clare College, framed by weeping willows dangling their fingers into the water. Such a day emphasized wonderfully the roles of trees in the built landscape. Where the architecture is good or hallowed by time, trees are complementary—just look at the great horse chestnut (that day laden with white candles) against the east end of King's College Chapel with James Gibbs' Senate House behind. Where some buildings are, shall we say, uncompromisingly modern, as at St. John's, seen through branches and foliage of mature trees, they take on a special quality. No doubt the architect intended such an effect.

That walk showed venerable trees in venerable settings as well as new plantings—Fitzwilliam College has the best young *Acer pensylvanicum* I had seen for years, even in its North American home. The day before was spent at the University Botanic Garden, which offered many of the trees described in the following pages, a few that are omitted for various reasons (such as *Trachycarpus* and *Cordyline*, which lack the branch pattern of proper trees) and one or two I had not met before. Why isn't the lovely fastigiate aspen more often seen?

Meeting good trees, thoughtfully used, is a great spur to personal planting, and a university town is often a good place to start. Even new campuses have much to offer, often boasting architecture and landscape planting of significance (the professionals know there is a tradition of quality in the field to live up to). In the traditional towns,

Trees beyond one's garden can be "borrowed" and brought into the design. Here, we just need to frame the idyllic view with one or two foreground trees to capitalize on the planting of a century or so ago.

the juxtaposition of plant and place has not only reached a fine art, it virtually defines them. Think of that great sycamore in Oxford—no species could be more ordinary—leaning out from Queen's College just where the High Street makes its slight bend on the way to Magdalen and the Botanic Garden. Nature's and Man's architecture become as one.

That other Cambridge, 3,000 miles to the west, near Boston, offers fine college campuses with similar felicities, and Harvard's associated Arnold Arboretum provides living collections of woody plants almost unrivaled in the western world. And the great virtue of such botanic gardens is that the plants are not only labeled but almost certainly labeled correctly! This is obviously vital for those of us wanting to plant trees. Tree-watching in advance of tree-planting is a necessary spectator sport, and a list of suitable spots may be found on pages 199–203. While written descriptions are desirable as *aides-mémoire* or inspiration, nothing can take the place of personal engagement with the living plant.

Such observation not only inspires the choice of species that are especially admired but also (and this is just as important, unless one is only concerned with a sort of stamp-album arboretum collection) reveals how they look in the garden or in the larger landscape. One can learn from great painters. Traditional artists composing a picture of garden or countryside are likely to show details of nearby trees, leaves, bark and even flowers; those in the middle distance are textural in foliage and habit, while in the distance, they are mainly shape and bulk. Often clouds beyond repeat those shapes. Gardeners play the same game, adding, if they are lucky, to existing plantings within or beyond their own boundaries.

As I write, outside our garden door, I see how fortunate we are to have been able to do just that. A couple of hundred yards away on a grassy knoll are a few mature beech and sycamores and one fine hornbeam. I guess they were planted when the house was tarted up in the 1820s and when the fields in which they grow belonged to it. They

still make our middle ground, and they frame views of the river below and distant hills beyond with their hedgerow trees and dark belts of coniferous forestry.

This is all a learning experience. Those great middle-ground specimens are to the south and provide summer shade for the cows and sheep in the field (all adding nicely to the picturesque scene), and the trees seem to stand anchored in pools of their own darkness. As the days move into autumn, the shadows lengthen until, in midwinter, should there be any low sun, they almost reach the house. But, and this is a vital factor, by then leaves are fallen, the shade cast is no longer heavy, and the elegance of the branch tracery is seen against the light. Had they been evergreens, the effect would be much less agreeable.

Within the garden and therefore within our gift is the foreground planting, and these, of course, are plants that demand close admiration for flower and foliage. Some we inherited, some we have added ourselves. Among the former are three youngish false cypresses (*Chamaecyparis*) starting to reach for the sky. During the decade since we've lived here permanently, they would have reached 30 feet (9 m) or so, cast daunting shade and dominated the scene unacceptably. An eminent garden designer staying for the weekend said we should bite the bullet—they'd have to go.

But one is always loath to cut down what has taken years to grow, and we'd already lost a fine elm from Dutch elm disease in the same area.

After a year or two of agonizing, we decided to treat them as topiary. They are now obelisks, controlled and adding a certain necessary formality, entirely satisfactory except when one is teetering with shears atop a tall ladder. There are several morals in this cautionary tale: Choose trees close to the house with great care, live with inherited trees for a bit before making any irrevocable decision, make that decision as a clear part of the overall design of the garden, be brave.

The intended scope of the book that follows should perhaps be mentioned here. It attempts to encourage gardeners on both sides of the Atlantic to plant trees for present pleasure and for posterity and in doing so to indicate potential that is shared as well as the differences in our gardening activities. These latter to a great extent revolve around climatic patterns: the moist, relatively mild oceanic climate of Western Europe and of maritime Western North America and the cold winter/hot summer continental climate to the east. Having spent a dozen happy years as director of a Canadian botanic garden on the north shore of Lake Ontario (zone 6b we used to claim, crossing our fingers all the while), I am acutely conscious of the possibilities of both sides. I am also conscious of grand gardeners from England on the lecture circuit who, when showing a slide of some ravishing plant, were apt to add in tired tones that "it probably wouldn't be hardy with you." Actually, often it was, or if not, good alternatives could be found. The reverse happens when North Americans in Britain illustrate their fall colors, some of which we can compete with. Well, quite.

Bridging the divide are hosts of splendid plants, natives of the Old and New Worlds and the Orient and their variants that succeed widely. The barriers are continually being pushed back. This is a recurring theme in the text that follows.

ABOVE LEFT: Not all inherited trees are perfectly placed. Ever-increasing and unacceptable shade cast by this handsome Lawson cypress is controlled by transforming it into topiary. RIGHT: *Acer palmatum* 'Atropurpureum' in maturity makes the perfect small garden tree. It has an open-branch habit and lightweight foliage, which is almost as colorful in spring as it is in autumn.

What must always be realized is the significance of planting and gardening with trees. These are not just pretty plants putting on a seasonal show, they are among the biggest of the Earth's organisms, their time scale is often far beyond that of their planters, and they affect innumerable other organisms to become ecosystems in their own right. In the garden, they either make possible or inhibit what else we wish to grow, and in the way they absorb or reflect the light and move with the wind seem to be a living part of everything that happens. They are not to be played with lightly.

On that subject, the writing of this book has concentrated the mind wonderfully. Dr. Johnson's use of that phrase, we all remember, concerned the prospect of "being hanged on the morrow," and though one hopes not literally relevant it does offer thoughts of mortality. One should always plant trees in the expectation, however unlikely, that one will live forever or at least see them in their maturity. With the smaller ornamental species, there is some hope of this, with the great forest trees not much, but where space permits, there is no better way of being remembered.

Thus in acknowledging thanks for help received, I can do no better than express gratitude to the unknown hosts of landowners, farmers, gardeners and plant collectors who have furnished our landscapes and gardens with native and exotic trees. More directly, I thank a number of friends who have helped with specific concerns: Jim Gardiner of Wisley, and Maurice Foster, whose magnolias in Kent are the envy of all; Anne Milovsoroff and Brian Bixley at the Royal Botanical Gardens, Ontario; Rodger Inglis, Douglas Chambers and Brian Bixley, also in Ontario, who share my enthusiasms. Elizabeth Scholtz and Judith Zuk of Brooklyn Botanic Garden were, as always, invaluable. At Frances Lincoln, Jo Christian and Anne Fraser have been entirely encouraging, and they involved Steven Wooster. Settling down to actually work on a book when there are things to do in the garden is never easy, so I am grateful to Mr. Andrew Ogden, orthopedic surgeon at Dumfries Royal Infirmary, for ensuring a period of relative immobility. Most thanks, of course, go to my wife, Penelope, and daughter Eve, who together turned my antediluvian pen-on-paper offerings into impeccable state-of-the-art floppy disks.

LEFT AND ABOVE: The autumn effect. The brilliance of beech and cherry leaves moves from sky to ground and defines the closing year. OVERLEAF: Rugged oak bark separates the exuberance of azaleas in full flower. The trees' high canopy provides just the right amount of summer shade.

understanding trees

understanding trees

We all know, or think we know, what a tree is. But the meaning of the word becomes extended when we refer to tree ferns and rose trees and tree peonies and eat the fruit of tree tomatoes and banana trees. None of these truly deserves the designation; for that, a plant needs to develop a framework of permanent woodiness capable of taking a spread of leafy branches above the surrounding plant growth. For all plants are in continual competition with other organisms (except those that have developed a sort of wary symbiosis, such as legumes with nitrifying bacteria), and extraordinary adaptations have evolved to succeed in continuing each species.

Variation in perennation is just one such. Ephemeral annuals race through their life cycle—seed to seed—in a matter of weeks, to capitalize upon sudden and short rainy seasons that provoke germination and growth. Those brilliant displays of African daisies in the semi-deserts of Namibia and Namaqualand are dramatic examples; our highly successful annual weeds such as groundsel and chickweed use the same technique within the season imposed by our cultivations. They even have the ability, if conditions become bad, to cut their losses, stop any more vegetative growth and immediately produce a flower or two. Imminent death has no sting (in the Biblical phrase) if even a few seeds ripen; posterity has triumphed. We have all seen the tiny, starved single-flowered poppy struggling in a gravel path that demonstrates the phenomenon. Once shed, those seeds can remain dormant but viable for many years, to germinate when conditions are right.

A step up the perennation ladder are biennials. These spend their first summer after spring germination in building up a body strong enough that, after a winter rest, they can send up a tall flower spike above their surroundings to increase the likelihood of effective pollination and subsequent seed distribution. Exhausted, the parent typically dies. Foxglove and mullein are examples in the flower border. The sequence is commoner in the kitchen garden, or would be if we allowed it. But of course we harvest the overwintering food stores of carrot and parsnip and so on for our own food, and buy seed for next year.

The planned and inevitable transience of annuals and biennials is rejected by other plant groups that commute intense adaptability for a longer life. Having once built up a permanent rootstock, herbaceous perennials can continue their half-year growth and half-year rest sequence until conditions become untenable. A peony may take three or four years to flower from seed, but then the clump can quietly expand for a further half-century producing seed—which is what it is all about—year after year. This pattern is characteristic of many species from the Russian steppes or American prairies, where the climate makes it sensible to get out of the way during the winter. Bulbs, tubers and corms are typical ways to survive below ground.

Shrubs and ultimately trees—these two categories exist in a continuum with no real divide—have exchanged the convenience of continual renewal for dominance of height and hence vital light. This implies supporting a permanent body over a long period of time, which has its own risks. Decades may elapse before a plant is mature enough to flower and seed, and it may never get there. But then the productive period, once attained, may be measured in centuries, and the gamble will have paid off. It is difficult not to think of trees in anthropomorphic terms; no wonder people hug them, for the human pattern of slow maturity but long productivity is strangely analogous.

Trees, then, are plants that develop one or more long-lived woody trunks to support a leafy canopy. Different conditions of climate, terrain and soil type have resulted in vast diversity of form. Tropical jungles are usually extremely species-rich; cool temperate mountainsides may be clothed by only two or three interacting species. But the point, of course, is the perfect adaptation to that environment of each, which makes the knowledge of origin so important if they are to be successfully grown in cultivation continents away from their homes.

As we remember from school (or should, because it relates intimately to our own human existence) plants have five prime requirements for life: air, light, warmth, water and food. Only the first is virtually unlimited, and so it is apt to be the availability in varying proportions of the others that determines the existence or success (ultimately these are almost the same) of a given tree species. Photosynthesis, as we vaguely recall from that same school biology, is the ability of plants to manufacture sugars from atmospheric carbon dioxide and water. Sunlight provides the energy source, and chlorophyll is the catalyst.

LEFT: Late October and the foreground oak canopy is only just starting to color, while the trees beyond are ablaze. RIGHT: Still water in the landscape doubles the value of unfolding foliage, as the trees still show their branch patterns. This effect will gradually be lost as the seasons proceed and the heaviness of midsummer foliage fills in.

So the search for light, especially in a forest situation, is critical. Woodland herbaceous plants at ground level adapt to a short spring season and go through their life cycles quickly before the developing tree canopy above cuts off the light and their ability to photosynthesize sufficiently; at this point, returning to some below-ground resting organ is the only thing to do.

Tree seedlings do not have this facility; either they can accept a lot of shade (which makes the hemlocks especially valuable when planting within existing woodland is required), or they have to wait until a forest giant crashes to the ground, often taking other trees with it, and a glade opens up. There is then a sort of botanical feeding frenzy as plants rush in to capitalize upon the opportunity, until eventually the status quo returns and a new tree canopy shades out the rest. The scene is particularly dramatic in the wet West Coast forests of British Columbia and Oregon, where the rotting trunks of fallen trees act as nurses to their successors, seeds germinating on the rich remains of each corpse, and one finds a straight line of young trees occurring as if planted by a forester.

There is a further dimension with regard to light and its availability. As the energy motor for the photosynthetic process, it is obviously only doing its job between dawn and dusk. In the tropics this can be a year-round 12-hour-a-day activity. As the equator is left behind and the poles are reached, winter day-length is progressively reduced to the point at which there is insufficient light to be of use. But this doesn't much matter, because water, carrying with it the soil nutrients, is locked up as ice. Indigenous trees must move into a period of torpor: deciduous species let go of their vulnerable leaves, coniferous needles' thick cuticles and protected stomata are able to survive in a resting mode. With spring thaw, it becomes all systems go. The leaves, the photosynthetic powerhouse, have got to get working.

The bigger the photosynthetic area, in other words, the bigger the leaves of any given plant species, the more robust and effective its growth. But as most plants don't grow in an environmentally controlled greenhouse protected from the vagaries of climate and terrain, each species has evolved to succeed in a particular ecological niche; it has adapted its form to function and to capitalize on what is available. The multiplicity of leaf shape and even behavior reflects this. Plants under the canopy of tropical rain forests need big leaves to catch all possible light; they can produce them because of ample moisture and protection from desiccating winds. In the open, they would burn and shred. Bananas (not really trees; morphologically, they more resemble giant leeks) do grow in the open and

Acer palmatum 'Ôsakazuki'. This is one of the most brilliant of the Japanese maples for autumn color, changing from green to fiery scarlet. One of dozens of cultivars available, it earns its keep as much now as when it was introduced to British gardens in the 1880s.

have huge leaves but have adapted their structure and leaf variation so that the inevitable tearing is parallel to the veins and not across them. Ragged they may become, but they still work. Such extreme examples of form allied to function are continually found throughout the plant kingdom, and therefore it must be presumed that it can be discerned, if less graphically, in all species. More difficult to understand is the reason behind the diversity of foliage type in a bit of northern mixed woodland; what gives the edge to the divided leaves of ash and rowan or the entire leaves of oak and beech? Each, we must accept, is perfect for its role and exquisitely adapted to its environment, yet to us they appear to share identical conditions. It is this that provides much of the fascination that trees hold for us—endless variations on a theme.

Most tree genera, even if they are spread widely around the world, are relatively constant in their leaf shape. The maples (*Acer* species, of which there are around a hundred) are native to North America, Europe and much of temperate Asia. In the moist, mild climate of western North America, the typical vine-like maple leaf reaches its maximum size with the Oregon maple, suitably named *Acer macrophyllum*. Here the five-lobed blade can be up to a foot across. That same pattern is repeated again and again, though the leaves

of the field maple, *A. campestre*, responding to exposed chalk uplands of southern England, may be only a tenth the size. The leaf lobes become longest and most delicately fingered in the Japanese maples. Both *A. japonicum* and *A. palmatum* have been cultivated for centuries in their countries of origin (the latter extends into China and Korea) and especially dissected leaf forms that look almost like filigree lace had been carefully selected and propagated and cherished long before they reached the West.

Against this general maple leaf rule, *A. negundo* from across North America has pinnate leaves, divided into segments off a central stem rather like those of ash, while a few oriental species have atypical undivided leaves. The Japanese *A. carpinifolium*, the hornbeam maple, does indeed look strangely like our common European hornbeam (*Carpinus*).

Though rare in maple, the pinnate pattern of *Acer negundo* is followed by lots of other tree genera, notably *Juglans*, *Carya* and *Sorbus*. There may be just two or three pairs of leaflets plus a terminal one, or many more: on young plants of tree of heaven (*Ailanthus altissima*), the whole compound leaf becomes a yard long. Secondary divisions also occur, giving the delicate fern-like foliage of mimosa and other, especially tropical, legumes.

An annual childhood pleasure, definitely demonstrating that spring had truly sprung, was to watch the day-by-day progress of a branch of horse chestnut in a school windowsill jam jar. From glistening sticky buds to dense-furred leaflets to the unfolded hands of the mature leaves. Soon this would be repeated on the trees outside, and followed by the candle-like flower heads, promise of chestnuts to come. Lovely though they are when young, common horse chestnut leaves coarsen as the season goes on. Other species, notably *Aesculus indica*, maintain a more elegantly manicured appearance to the end. Obviously the palms, whose very name is derived from the leaf shape, take it to the extreme. Only *Trachycarpus fortunei*, with its great leaf fans, is generally hardy in the cool temperate world.

Undivided leaves, species by species, seem to exhibit every variation that it is possible to imagine, from the almost circular leaves of the Judas tree to the pencil-slim sprays of willow. Whether in permutations of the oval, whether they narrow to the tip or to the petiole, or how the blades are toothed have provoked morphological botanists into compiling a huge glossary of specific terms by which every type can be referred to as an aid to identification. Pattern seems to have no relation to size; simple leaves of any type may be tiny—an attribute that gives some of the southern beeches (*Nothofagus* spp.) an extraordinary delicacy on a big tree—or huge, as with *Catalpa* and *Paulownia*. Hard-pruned for foliage effect, these produce velvet dinner plates to rival denizens of the deepest rain forest.

Within the world of trees, no leaf shape or pattern seems to be restricted solely to the deciduous or evergreen habit, except that, obviously, as autumn leaf fall is a response to cooler climates, the range of cold-tolerant, broad-leaved evergreens is necessarily small. Hollies, laurels and holm-oaks have given year-round foliage to cool temperate gardens and landscapes for centuries, and the great glossy leaves of *Magnolia grandiflora* since the 18th century—though the magnolia needs its native Georgia or the South of France to reach its potential forest-tree size. In recent decades, eucalyptus seeds from high altitudes in Australia and Tasmania have also provided distinctive evergreen foliage for cool temperate zones.

A pure stand of European beech (*Fagus sylvatica*) regenerating freely. The young plants in the protection of their parents leaf out early and are able to put on some spring growth before the inhibiting canopy above reduces the light availability.

However, that role has traditionally rested with the vast range of conifers whose evolutionary success has been most marked in high latitudes and high altitudes, often both. Because of this, wide leaf blades are never a feature, leaves being typically long and narrow, as with the pines—though with a variation in length from an inch or so to 10 times that. Spruces, firs and yews have similarly narrow needle leaves arranged in sprays, while the foliage effect of cypresses and their cousins, thuja and chamaecyparis, is provided by a solid massing of tiny scale-like leaves.

Warmth, another of the prime desiderata of plant growth, is obviously also sun-given. Warmth is affected by latitude, by altitude, by aspect and by the angle at which the sun's rays meet the ground. Soil warmth in spring, much of which in high latitudes is initially used in thawing out winter frost, is the spur to the annual renewal of growth. Seeds in the surface layers, which may have needed the winter cold as a part of a dormancy-breaking sequence, begin to germinate. Water that had been locked up as ice becomes available, and the shallow roots of the herbaceous layer are activated and start into growth. So, too, on the woodland floor do tree seedlings; one notices young beeches in leaf long before the mature tree canopy unfolds. Presumably that vital spring warmth takes longer to penetrate to deeper soil levels, and thus the big trees lag a little behind, leaving time and space for essential regeneration.

The regular pattern of seasonal warmth and cold is that which has determined the natural tree flora in most parts of the world. In the tropics, with little variation in light or temperature levels, rainfall patterns are greater determinants and provide, in human terms, some indication that it is December, say, rather than August. Some trees have a sort of facultative ability to drop their leaves in order to reduce transpiration and stress in times of drought, but the clear four-season sequence with which we from the temperate world are familiar—and which we can miss terribly in lands of perpetual summer—just does not occur.

In higher latitudes, it seems that humans have developed a relationship with the rolling seasons in which, from the earliest times, agricultural practices, built upon what has been gradually shown to be effective, become linked to myth, religion and the whole culture of evolving communities. The turn of the year, the end of frost, the phenomenon of growth and the prodigality of harvest were all reasons for celebration and thanksgiving. These, linked with observations of the heavens, provide the calendar we still live by. Today's supermarket availability of French beans, strawberries and asparagus throughout the year may have deprived the seasons of much of their power and significance. But not for gardeners, the essence of whose (non-gardeners might say dotty) activities lies in the actuality of place. We can ameliorate the conditions in which we grow plants—improve the soil, add nutrients, irrigate, protect, we can even move somewhere else—but ultimately we are constrained by climate. This is especially the case in growing trees; while it is possible to build a palm house at Kew or a biodome in Cornwall in order to cultivate tropical trees in a temperate land, their enclosure in buildings deprives them of their essential "treeness."

All of which is why it is essential, for effective tree-growing, to know first the constraints and potentials of the climate of one's own garden and, secondly, something about the conditions the chosen plant experiences in its original home. Climate, of course, is a complex interrelationship of many factors; this is discussed further elsewhere. Sufficient to note at this stage in considering warmth to permit and promote growth that it is not necessarily what temperatures are attained but when and with what constancy. In the notes on individual species, there is a continual subtext that hints at the unpredictability of the British climate—a mild February spell in which early spring flowers and leaves burst from their protective buds, followed by unseasonal (as we like, against all the evidence, to describe them) frosts in May. In eastern North America, though winter temperatures drop far lower, there is a progression to be expected: when spring does eventually come, it will not turn back and return to winter.

Availability of water and food is intimately linked. The three main elements, nitrogen, phosphorus and potassium,

A quartet of conifers demonstrates just some of the diversity of this distinctive group of plants. They are (clockwise, from top left): *Picea abies* 'Cranstonii', a curious, semi-weeping form of the common Christmas tree; *Chamaecyparis lawsoniana*, Lawson cypress, with its pea-sized cones, which have opened and shed their seeds; *Thuja plicata*, Western red cedar, in one of its variegated forms; *Pinus patula*, a rather tender Mexican species that has needles over a foot in length.

are vital for all plant growth—nitrogen is involved especially with vegetative growth, potassium with the ripening of fruits and seeds, and phosphorus with root growth and the general health of the plant. Plants also react positively or adversely to amounts of the so-called trace elements, which include magnesium, molybdenum, boron, sulfur, calcium, and so on; most are needed in minute amounts for effective plant growth, but excess, either naturally available or added unnecessarily in fertilizer form, can be toxic.

It has to be remembered that the availability of plant nutrients—apart from those produced by the photosynthetic process in green aerial parts of the tree, and even here the translocation systems are the same—is dependent upon water at the root. "Artificial," that is inorganic, industrially produced fertilizers are decried by the organic lobby (which makes many vital points about soil fertility—but this is not one of them). Plants obtain most of their nutrients as elements dissolved in the soil water, regardless of their organic or inorganic origin.

What is truly astonishing about trees is their ability to distribute those required nutrients to the farthest parts of the organism. If one accepts that the root system below ground is almost a mirror image of what we see stretching a couple of hundred feet up towards the sky, it becomes possible to realize what a miracle of perfect plumbing this is. Soil water with its dissolved nutrients is taken in by literally astronomical numbers of minute root hairs and passed cell by cell, throughout the tree. (Rather as it can be proved that, aerodynamically, bumblebees cannot fly, so trees have no right to be 300 feet [90 m] high.) In fact, vastly more water is used as a food conduit than is actually required to maintain cell turgidity and take part in the photosynthetic process. Hence the continual transpiration of surplus moisture in the form of water vapor from stomata on the undersides of leaves and the young shoots. This in turn affects the environment in which the tree grows, with all these endless ramifications to micro- and macro-climate that make possible the complicated ecological interactions of interdependent plant and animal worlds. To some extent, then, trees make or at least strongly

Katsura (*Cercidiphyllum japonicum*) begins its autumn show in late September, the leaves changing, on different plants, from green to shades of yellow, red and orange.

influence the climate in which they themselves—along with the rest of us—flourish. Such statements start to sound like one of the more shrill tracts from environmental campaigners that are apt to make one reach for the "off" switch or turn the page, but it is worth—even, selfishly, just to grow your own trees better—trying to comprehend what is involved in "the world of the tree."

What is significant in ecological and cultivational terms is the quality of the soil that makes available the immense amounts of water needed. Soils are complex amalgams of rock debris built over geological time, modified and moved about by glaciation and water and continually affected by climate and the transience of weather. The whole process is known as "weathering," and it leads to the different sorts of soils in which we grow our trees. The type of flora of any given area is an adaptational response to the soils and underlying rocks continually in the process of weathering, releasing the elements contained within, and this makes it essential that our choice of species and methods of cultivation are in sympathy with our own soil.

The most obvious example is that great divide between calcifuge species and those which are described as calcicole: lime-haters versus lime-accepters (in Britain, the phrase "lime-lover" is often used but is an exaggeration). Many species will grow happily in either limy or acid soils. In this context, soils are categorized on a 14-point pH scale of increasing alkalinity. The center point at pH 7 is neutral, and though it is unusual for garden soils to be more than a couple of notches either way, it is this variation that permits or discourages the growing of whole plant families. Most members of the *Ericaceae*—the vast range of rhododendrons and their relations the heathers—demand a high acidity/low calcium reading of around pH 5. This doesn't at first sight take much away from our garden tree flora—a few rhododendrons and arbutuses get a mention in the following directory—but the tree species where rhododendrons grow as understory or forest-edge plants are likely to require similar soil conditions. All are part of a plant community evolutionarily programmed to succeed there. Thus we see that most Western North American trees and many Himalayans—from that epicenter of rhododendrons—are intolerant of limestone. We can play

around with lowering soil pH on a small scale, but the bigger the plant, the more impractical the game becomes. Trees from areas of high pH may do less well in very acidic peat soils, but they are usually unfazed by a neutral or slightly acid situation.

The remaining essential for plant growth is air. It might be casually presumed that this is something which is always with us. But we are apt to forget that aeration at the root is as vital as for the foliage. Badly drained soil leading to waterlogging is the reason for many plant deaths. Either it must be remedied, or species must be chosen that can accept the usually unacceptable.

Some basic understanding of the workings of a tree leads directly to considerations of successful cultivation. Often some recommendations can seem arbitrary, while others seem to relate more to tradition than to current practice. It is helpful to keep in mind what is known about how trees, as living organisms, arrange their lives. Success depends more than anything upon choice of species, which is what at least half this book is about, but that decision made, relatively simple garden practice takes over. What this does in essence is to reflect what happens in nature.

LEFT: Moss-covered boles of old sycamore trees (*Acer pseudoplatanus*) and soft leaf litter indicate the moisture and the organic soil the distant rhododendrons enjoy. BELOW: Another fine Japanese maple is *Acer japonicum*. Any of this species would be happy in the woodland glade shown at left. *A. j.* 'Aconitifolium' is an old cultivar with a distinctive leaf form that has a brilliant color in the autumn. OVERLEAF: October in Ontario. With winter snow only a month or so away, the native birch, maples and oaks put on their finest displays of the year.

landscapes with trees

landscapes with trees

In spite of a century of films and 50 years of television that have depicted North America more than any other land, first-time British visitors are conventionally surprised by the size of that continent and by its diversity. In the north, Canada is itself one of the biggest countries in the world with a 3,000-mile-long (4,825 km) southern boundary that follows the 49th parallel from the West until it meets Lake Superior halfway across. Then, taking the center of each of the Great Lakes as the divide, it dips southward until, below where Lake Erie drains into Lake Ontario at Niagara Falls, it is on a line, if one follows on due east, not far short of New York and Madrid.

Canada's northern boundary is neither political nor clearly discernible but dissolves into a maze of islands divided by the fabled Northwest Passage from the erratic Arctic ice mass. The North Pole is not far off. Not surprisingly, therefore, the concentration of population, where gardening exists as a landscape-affecting activity, is mainly in a variously narrow band along that southern boundary where climate conditions are as kind as the latitude—affected in turn by longitude and altitude—permits.

This, of course, is where the United States of America begins. This border, considered by Canadians to be relatively benign and climatically as good as it gets, is to their neighbors the clear manifestation of ultimate north. That innocent British traveler watching an American television weather forecast is bemused to be shown maps of the continent which stop short at that line as if nothing further exists. They are like Ptolemaic maps marking the known world; beyond there be dragons, and Boreas blows out his cheeks. The hoary jokes about Americans arriving in Vancouver in August with skis at the ready are not entirely unfounded, at least attitudinally.

Apparently impervious to the full force of Pacific Ocean gales, the Monterey cypresses (*Cupressus macrocarpa*) and Monterey pines (*Pinus radiata*) cling to the rocks of Point Lobos, overlooking Monterey Bay, California. No wonder they are planted for wind shelter in mild maritime gardens.

Then, within those 48 states (most of which are bigger than the British Isles, with a couple the size of the whole of Continental Europe) are variations and extremes of climate and topography that from the point of view of growing plants vary from the arid to the subtropical.

Early travelers were impressed, even appalled, by the immensity of North America. It was not until 1853 that Lewis and Clark made the first crossing of the continent. The rail journey takes three days coast to coast but it is from the air, even at 500 miles an hour, that, clouds permitting, an overview of terrain and flora becomes possible. It is also possible to appreciate early European travelers' surprise and indeed despair with the new land they had laboriously sailed across the vastness of the Atlantic Ocean to inhabit. The chronometer and the ship's log told them they were far south as well as west of home, but if it were any month from October to April, they might as well have sailed eastward to the Baltic and beyond for similar cold.

Today's Easter holiday traveler from London to Toronto, for instance, will leave an England awash with daffodils and spring blossom to meet the New World landfall covered with ice and snow. It takes an hour for thin forests to begin to appear below and yet another before landing in a southern Ontario still sere and brown from a wicked winter. Stay the night, and then the next day cross the continent to Vancouver. As you look below, there passes an hour of farmland and woodlots, the remnants of indigenous forest, three hours of prairie with poplars in the frozen river valleys, still a couple of months from leaf-out, and then, after a Rocky Mountain alpine experience, a wholly green scene again: the great evergreen forests of British Columbia.

Going south, further transects might be made every couple of hundred miles or so. From Boston, Massachusetts, perhaps, Washington, D.C., or Savannah, Georgia, and in each case, the first sight would be of majestic forests rolling on into the far distance, hinting at the incredibly

rich native flora, woody and herbaceous, that is still present—such is the extent of the land—after centuries of exploitation. Here are the plants painted by Catesby and collected by Bartram that so excited 18th-century gardeners in Britain—the American oaks and maples and pines, the tulip tree and swamp cypress and liquidambar.

This is a flora adapted to the continental climate on the eastern side of a great landmass, a climate of hard winters and hot summers where seasons know their specific roles and keep to them. Trees leaf out when it is safe to do so, in a spring that is unlikely to do the sort of wintry volte-face that can happen from February to May in Britain. Certain, too, is a wood-ripening summer, and thus it is not difficult to see why so many of these trees were a deep disappointment to those first 18th-century British planters and why they have been unable to fulfil expectations. Many much prefer eastern continental Europe, which has a similar continental climate.

Fortunately, from the British perspective, with Captain Vancouver's exploration of North America's West Coast from California to Alaska in the 1790s, the continent's hoped-for plant potential was at last richly fulfilled. Here is an ocean-fringed land backed by great mountains. High rainfall and the moderating effect of the sea produces a distinctively though not exclusively evergreen-tree flora. It

is the sort of flora the British Isles might have recovered after the Ice Age had not the species base been so reduced and then its replacement possibilities scuppered as it was cut off by the rising sea levels from mainland Europe. As a result, Britain was a small country amazingly ready, by force of climate, cultural expectations and horticultural expertise, to benefit from the huge consignments of seeds that David Douglas and other collectors soon sent. How fortunate, too, that these islands' position in the North Atlantic was ameliorated by that other great benefit from across the seas, the Gulf Stream Drift. Thus Britain's amazingly diverse garden flora flourishes at what might reasonably be expected to be impossibly northern latitudes.

Our hypothetical aerial tourist (and it could be any of us, looking down with intelligent inquiry) crossing the continent observes the changing terrain below and the flora responding to it. Vast areas have been cleared for agricultural cultivations, and there are huge populous conurbations. Nonetheless, what is seen below still reflects the original, native flora—and we will be especially struck by the trees, because, being bigger, they are recognizable from 30,000 feet (9,000 m). Only perhaps in the far south and especially in California do exotics make any major impact: Australian eucalypts have developed a positively dangerous dominance in many areas with the Mediterranean-type climate they enjoy.

It is worth playing this game of botanizing from the sky in the other direction now, with North American eyes fixed on the British Isles. Of course, many of the common preconceptions immediately apply. It's a small land. It can be crossed by airplane in an hour or so from west to east and from south to north in a couple. There are the expected great cities with their surrounding suburban sprawl—though few on the scale of those that have been left behind. But the great surprise, knowing that 50 million humans populate this little space, is how much open countryside there seems to be. To the west and north, uplands appear of baize-green grass or some sort of low herbage impossible to

ABOVE LEFT, AND RIGHT: Native deciduous and coniferous trees that grow on the banks of a small river which flows into the western end of Lake Ontario are still under snow in March. Leaves begin to emerge in April, and the carefully conserved view is framed by a mass of yellow forsythia.

identify from this height (though if it's August and purple it must be heather), interspersed with areas of dark forest with obviously contrived rigid boundaries. Farther south and east, while some such similar forests can be seen, the terrain is intricately divided. Arable fields and pasture are mixed with woodlots (to use a North American term). The narrowest of these are presumably hedges enclosing fields often of apparently illogical shape. In summer, it is a quilt of every conceivable shade of green, in winter the dark of conifers becomes apparent—the swaths of forestry, the dots in parkland and gardens.

This is all in contrast to North America, where it still feels as if the towns and cities, gardens and farmland have been carved out of a land whose natural constituents of terrain and flora remain dominant. In Britain, the converse is the case. Millennia of human activity, first working on the almost bare slate of recent glaciation, of gradually more sophisticated agriculture, of conquest and re-conquest, have affected and changed almost every scene. Those bare hillsides have lost most of their native trees (small and scrubby as most were, and of little economic use) to sheep. Those swaths of dark forest are recent additions, probably species from British Columbia or Washington State. In the

south, that erratic patchwork of arable land and mainly deciduous trees reflects the changing forms of agriculture and even the artistic culture of the country over the past thousand years. This is landscape made in man's image.

The country that became a northern outpost of the Roman Empire for 300 years or so, from just before the birth of Christ, was a wooded land. Bronze Age and Iron Age agriculture had only been able to work the easier, well-drained soils, mainly in the south, and here on the chalk and limestone hillsides native forest began to be cleared. Cereals and beans were grown, animals were pastured. Then came Roman domination and a more sophisticated Roman culture was able to take root, and it becomes possible to see in the villa system both the first essays in esthetic gardening in England and the blueprint for the manipulation of the countryside still evident today.

This is based upon land ownership or long-term tenure from an absentee owner. It is centered on a house of significance and quality (the luxury of the floor mosaics and hypocaust underfloor heating systems that have been excavated at a number of Roman villas attest to that), and its attached or adjoining farm buildings and the immediate enclosures form space for horticultural rather than agricultural activities. The wonderful villas of Andrea Palladio in the Veneto, built in the 1500s, show the pattern, for it was still valid many hundreds of years later. In essence, it still is.

Even after the Roman legions were pulled out in the fourth century, a Romanized Britain was able to maintain some aspects of what had been achieved, with prosperous landowners managing to retain a civilized life. The famous palace at Fishbourne in Sussex, excavated over the last four decades of the 20th century, demonstrates great style. Though there is no clear continuum, some of this was carried on, as waves of invasion from Scandinavia and Europe broke up post-Roman life, in the increasingly significant religious houses. The abbey or friary took on the role of great house with its dependent properties, lands and inhabitants.

Our history books take us inexorably through the ages, a story of conquest and plague, baronial wars and kingly strife. But there is a subtext which continually affects the land, and that is not paid much attention. In spite of the social rigidities of the feudal system, boundaries of forest are pushed back as more land is needed for food production; it is worked on a rigid system of strip cultivation whose imprint can still be seen today throughout Britain. In essence, it was a type of slash and burn agriculture; to peasants scratching a subsistence, living trees were a nuisance. The result was acres of almost prairie-like landscape between the forested areas. Trees were also the main source of domestic fuel, charcoal for iron-smelting and glass-making, wood for ship- and house-building, all of which as industry increased contributed to a steady diminution of woodland.

With 20th-century egalitarian hindsight, we are apt to see the imposition of the strict Norman forest code from the 11th century as inhuman. How dreadful, we cry from the comfort of our centrally heated homes, that the king and nobles were able to preserve great tracts of land purely for hunting, where even wood-gathering was severely punished. In fact, we might applaud the fact that remains of the five royal forests listed in the Domesday book still exist today and that, for example, the New Forest and Windsor Forest give at least an impression of true natural landscape as well as huge pleasure to today's populace.

But as time went on, the forest laws were imposed less strictly, and during the 14th and 15th centuries, deforestation increased to the point where it began to be seen as a threat to the national economy. Toward the end of the 15th century, necessary legislation was passed to encourage landowners to enclose woodlands and therefore help protect what remained. The exemption of timber from tithes, also enacted toward the end of the 15th century, can be seen as an early form of the forestry subsidies that government provides today. Trees matter; then as now.

Nevertheless, it became clear that enclosure and the expectation of natural regeneration was not enough. The 17th century saw the start of serious tree planting. It is an age of interest in new plants for gardens and parklands. John Parkinson's *Paradisi in sole Paradisus terrestris* of 1642 is the first English language encyclopedia of gardening. Twenty years later, the diarist and scholar John Evelyn lectured on afforestation to the newly formed Royal Society, and from this grew his famous book *Sylva, or a Discourse of Forest Trees*.

Sylva is addressed to landowners large and small: Evelyn describes the virtues and values of available species, a relatively small list that was

The oceanic climate of most of Britain encourages a woodland ground flora that has no need to disappear completely during winter. Broadleaf evergreens such as holly and ivy (here trying to grow high enough up the beech trunks for light to permit flower and fruit) furnish the scene throughout the year.

just beginning to grow with foreign importations, and he recommends that horse chestnuts, tulip trees, planes, laburnums and cedars be added to the planting of native species which provided the backbone of it all. Evelyn writes with three main motives. It is patriotic to plant trees that in time will help maintain an increasingly important navy ("Hearts of oak are our ships/Willing tars are our men"), and it makes economic sense for landowners to capitalize upon their inheritance. Running in parallel to both of these is Evelyn's clear esthetic sense. He recommends elms for hedgerows, alders for riverbank retention, limes for avenues and hornbeams for pleached walks.

These last two remind us of the then current fashion for formal French-type gardens around royal palaces, as at Versailles and later at Hampton Court and for framing great private houses throughout Europe. The change of taste from 17th-century formality to the full-blown informality of the mid-18th century made a sea change in tree planting. It was William Kent who, said Horace Walpole, "leaped the fence and saw that all nature was a garden" and who popularized the use of the ha-ha, or sunken fence, which makes visible fences and therefore the visual divide between garden and parkland unnecessary. This brought the trees of the countryside into conscious view and appreciation.

This is not the place for philosophical discussion as to how this led (or followed an inherent interest) to a British idealization of (ostensibly) natural countryside, nor of its possible origins in paintings and literature. It is enough to accept it as a part of the spirit of the age most wonderfully supported by the developments in agricultural practices, economy and increased rent-rolls that made further developments possible.

As long as strip cultivations in vast open fields, virtually unchanged since Saxon times, were predominant, agricultural progress was not possible. Everyone had to follow the same pattern: two years of crops and a third fallow to help the ground to recover. Animals were turned out

LEFT: Trees as architecture. Trees have long been used to complement and extend the built landscape. Avenues of lindens (*Tilia* spp.) recall a pillared cloister with a fan-vaulted ceiling. ABOVE AND OVERLEAF: A rondel of hornbeam provides a garden theater. It might be peopled with a cast of actors of all shapes and sizes, clipped in topiary obelisks, balls and finials like those shown overleaf.

at random with breeding no more than "the union," it was said, "of anybody's daughter with nobody's son." But this winter grazing was too thin to feed the full flocks and herds, and many animals were killed in autumn; this diminished the quantity of available manure and in turn caused a reduction in soil fertility. The introduction—from Holland, in the early 18th century—of turnip growing, which provided winter fodder for livestock, was one of the major spurs to change; such innovations could only occur on a controlled basis and led to the need for the division of the open fields into smaller areas, enclosed by hedges. Each landowner with plans to divide his lands had to steer an individual enclosure act through parliament, a slow process, but by the end of the 18th century, the face of the English landscape had changed. It all made economic sense and gave esthetic pleasure into the bargain.

So the idea that pastoral calm, a sort of Virgilian idyll, could exist in parallel to agricultural improvements also took hold. In a perfect world, farm laborers would live an Arcadian life and add to the picturesque scenes being developed around great new classical houses—they might even, it was suggested, "be prettily disguised as shepherds, to keep the flocks from straying." Increasing numbers of landowners began to embellish their lands in this manner. Charles Hamilton's Painshill was famous in his time; at Woburn, also in Surrey, Philip Southcote turned his small estate into what he termed a "ferme ornée."

A new breed of professional men was necessary to be able to turn these literary, painterly, philosophical desiderata into fact. At the turn of the 18th to the 19th centuries, Humphry Repton coined the term "Landscape Gardener" to describe himself, but it was his famous predecessor Lancelot "Capability" Brown, working in the mid-18th century, whose designs, along with those of his followers, molded much of the English landscape we see today. His projects are all variations on a similar theme:

LEFT: Here in an Irish garden, a fine beech (*Fagus sylvatica*) 100 feet (30 m) high shows how to become a giant. A forest tree, it was planted in the 18th century in parkland where it enjoyed space to develop and no competition. RIGHT: Against the light, walnut (*Juglans regia*) foliage is palest green. Late to leaf out and early to lose its leaves, this tree is ideal where not too much shade is needed. Grafted plants of named cultivars will soon provide delicious nuts.

idealized countryside, planted with clumps of trees in pasture, is brought up to the very walls of the house, though of course an unseen fence usually protects it. Belts of trees conceal the boundaries, walks and rides contain viewpoints from which the house or other eye-catchers are framed. Streams are dammed to form serpentine lakes whose extremities are hidden to give the impression of great winding rivers. Landforms are changed to emphasize differences in terrain. For 40 years, Brown worked on innumerable great estates and their parkland throughout England, and the 18th-century ideal pastoral scene he produced has come to be seen not as contrivance but as untouched countryside in which trees are a vital part.

Brown's planting palette today seems very limited. It is based, as was Evelyn's a hundred years earlier, upon native species usually indigenous to the specific area concerned, which therefore links each scheme to its surroundings. (Exactly the same principles are followed today in motorway and trunk road planting.) However, it has now been shown that 18th-century parks were not the flowerless wild-tree and grass expanses that have become the common concept; such simplification and hence falsification derives from the fact that the shrubs and herbaceous plants actually

used are short-lived and that exotic trees (with a few exceptions, such as sweet chestnut, cedars of Lebanon and European larch) tended not to settle down to become major specimens.

Brown was not without his critics in his own time: they variously complained that his landscapes were too bland or too conventionally similar. And recently, with renewed interest in the formal layouts of the 17th century, he has been derided as the anti-gardener of all time, tearing down terraces, felling avenues and generally turning back the clock to a time that predates sophisticated gardening. But there were among his contemporaries some who appreciated the true elegance of his own work. With splendid prescience, the then poet-laureate William Whitehead wrote an amusing pastoral on "The Late Improvements at Nuneham" (Brown worked on Nuneham Park, the seat of Lord Harcourt; as it overlooks the Thames just south of Oxford, he had no need to construct a mock river there). In the poem, Dame Nature meets "Capability" Brown, and they argue as to which of them has had the greater effect upon the beautiful scene around them. Brown lists what he has done and seems to win the debate hands down until Dame Nature

> . . . blushing withdrew.
> Yet soon recollecting her thoughts, as she pass'd
> "I may have my revenge on this fellow at last;
> For a lucky conjecture comes into my head,
> That, whate'er he has done and whate'er he has said,
> Each fault they'll call his, & each excellence mine!"

Two hundred and fifty years later, the fine Palladian house of Nuneham Park still sits on its wooded eminence above the river, its eye-catchers are still surrounded by great trees in the parkland, the planned views to Oxford's "dreaming spires" and the Berkshire hills are still elegantly framed. Apart from the buildings it's all entirely "natural."

"Capability" Brown's influence continued, after his death in 1783, to the end of the 18th century and well into the 19th. Successors such as Humphry Repton and Thomas White (working mainly in Scotland) continued to plant trees in the "clumps" and "belts" of the picturesque fashion. By the mid-19th century, its earliest essays had had a century to mature on the ground during a critical period for the landscape. The great industrial conurbations had sucked into their maw vast numbers of the working population who could look back to a rural past, even as landless peasants, as a lost golden age. Its place in national mythology was secure—England's "green and pleasant land," which William Blake asserted was everyone's birthright rather than the "dark Satanic mills" among which they lived.

Landowners and gentleman farmers continued to plant trees in the traditional fashion, for amenity and for profit. Though they had less space at their disposal, so did a burgeoning middle class in the ever-widening suburbs around big towns and cities. As for the cities themselves, only London had a "green tradition," around the royal palaces of St. James's, Kensington Palace and later Buckingham Palace. Amazingly, St. James's Park retained its formal Franco-Dutch formality of avenues and promenade walks until the 1820s, when Repton transformed it into its present picturesque scene. *Rus in urbe.* Speculative builders of fashionable houses, in association with the noble owners of London estates (Bedford, Russell, Westminster, Cadogan, et al.) responded with tree-lined streets and the communal gardens of residential squares.

It took almost until the mid-century for philanthropical industrialists and the first public health acts to promote public parks for the use and benefit of the working population, and the many fine urban parks reflecting the designs of John Claudius Loudon and Joseph Paxton have acted as the lungs of industrial cities for 150 years. It is heartening that in Great Britain today, after several decades of positively criminal neglect, their value to inner-city living is being newly appreciated and some restoration is taking place.

Nineteenth-century urban parks were naturally affected by what was new and fashionable in landscape design, attempting to combine the broad sweeps of picturesque countryside with the *multum in parvum* essays of the smaller suburban estates. Both were quick to try the range of exotic trees flooding into Britain, first from the Pacific coast of North America and then from the Orient. This, combined with the typically Victorian belief that the study of botany was itself morally uplifting, moved a number of such parks into the category of arboreta or botanic gardens which maintained really significant plant collections.

Across the Atlantic, there was, initially, no need to plant a landscape—though it is amusing to see those early publications designed to encourage the opening up of the West that show prospects of doubtless highly desirable virgin land elegantly framed in wholly imaginary trees; the picturesque idyll traveled far. It was more a case of carving one out of the almost impenetrable indigenous forest; that well-known image of the bluff on which General Oglethorpe was to found his planned town of Savannah could be repeated up and down the East Coast. What seems so extraordinary today is how quickly and apparently seamlessly the fashions and cultivated lifestyle of Europe were translated across the ocean. Thus by the mid-19th century, the classic circle already starts to be completed: forest clearance for agriculture, industrialization and increase in population, the prosperous move to country

ABOVE: Old top-grafted trees of *Prunus* 'Accolade' look like vast pink sea anemones. The flowering profusion is inevitably short-lived, but summer shade and good autumn leaf color earn it a place even in a small garden where it might be the only tree. OVERLEAF: A cascade of cherry blossom epitomizes spring. It may be fleeting on the tree, but the image remains in the mind.

estates needing gardens and amenity planting and the emergence of designers to do it. A final component is, hopefully, ongoing—the tree-planted reclamation of land despoiled by the industrial processes.

Although his life (1815–52) was tragically short, Andrew Jackson Downing moved forward the North American landscape movement in very significant ways. He had studied Repton and other British exemplars, taking Loudon (d.1843) as his most important contemporary influence. Downing worked on many estates, especially in the Hudson Valley, designing landscapes, garden buildings and houses in classical and picturesque modes but emphasizing that his designs were not mere transatlantic pastiche but truly American in response to the site, its endemic flora and local climate. He assured smaller clients that single trees perfectly proportioned and positioned could provide visions of beauty that did not necessarily demand broad acres.

Downing's influence continued in the hands of Calvert Vaux, whom he took on as an assistant in 1850 and with whom he laid out spaces of national importance such as the Capitol and the White House in Washington, D.C. The fact that Vaux went on to join Frederick Law Olmsted ensured the continuity of Downing's vision and led to celebrated landscapes in the public domain—cemeteries, city parks and (an Olmsted innovation) parkway systems even before the age of the automobile. Deservedly famous planted scenes include Central Park in New York City, with its then unique system of up-and-over transverse carriageways; Mount Royal in Montreal, Quebec; and in Ontario, Canada's Niagara Parkway System. As in Britain, the strong ethical concerns of mid-19th-century society are seen in the use of such public plantings to instruct and educate and demonstrate. Toronto's Mount Pleasant Cemetery, for instance, proclaimed that it grew every tree that the Great Lakes climate would permit, and it is still a valued resource for gardeners and students of landscape architecture.

Such collections point to the problems we face today in the multiplicity of choice. It is pertinent to wonder whether Brown's "natural" English landscapes would have developed as a national impression of perfect countryside if he had been able to use the worldwide products of the great plant collectors that have flooded in over the past 150 years. This is not really another skirmish in the age-old battle between formal and informal garden styles. Of course, it is worth recalling Joseph Addison's praise of orchards in bloom or ideal gardens in which "Nature and Reason" go hand in hand and the effect his thoughts had upon Alexander Pope ("In all let Nature never be forgot" and the need to "Consult the Genius of the Place"). Perhaps it moves us on to the phrase of a very un-gardening writer E.M. Forster, who advises "only connect." Trees, because of their scale and their eventual ability to dominate almost any scene, deserve our greatest care in their selection and in their relationship to what is already in place.

Great gardens that use trees sensitively can be works of art as well as monuments to fine horticultural practice, but their artifice is usually obvious, just as their contents are clearly exotic. Seldom are they integrated into their surroundings. A model exception is Crarae in Argyllshire, Scotland, where the glen garden with its burn rushing down into Loch Fyne is a perfect evocation of a Himalayan gorge. Here the rhododendrons and magnolias and their companions merge seamlessly with the Highland hillside on the edge of the garden.

trees and man

trees and man

There is not an advertisement for garden furniture made from tropical hardwoods that does not protest that the wood is from some ecologically "renewable source." Counter protests follow fast.

This sort of polarity develops whenever an indigenous population becomes too large to be sustained by the natural resources around it. Of course, in undeveloped, uncolonialized communities—the kind of land in which Rousseau's 18th-century ideal of the "noble savage" could flourish—there is a sort of equilibrium between what the environment can provide in the way of food and other necessities of human life and the size of population. There are still, just, Amazonian tribes who live thus and whose traditional knowledge of the plant and animal resources with which they share the land enables them to maintain a simple subsistence civilization. Their survival into the 21st century is less to do with worthy Western anthropological concerns than the fact that their numbers are small in huge areas, that their footprint upon the land is light, and that rapacious incomers have not yet used up resources nearer to hand and easier to exploit. As, one fears, has always been the case.

Enlightened people, which of course means us, rightly have intellectual worries about the situation but probably do little about it apart from remembering that John Donne has already worried more eloquently about no man being an island. Our interest in trees, however, can bring it all very much home to our own surroundings. Existing bristlecone pines and redwoods living in America today were already flourishing trees when the local native peoples (though not necessarily co-existing in happy harmony)

knew what the land offered and had lived off it for untold generations. There are yews in English country churchyards that predate the Norman church they shade. They began their life cycle at a period when, in spite of waves of human invaders of varying unpleasantness, a small population lived off its land and knew what its flora and fauna could provide, just as do those Amazonians today. These were pre-industrial communities in which native trees were essential to survival. They were the universal providers; what is extraordinary is that that which they offered to mediaeval man has not been superseded in any way.

In Britain, there may be virtually no wild woodland left, and what comes nearest to it—Wystman's Wood on Dartmoor with its age-old contorted oaks and the remnants of royal hunting forests—is carefully conserved, so it has become necessary to grow as crops the trees needed for different purposes. No building construction takes place without wood; even in the most excessive mode of 1950s and 1960s brutalist building, the "honesty" of concrete walls carries still the grain of the wooden shuttering between which the slurry was poured, like the passing breath of a sympathetic ghost.

In earliest times, wood was *the* building material. Shelters were made of a framework of thin branches woven together and covered with skins or, more permanently, with turf or puddled clay. Even when stone could be employed, wood still permitted wider spans for roof support, as well as providing flooring, paneling, furniture, and so on. It is a happy suggestion that the builders of classical Greece and Rome, in their use of constructional pillars and ornamental dentil cornice, were intentionally paying homage to the tree trunks and cross beams of their cultures' first buildings.

LEFT: Wood in a wooded garden. Natural materials associate happily in the garden scene. Furniture made from Western red cedar from North America and (environmentally forested) teak from the tropics can stay outside throughout the year. RIGHT: Matched pairs of Irish yews, *Pyrus salicifolia* and polyantha roses in the front garden of a clapboard house. It could be Kent or New England—but not with that Norfolk Island pine behind: this is New Zealand. Good planting and design travel well.

Such motifs have been hallmarks of the neoclassical tradition from the Italian Renaissance to the present day, and nowhere has it been stronger than in North America, where it remains a living tradition even for corner stores and—wonderfully—gas stations. How suitable in such a forested land.

Throughout early times or in early colonial periods, a wooded country was the most valuable. In temperate regions, the ability of land to support especially deciduous woodland is an indication of its potential acceptance of man: soils must be relatively rich and climate amenable. Early settlement, over millennia in Europe and in a remarkably short time in North America (accepting that the native peoples had traditionally a less aggressive use of land), gradually clears forest for grazing animals and arable crops. In our chainsaw age, it is easy to forget what incredible labor, with primitive tools, was needed—perhaps gardeners are of the few with some appreciation of it when wishing to remove even a small tree planted in the wrong place. (When it's a whole grove of elms struck dead by the dread disease, the age-old problem is brought even closer.)

Nonetheless, such woodland clearing also provided materials for use—those branches for primitive shelters, wood for fuel and, with greater sophistication of tools, timber for constructions of all types. Nothing was wasted, and one can still see today, for example, across rural Ontario, in Canada, lines of great tree boles with the roots attached like the spokes of cartwheels marking field boundaries and stock enclosures. They have done their job for a hundred years and more.

It is possible to guess at how various uses and techniques evolved over time: charcoal, left behind through poor combustion, is found to burn subsequently at higher temperatures. Its commercial production for iron smelting in the Middle Ages led to huge deforestation throughout the Sussex Weald in England. (Exhaustion of iron ore and the fact that the heavy clay soils were difficult for farming has in turn led to that county's dense woodland recovery—as can be seen flying into Gatwick airport.) Similarly, it was found that some trees, when cut down, resolutely refused to die and sent up suckers that grew quickly enough to be of use in a very few years. Coppicing, very much a part of

those same Sussex woodlands, of hazel and chestnut provided a country industry that was almost ideally sustainable. It is enjoying a quiet renaissance today: well-shaped oaks cropped at around 100-year intervals shelter the coppice plants, with a 10-year turnaround, which are used for hurdle- and fence-making, basket-weaving and simple furniture construction done by "bodgers" who turn struts and legs by primitive foot-lathes.

From such basic skills, wood-based local traditions grew. Windsor chairs are a typical product, as are the Shaker designs of New England, never out of fashion and holding faithfully to the forms of a simpler age. Long predating our global economy, local knowledge built upon the natural attributes of different timbers: the water-repellent wood of alder was used for clogs; oak bark for tanning leather; the close grain of ash for tool handles; strong boxwood and holly for small implements and "treen"; these and laburnum for intricate inlay on furniture; weavable fiber was derived from bass wood.

For domestic furniture over the past 500 years—a period from which plenty of actual examples still exist in historic homes and museums—it is possible to trace a hierarchy of woods affected by fashion and availability. Country pieces have no doubt always been made with what comes easily to hand, but with increasing sophistication, certain species begin to predominate. In turn, they define the age.

With its strength and durability, oak has never ceased to be used, the timber being sawn in different directions to obtain different effects. But at the top end of the market in Britain, one sees walnut used from the mid-17th century, to be overtaken within less than a century by mahogany from the New World tropics. Other exotic woods soon followed. For the hugely increasing general population of the 19th century, furniture in Britain was mainly made of "deal," a word referring to "softwood" coniferous timber—usually pine, spruce or fir. Often such furniture was painted or stained to resemble more expensive

ABOVE, FAR LEFT: Alder is a waterside tree whose timber was turned into clogs. Here are its lamb's-tail catkins in March. ABOVE, LEFT: Iron-hard holly was used to create small tools and inlay in furniture. This trunk shows branch scars healing over. ABOVE: English oak, *Quercus robur*, is one of the world's great timbers, used to make everything from ships to sideboards, buildings to bookcases.

materials: today, the disguise removed, it is the stripped pine of smart antique shops.

Frequently, pine was used for the carcass of ultimately expensive pieces covered with thin veneers of rare woods and especially finely figured grains; ornamental inlays and complicated marquetry, sometimes embellished with ormolu mounts and porcelain plaques, move utilitarian objects into the realm of exquisite works of art. French *ébénistes* and famous British cabinetmakers such as Chippendale and Hepplewhite produced streams of objects to furnish royal palaces and great houses throughout Europe.

These fashions were adopted at astonishing speed in the young colonies of North America. Equally impressive is the elegance of what was soon produced. The wonderful range of native hardwoods—cherry, oak, maple and hickory, plus local softwood—was a rich resource; Cuba and the south provided mahogany. Highly sophisticated indigenous cabinetmakers such as Duncan Phyffe rivaled the grand London names, and their products are just as covetable. The traditional furnishing of fine 18th- and 19th-century houses in old U.S. East Coast cities such as Charleston and Savannah is exquisite. Moreover, quality furniture is still being made in traditional ways from the native woods without any hangups about the pejorative

word "reproduction." The dependence on timber for the houses themselves is still wonderfully evident, though over time it has made them so vulnerable to fire damage. One can only wonder what was lost during the Civil War; it was said of General Sherman that he was such a nice man, really, but very careless with fire.

If timber constructions, from a mansion to a matchbox, are trees' most obvious benefit to man, the provision of food runs neck and neck. Throughout the world, that which these plants have evolved for their own species' success has contributed to the similar success of innumerable animal species that feed upon them. Tree fruit is a staple food for many birds and mammals, including ourselves.

The juicy flesh of fruit, evolved to assist in the distribution of the seeds inside (whose subsequent germination may be dependent upon a period in the gut of the distributing agent), has generally a short life and is therefore a highly seasonal food source. The amazing availability of every common fruit in our shops today has

LEFT AND ABOVE: Apples in flower and in fruit. Trees of the rose family contribute the vast majority of temperate-climate fruit. Different root stocks of varying vigor offer fruit trees for every size of garden. OVERLEAF: Pears combine beauty and economy to the most perfect degree.

been made possible by advances in storage of homegrown crops and rapid transportation from the other hemisphere. This is a relatively recent development; over previous centuries, the trick was to select and then breed cultivars that mature early or late and also store well without chemical help. There is no doubt that with globalization of production and distribution, the excitement when the first apples of the year's scarlet 'Jerseymac' suddenly ripen in August or the thankfulness that the 'Stayman' in the apple rack are still good at Easter has been lost. This is not mere nostalgia for an age that has passed: that was not all good news, as anyone knows who discovers that his whole 'Williams' Bon Chrétien' pear crop seems to ripen at 2.25 p.m. on 23 September, or whenever. But there is a satisfaction in seasonality that comes from actually growing the stuff and using simple means to extend its use.

Across the world, then, tree fruits support human cultures. They vary from the common cool-temperate apples, pears, cherries, peaches and so on—all variations within the amazing *Rosaceae* family—to the citrus range— tiny calamondin to monstrous grapefruit and pomelo—and the huge range of tropical fruits not yet in worldwide availability, such as rambutans and mangosteens. Some have a very limited appeal: there used to be signs in Singapore prohibiting ripe durians from being carried on public transport, such is their stink. The ultimate acquired taste perhaps. Others have been similarly unwelcome. How ironic that the famous mutiny on the *Bounty* was provoked by Captain Bligh giving less care to his crew than to the cargo of breadfruit trees aboard. They were being shipped from their native Tahiti to the West Indies where, it was hoped, the fruit would provide cheap food for the slave population, who were less than enthusiastic.

It is interesting to observe how quickly certain fruits move into popular use. Fifty years ago, subtropical avocados were virtually unknown; now they will be on a mini-market shelf in rural Scotland where you cannot find a decent apple. How unfortunate that the seed inside—at least half its weight—is not edible; the way it germinates with abandon in the compost heap always seems something of a reproach: surely it's got some use. That seed, of course, is what in many other species we designate a nut, invariably having to discard the

inedible juicy surround (nutmeg is a famous exception, with the fleshy aril producing another spice, mace) and thus of course walnut, hazel, chestnut, pecan and hot-climate macadamia, and the rest, become foods of importance.

Several nuts are also the source of specific oils. Olive, especially, has been a staple since classical times, both for the ripe flesh and for the oil obtained from the whole ground-up fruit. While *Olea europaea* is a classic tree of the Mediterranean basin, it is now widely cultivated in California, South Africa and parts of Australia and Chile where a Mediterranean-type climate is also found. Whether apparent "global warming" is a long-term fact or a blip, its effect can be hinted at by the numbers of olive trees brought from the south and used in recent Chelsea Flower Show designs and smart London courtyard gardens. But the well-recorded picking of seven pounds of ripe olives in December 1976—admittedly after a famously hot summer—from the old tree in the Chelsea Physic Garden may indicate that they just hadn't been tried much before.

Pressings of nuts give us oil. Pressings of whole tree fruits provide fresh juices, now with refrigeration able to be stored for long periods, and drinks in which sugars converted to alcohol aid preservation. In turn, the distillation of cider and perry leads to liqueurs. Liquid obtained directly from certain tree species—the spring-rising sap in maples (especially *Acer saccharum*, whose maple syrup is still of great economic importance in eastern North America) and birches—has long been employed. Its appearance at the end of winter when stored food was running short and before any new crop was available made it especially significant to early peoples in cold climates. But perhaps the most remarkable exudation is the white latex from the rubber tree, *Hevea brasiliensis*, now grown throughout the tropics.

With our understandable obsession with food and drink, it is a cause for regret that one of the main parts of trees offers us very little, though at one remove mulberry leaves do give us silk. Apart from that inordinately wasteful and

Olives have been a staple food in the Mediterranean region since classical times and are now cultivated all over the world wherever a similar climate is enjoyed. Sheltered London gardens currently seem to be warm enough, but while the silvery domes of olive foliage are a not uncommon sight there, ripe fruit is a rare treat.

extravagant salad made from the growing point of a palm, tree foliage is not much eaten by humans. Yet as factories for the processing of soil nutrients and for gaseous exchange, the leaves build up sugars and carbohydrates. In the process, species by species, other chemicals are produced that have been discovered to be of use to man. What salicylic acid does for willow is less clear than the inestimable value of aspirin, its derivative, in relieving human ills. The recent use of taxol in the fight against cancer puts an entirely new light on a heap of clippings from a yew hedge. Many more such instances are found, especially in tropical forests where traditional remedies are still a normal part of native peoples' lives.

There is, however, one further major dimension, especially with deciduous trees. While much of that "leaf-factory" food is passed back into the body of the tree in autumn (compounds remaining, worked upon by sudden cold, provide the dramatic fall colors we so admire) what drops to the ground becomes part of humus, that endlessly renewable and endlessly necessary resource that maintains soil fertility. Left alone and worked upon by fungi, bacteria and other micro-organisms, fallen foliage breaks down, giving that soft ground layer in which the woodland herbaceous plants are able to have a quick-run life cycle and by which the trees themselves are fed. Some gardeners are obsessed with tidiness—grizzling on about dirty trees and messy trees (it's like blaming Newton for gravity)—but bagging up leaves to be sent to the dump is a sin against nature. Even in the smallest garden it is possible to preserve and develop this resource to return to the soil. And in both practical and esthetic terms, a leaf pile with a tight wire-netting surround on stout stakes is less obvious and infinitely preferable to those expensive high-tech plastic bins.

This is not the end of that story entitled "Trees and Man." Indeed there probably is no end to what has been an interrelationship since time began. Trees have been enemy and friend, refuge and hiding place for humans and from humans (go to the Chelsea Hospital by the Thames in London on Oak Apple Day, and with the red-coated pensioners, wear a sprig of oak leaves to commemorate Charles II's avoidance in an oak tree of the searching soldiers after the battle of Worcester in 1651). Trees have been the homes of the gods and for some cultures, the gods themselves. Even in an irreligious age, we recognize in the pillars and fan vaulting of great Gothic cathedrals the architecture of trees.

LEFT AND RIGHT: The diversity of leaf shapes is a part of the evolutionary development of every tree species, and each shape is as efficient as possible in its environment. Their annual unfolding, fall and decay are both product and producer of deciduous woodland.

Enchanted forests are a part of the arts of all cultures. The magical goings-on of *A Midsummer Night's Dream* could have happened nowhere else; Mendelssohn's incidental music and Britten's opera add to the scene. Children in Hans Christian Anderson and the Brothers Grimm are lost and found in the forest, and in Arthur Rackham's illustrations, the trees themselves take on human form. Macbeth's Birnam Wood comes to Dunsinane: early camouflage, but with Tolkien's terrifying tree-like Ents, the forest itself can march.

The whole genre of landscape painting, it could be said, is tree-based. They are foreground and background, they frame and balance, and just as in the garden, they give shade and shelter. Uccello's great 15th-century hunt scene takes place in the Wildwood, the trees as important as the hunters. Nicholas Hilliard's famous miniature of a melancholy young man leaning against a tree is just about contemporary (1590s) with *A Midsummer Night's Dream*. That same sort of relationship of trees for refuge, not from physical danger but from the press of the world, heigh-ho, is seen in Joseph Wright's portrait of Brooke Boothby—a picture that never fails to raise a laugh: surely he can't be serious—lying on a shaded bank in a floppy hat, ostensibly reading his book.

It is generally accepted that Claude Lorrain's idealized views of the Roman *campagna*, where he sets Biblical or Classical incidents in lovely landscapes, had a great influence a century later upon garden-making in 18th-century Britain. The great trees framing carefully contrived scenes of a winding river and artfully placed ruins are still seen throughout the country. Landscape painting and landscape-making gather momentum and eventually seem to go hand in hand as artists depict patrons' Claudian views in the making. How they have survived is splendidly shown at Petworth House in Sussex, where you can look at Turner's images, then turn to see that very thing outside the window. Only the deer have moved and the elms are dead and gone.

By the late 18th century, perhaps both painting with trees and landscaping with trees had become somewhat formulaic. "Capability" Brown became criticized in part, not just for repeating himself, however beautifully, but because lesser people could learn only some of the tricks of his trade, and less inspired creations resulted. In landscape painting, the "rules" that made up a "picturesque" composition became similarly stuck—warm, golden colors in the foreground fading to pale blue distances—so that Constable's 1821 *Hay-Wain* caused a sensation. Revolution is in the air, and what is being shown here is a working landscape in which the trees do more than frame, they are a part of the lives of that peasant community involved with Flatford Mill; they are the recognizable oaks and elms of Dedham Vale.

What painting does is cause us to look closely at an object or scene to concentrate upon an image consciously chosen by the artist for that express purpose. Constable's pictures show East Anglia as it was in an entirely pre-industrial age, quietly getting on with its life, but without false intrusion or sentimentality. Yet we are being shown distillations, scenes heightened by a great artist that help us to see in a new way. The Victorians' ever-increasing insistence on verisimilitude may be seen to have provoked the Impressionist backlash. Very different images appeared and have become indelible parts of our cultural memory. Again, we see trees through the eyes of the artists, not, in this case, predominantly as mass and shape but in the way that leaves play with light, absorbing, reflecting and dancing in it. Monet's weeping willows evoke the whole world of water gardens; Van Gogh's cypresses and olives seem to twist and turn in the roar of a continual mad Mistral.

Other cultures develop their ideal of treeness differently, their artists both defining and recording those ideals in their native idiom. No doubt our Westernized impressions of oriental painting are pretty superficial—a sort of Madam Butterfly/willow pattern oversimplification which misses many of the nuances and much of the symbolism, but we can appreciate the obvious importance that certain species have. Flowering cherry and plum and pines have shapes and textures that seem to define the east.

That same essence of place is constant on the other side of the world with the band of early-20th-century Canadian painters known as the Group of Seven. Tom Thomson, Arthur Lismer and company use native *Pinus strobus*, paperbark birch and flaming maples to define and celebrate a very specific land in a way that had not been attempted there before. Australian painters working today find their extraordinary eucalyptus, so perfectly adapted to the climate, equally defining of what it means to be there. Wherever artists paint, it seems, these huge organisms are used as symbols of beauty, fecundity and permanence, and the artists' attuned eyes help us both to appreciate and to use trees more effectively in our gardens and landscapes.

It is not too extravagant a claim to suggest that the planting of a tree today is a tiny part of that amazing historical, cultural and esthetic continuum. In turn, that tree, giving pleasure as it grows, may well continue into the future far beyond the lifetime of the planter, contributing to the country's heritage. The following chapter suggests ways we might go about it.

LEFT AND BELOW: Artists across the centuries and across the continents have painted trees, shimmering against the light as with this beech (left) or darkly looming as they dominate every landscape. *Prunus* x *subhirtella* (below), silhouetted in front of a lattice screen, evokes the oriental tradition, in which cherry and plum blossom have an almost mystical symbolism. OVERLEAF: The potential for floodlighting a significant garden tree is enormous. Branch tracery against the night sky turns into filigree silver.

choosing trees

choosing trees

The first question we need to ask is: why plant trees at all? One could say, philosophically, that it is because we inhabit lands where trees are central to the life of all organisms, plant and animal. Even 21st-century humans are affected in basic environmental ways. Planting or replanting even on the most cursorily utilitarian terms goes some way to acknowledge the fact.

Trees are vital to the land and its well-being. Where, in the search for ever more profitable farming practices, woodlands, woodlots, hedges and the trees that grow in them have been inexorably torn out, it is now being recognized that this is good neither for farming nor for the countryside. In Britain, the financial grants that only recently were available to increase field sizes are now offered for hedge and tree replacement. The pro and con arguments whirl around, like Florida in the hurricane season, the conflicting concerns of economics, environment and nature conservation.

However, most of us, when we wonder whether or not we should plant a tree, are thinking more about what the tree will do for us personally. Altruism is apt to be a subsequent justification. For while annuals offer quick color, perennials quick height, only woody things have winter presence, and only trees give scale. The only natural organisms that compete with man's works and put them into context, trees can complement our buildings and even our way of life. So it is wise to make considered decisions.

Owners of large properties (even those whose agricultural lands beyond have succumbed to the modern mode) plant to frame or enhance views from the house, to hide encroaching eyesores, to dampen noise from the new bypass, to plan for a succession to those aging trees planted to deal with the similar threats current a couple of centuries ago. Overall are the desirable virtues of providing enclosure, wind protection, shade and, in all its manifestations, beauty in the eye of the resident beholder.

These same considerations apply regardless of the size of our gardens, even to the tiny city courtyard that can take only one tree. Indeed, in many ways, the smaller the space

available, the more crucial the choice. Shade in summer is highly desirable; shade in winter, when we cherish every gleam from an often reluctant sun, is unacceptable. So, when it comes to the small town garden, evergreen trees, on the whole, are out.

As also, for the most part, are those trees graphically described as "weed-trees." These may well be fine plants in other situations, even desirable, but city conditions often imply higher ambient temperatures and lack of competition, which can turn them into thugs. Sycamore in London, tree of heaven in New York City, Manitoba maple in Toronto, every place has its pariah. They grow too fast for small gardens, get too big too soon and cast seed around with gay abandon. Their offspring can be seen sprouting happily from cornices, eaves-troughs and downspouts, to the detriment of all.

Such strictures must not be exaggerated, however. The elegance of 18th-century terraces as far apart as Edinburgh's New Town and Washington D.C.'s Georgetown is vastly enhanced by the trees in the streets and communal garden squares in front and those in the private spaces behind. Modern building regulations, heavily influenced by

an increasingly litigious society, worry about tree roots undermining foundations and generally behaving badly; but these historic houses stay up and remain, embowered in branches, supremely desirable for city-center living. And though in a small space it is certainly as well to avoid deciduous species which reach for the sky as if they are atavistically fighting it out in their primeval forests, it should be noted that, once mature, many forest trees are entirely suitable for town planting: think of the London plane trees of Belgravia, in perfect scale with the great houses around. By maturity, the canopy is high, so low winter sun gleams on the marbled trunks, and judicious surgery may have thinned the branches. Architecture of man and of nature are wonderfully attuned.

While it is seldom that individuals today have the opportunity to plan and plant on such a scale, the ideal remains valid. Small spaces do not necessarily demand

ABOVE, LEFT TO RIGHT: The diversity of choice in garden trees. We might plant for fall color (*Acer rubrum*), delicate spring blossom with fruit to follow (*Amelanchier canadensis*), architectural effect (*Araucaria araucana*) or huge scented flowers in May and June (*Magnolia* x *soulangeana* 'Lennei'). All have presence throughout the year.

small trees. It is height without weight, a delicate tracery of branches that is required. Also, the lighter the winter pattern, the better. Mount Etna broom (*Genista aetnensis*), for example, makes an excellent tree for a small city garden, because it is completely leafless: just elegant green wands of growth that develop a showering habit. Its early summer display of yellow pea flowers is a summer bonus. Reaching no more than 15 feet (4.5 m), the Chinese angelica tree (*Aralia chinensis*) ensures winter light in a different way. Here what appears to be the whole branch canopy falls away in autumn (in fact, it is the huge thrice-pinnate leaves), leaving just a slim trunk and a few sparse stems. The Kentucky coffee tree (*Gymnocladus dioica*) plays the same game on a bigger scale.

Such thoughts on small courtyard gardens also have relevance to many somewhat larger plots, whether the long and narrow suburban strip or the country garden up to an acre or two in size. For courtyard read terrace or patio, the vital extension to the house that we use more and see more of than any other part of the garden; the room outside may well need that one elegant architectural tree.

Beyond this, there will be room for more, though almost certainly not enough for all those one would like to plant and own (the urge for tree possession—mine, mine—can become almost obsessive). In the situation where there are neighboring gardens on either side and probably others backing on at the end, it makes sense to try and see the space as a single entity, though one which is viewed most importantly (of course) from one's own windows and one's own space. There may well be good trees in the surrounding gardens that it would be foolish to screen; the concept of borrowed landscape is just as valid here as in a British country garden where one plants or fells to point a view to the church tower in the next parish. And the effect is reciprocal. One's own planting influences the surrounding gardens and houses. A large

LEFT: Weeping willows (*Salix babylonica*) in a traditional site. These willows are planted close to an expanse of water, and their branches will soon trail down to meet it. In leaf and without, the effect continues throughout the seasons. ABOVE: On a much smaller scale, the Mount Etna broom (*Genista aetnensis*) has a similar showering habit. This is an ideal small tree for a protected courtyard.

species placed against a boundary may give unacceptable shade on the other side within a very few years, building understandable resentment next door.

At least in the country proper this is not a problem, though boundary planting where there is farm stock has to be done with care. A hungry heifer seems to develop an almost prehensile neck and will lean across barbed wire to get at new tree growth and do serious, lasting damage. Again, even with more space, there is the temptation to plant too closely; if it cannot be resisted at this stage, it is unlikely that the planter will be strong-minded enough to thin sufficiently later on.

Throughout, regardless of the size of one's garden, it is vital to decide what is wanted—shelter, screening (it's interesting to note that when houses are close together, neighbor noise is less disturbing if it's not actually visible), fine foliage, flower, fruit. The answer is probably all of these. The lists on pages 196–7 will help to show what is possible. Then the A–Z entries discuss the virtues in more detail.

But the decision about what species or cultivar to plant is not the end of it. Say, for example, you have decided that the winter-flowering cherry, *Prunus* x *subhirtella* 'Autumnalis', will look particularly fine against an existing evergreen background of Portugal laurel. This will not only help the flushes of little flowers to show up throughout winter and early spring but will also give a bit of protection and help to extend their season. Further choices emerge. What form is this tree to take? How big a specimen is to be bought? When should it be planted? Where will it come from?

For most people (answering that last question to begin with), a local garden center is first on the list. It reflects our current penchant for impulse-buying only too well—we go in for the winter-flowering cherry and come out with a purple plum because that's what they've got (perhaps it is irresistibly on sale as well), but what a pity it's going to look so dull with those dark laurels for the next 25 years or

CLOCKWISE FROM TOP LEFT: The bark of paper birch (*Betula papyrifera*), *Eucalyptus gunnii*, *Acer rufinerve* and Scots pine (*Pinus sylvestris*). Many trees are immediately recognizable by their bark, which varies in color and texture, and a number of trees are planted especially for their bark; smooth or rugged, it has evolved to protect the living tissue beneath.

so. This is not to knock the convenience of the local garden center, for it is unreasonable to expect it to stock exactly the plant on which you had set your heart just when you want it. Fortunately, many garden centers have close links with the propagating nurseries (several chains are in fact the retail outlets for such nurseries) and can obtain by request all but the most esoteric species with relative ease.

An alternative is to go to a specialist grower who sells by mail order (the way in which plants are packed for distant delivery can be an art in itself) or, better still, can be visited by appointment and the planned plant taken away—with the others that you had originally no intention of buying. the *RHS Plant Finder* in Britain and *Andersen's Source List* in North America will tell you who is offering what. Growers' catalogues are usually circulated in autumn and sometimes in spring as well, listing what is available with their size and price. Often there are unusual cultivars and selections made by the nursery itself. In the search for the winter cherry, one may find its pinker cultivar (*Prunus* x *subhirtella* 'Autumnalis Rosea') being offered. Descriptions are of necessity short but may well offer some personally observed hints on cultivation. Sometimes, too, there is an announcement that a particularly desirable plant is currently being propagated and will be available in a couple of years. Put your name down quick is the underlying message. The other great virtue of obtaining nursery catalogs, apart from happy dreams of summer beside a winter fire, is the time it gives to planning and designing around the choices being made. However good a garden is, it is the gentle musings over time that build up the plant associations which make it special.

It is always comforting to know that your chosen supplier has actually grown the plants you order in an area of the country similar to your own, and thus, we are apt to fondly believe, the plants are already used to what they are about to receive. While this would be so if they were grown entirely outdoors, that is not necessarily the case. Nurserymen have businesses to run and livings to make and that sort of altruism seldom pays off a mortgage; therefore, they are bound to adopt production methods that are as efficient as possible. British nurseries may bring stock in from specialist producers elsewhere in the country or

abroad. Dutch growers, for instance, have been famous for plant propagation since the 17th century and, with faster transport within the EU, vast numbers of plants are now imported from the South of France and Italy, where a longer growing season enables bigger specimens to be produced more quickly. North America has its own warm-climate nursery areas, which may fuel outlets in the northern states and some in Canada. Stock that survives lengthy cross-border examinations demonstrates its determination to live.

This is not to imply that such stock is inferior to the home or locally grown product: if they are true to name, the plants are genetically identical and are able to succeed equally well—presuming, of course, that they have as good a root system as the encouraging top one sees. What is vital is good acclimatization and ongoing care until the plants are sold. Small specialist nurseries are more likely, if they do not propagate all their own product, to buy in "liners" (that is, young plants which are to be lined out in nursery rows) or other small stock that is grown on for as long as it takes to develop a good specimen, and prices must reflect what may have been several years of care. On the other hand, the local garden store may be no more than a horticultural distribution depot with little cultivational backup. Plants will be cheaper, certainly, but may represent false economy. One must choose with care: *caveat emptor* and all that.

Over the past half century, there has been a revolution in garden plant production—or perhaps the developments should be seen more as ongoing evolution as, for instance, the peat-based composts that fueled much of the early innovations are now themselves in the process of change in response to environmental concerns of peat-bog loss. The new composts, combined with plastic pots of ever-increasing size, have led to containerized stock that can be planted at virtually any time of year and therefore offers availability to a gardening public unused or unwilling to plan ahead through the nursery catalog pattern described above. From a purist point of view, this may be considered unfortunate. In fact, it has put a host of good plants in front of a potential gardening public who buy what they can see. Sophistication can flow later.

It is inevitable that most of us think of spring as planting time par excellence: the vegetable seeds are sown, and with the end of the frosts, the tender annuals go out in every garden and window box in the land. But for woody plants, and trees in particular, it is not the first choice of planting season. It is often difficult to keep the pot-shaped root ball moist enough so that the roots can reach out and supply the unfolding leaves above or, even more, the full existing foliage of evergreen species. In Britain, where April and May are often the driest months (perhaps it was different in Chaucer's time, with his "shoures sote"), better to plant in autumn. Today's weather pattern tends toward a moist and relatively mild October and November when the soil is still warm enough for a bit of root growth to take place before winter sets in. Come next spring, young trees are ready to move with the season without too much help.

Although the trend continues to be in favor of containerized trees (and to be honest, the favor is more on behalf of the garden center and the buyer than the tree itself) some nurseries do offer plants dug straight from the open ground. They are then sold "bare-root" or wrapped in sacking (balled and burlapped was the old phrase) to hold a fibrous root ball together. This is, of course, a seasonal operation and, equally seasonal—during dormancy—is the time when bare-root trees are planted. Ideally, evergreens are planted in October and deciduous species as soon as the leaves have fallen. In practice, planting will be as soon as the plants are available, which is another reason to deal with the actual grower, who will be able to say when lifting and delivery is likely, weather permitting, to take place. Equally, the buyer can warn against delivery when he is going away; there is nothing more dispiriting than to find a package of plants drying out by the back door on one's return.

There is a further dimension to the container-grown versus bare-root debate where the systems overlap rather unsatisfactorily. Many plants, a bit like battery hens, spend their lives enclosed. They are potted up as rooted cuttings or as seedlings and are moved on into larger containers from which they are eventually planted out. Others, however, are grown in the open and are then lifted when dormant, potted up and sent off to the retail outlet—the garden center—for sale. If bought quickly—and it is perfectly obvious when you've bought something that has just been potted up, as the compost simply falls away when the container is removed—the effect is of a bare-rooted plant, except that to get it into the container, roots may have been cut away or damaged. If, like wallflowers at a dance, plants are not snapped up by springtime, they do their best to come into growth. Looked after with care, they remain perfectly desirable plants and may be planted over the succeeding summer months—though with the disadvantages already mentioned— or in the following dormant season in the normal way. Some, however, resent that sort of summer-long slave market and gradually lose condition. One must choose.

CLOCKWISE ON THESE PAGES FROM TOP LEFT: *Malus* 'Wisley Crab', *Cornus controversa*, *Magnolia* x *soulangeana* and *Prunus* x *subhirtella* 'Pendula'. Unfolding leaves and opening flower buds begin to excite us long before the full display occurs.

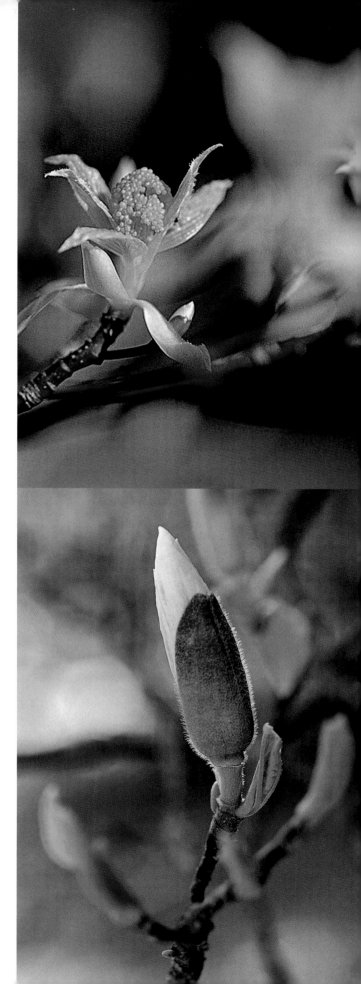

The above is generally the pattern in Britain or the West Coast of North America, where in most winters, nurseries can lift woody plants, and gardeners can plant them from late October to early April. On heavy soils, a wet period can make planting undesirable, and cold snaps and snow stop it altogether for a bit, but generally, work goes on. In continental-climate North America, winter planting is not possible and planting seasons each side of real winter are rather more constrained. Deciduous trees have only just dropped their leaves when hard frosts begin and the ground starts to freeze. Lifting becomes difficult and planting unwise. The cliché that those areas also have no spring—that winter breaks suddenly into summer—is an exaggeration but in some years not much of one.

This continental-climate spring is a frantic time in the garden when everything suddenly needs to be done and woody plants need the most immediate attention of all. During that ideal window of opportunity (this can occur at any time from the end of March into May depending upon region), specimen trees can be lifted and replanted and they will hardly notice the move. Buying plants small and growing them on in a corner of the garden for a year or two facilitates this wonderfully. For the nurseryman and his retail center, things are less calm. Many plants are lifted in autumn, potted and kept in plastic tunnels throughout winter. Others are bundled and stored in cold stores and containerized in early spring. In both cases, the planter buys what are in effect bare-root plants that need to get into the ground as soon as it is workable. Sun and accelerating air temperatures provoke rapid leaf growth, and root development to support it must be in parallel. If not, the effect will be like bringing a vase of dormant horse-chestnut twigs to open indoors: lovely, but temporary.

So far, the unstated assumption is that a tree is to be chosen, ordered or directly collected and planted by the person whose own garden is going to be improved by it. And that, by definition, it is not too big to be lifted and put in the car—perhaps with the tailgate up—and brought home. Size is worth some discussion. Mature trees are big, living organisms, which is why we want them—to enhance our house, screen the neighbors, frame the view, provide shade. And, of course, we want all these things now. How fortunate are they who inherit good trees with the house they buy; how bare, by comparison, is the new housing development, which only time can really help. The temptation, inevitably, is to buy as big as one's budget will allow. At a price, it is possible to buy semi-mature trees 20 or 30 feet (6–9 m) high and plant an avenue in the country or install a focal-point specimen in a city garden. Too big to go through the house? Well, then, an extending crane will swing it in over the roof.

This, obviously, is a job for professionals—the garden designer who will oversee the specifications for planting, the preparations and the supplier of the relatively restricted range of trees that can be grown in huge containers or can accept being moved with a mechanical tree spade. Splendid instant landscapes (and especially cityscapes) can be designed and planted within months—the vast developments of Canary Wharf in London and North American examples across the continent show what can be done; only with trees can a human dimension be brought to such sites. But it must be agreed that this is really engineering with plants rather than gardening; it is a part of an enormous financial package—for financial return—though, ironically the project's expected life span may be shorter than the natural span of most of the trees. Here, however, they are not grown naturally. They will do their job magnificently but, as a modern form of Louis XIV's instant forests at Versailles, are

ABOVE LEFT: Rhododendrons ready for planting. These have been lifted from the open ground and their fibrous root balls held together with a piece of burlap. Such plants will often flourish at a better rate than those planted out from pots. RIGHT: *Robinia pseudoacacia* 'Frisia' is one of the brightest of golden-leaved trees. It is especially effective when contrasted against the darkness and solidity of conifers.

unlikely to be long-lived. Perhaps in such a context it doesn't matter, though it is still rather shocking.

In the personal, private garden scene, the situation is different. Certainly the big trees can be obtained, but are there the facilities for soil amelioration, drainage, irrigation and so on? Is the long-term view important? It should be. For most of us, however, the options do not include the instant effect of semi-mature trees with all they entail. The choice is between small plants two or three years old and somewhat bigger specimens. The latter look encouraging, but again, it must be emphasized that young plants which have lost few roots in the transplanting process grow far more quickly and develop into better trees. In a very few years, they will have overtaken the expensive specimens. Granted, there will be no immediate shade on a hot afternoon, but to compensate, there is huge satisfaction in watching their development—and in a new garden, there is no time to lounge back anyway.

As may be noted in the directory, some species, such as eucalyptus and most conifers, absolutely must be planted when small. Apart from resenting root disturbance, the gums grow so quickly that unless new root development is in balance, they are sure to blow over and no subsequent staking will hold them. Conifers' heavy tops make them also prey to strong winds.

In essence, then, those two inevitably conflicting requirements of quick effect and well-grown permanent trees must be kept in mind. Screening an unwanted excrescence with a row of Leyland cypress may be a perfectly reasonable thing to do, as long as other, slower, but more desirable trees are planted within the garden and the cypresses are taken out when they are no longer necessary.

As is becoming clear, choosing one's trees is no simple matter; there are so many wonderful choices to be made. Trees develop into many sizes and shapes. Size is heavily influenced by site and by the sort of conditions and care we provide—a common rowan growing out of a rock crevice

LEFT: Known as the scholar tree, *Sophora japonica* has the pinnate leaves typical (as those of *Robinia* and *Gleditsia*) of the pea family, but it is especially valuable for its August cloud of creamy flowers. RIGHT: A young honey locust (*Gleditsia triacanthos*) arches over an informal path. A triple-trunked specimen like this is often more attractive than one with a rigidly upright "standard" form.

by a rushing Highland burn seems an entirely different species from one in the back garden. Shape is largely a concomitant of species. Wild plants of rowan or bird cherry or balsam poplar in similar conditions will share a similar shape and outline, and if one observes trees with care, one builds up in the mind a sort of dictionary of tree silhouettes with their variation in outline and visual weight. But trees do not commonly grow as isolated specimens. They are often part of woodland and forest, plant communities of individuals all in competition for the necessities of life, and the race for light produces a narrow head and tall straight trunks bare of branches for 30 feet (9 m) or more. Obviously, there were once lower branches when the trees were small, but gradually these are shaded out, die and fall off—only a well-healed scar in the bark and knots in the timber mark the spot. Such trees are the forester's ideal —but not necessarily that of gardeners.

To some extent, by sensitive early pruning and subsequent tree surgery, we can create the shape of tree we want, but only if the subject can accept it without losing its natural individuality. Successful choice is ultimately the right plant in the right place.

In addition, selections have been made of naturally occurring variants that have caught someone's eye—narrow Lombardy poplar and cypress oak, pendulous birch and weeping beech. It is amazing how many variants have occurred in nurseries—no doubt because they are in constant view of discerning plantsmen; one can only speculate what desirable one-off forms have come and gone. Thomas Gray's lines are apposite: "Full many a flower is born to blush

unseen/ And waste its sweetness on the desert air." What have we missed?

But even a genetically typical plant may develop erratically. The tip of a seedling chewed off by a rabbit may re-grow with several shoots: apical dominance then is shared as each shoot gets to trunk size. The ultimate tree may be a forester's nightmare, but as a picturesque form in the landscape, it may be ideal. In embellishing "Capability" Brown's ideal of regular clumps of trees, Humphry Repton invariably proposed a few misshapen specimens for just this reason. The popularity today of multistemmed silver birches where one buys a clump rather than a single-stemmed plant is another example. If such an effect is required, it is always possible to plant three or five two-year-old seedlings (or whips, as they are often called) in the same hole and stake them to lean elegantly outward. Almost any species can be grown in this way, and those with good bark are especially welcome.

Typically, however, trees are supplied, unless you state otherwise, with a single trunk, bare for five or six feet (1.5–2 m) before the head of branches begins. These are called "standards"; half-standards have only three or four feet (1–1.2 m) of clean stem. Within the natural capabilities of the plant, one chooses by judicious pruning what sort of ultimate outline and canopy is wanted. But gardeners have never been satisfied with those. In the great age of formal gardens in 17th-century France and Holland (and to a lesser extent Britain and pre-revolutionary America), whole avenues of full-sized trees were maintained as extensions to the architectural scene—the great topiary yews at Levens Hall in Cumbria date from that period. Today's beech hedges reduce what is in fact a row of forest trees to a green wall six feet (1.8 m) high evoking Versailles in a suburban strip.

Another 17th-century conceit that has enjoyed a recent renaissance in Britain is the "hedge on sticks," where a row—or more usually a double row, to form an avenue—of standards is planted and the branching heads are trained and pruned to form a hedge six feet (2 m) or so above ground. There are famous examples at Dumbarton Oaks in Washington, D.C. and at Hidcote Manor in Gloucestershire.

Beech, lime and hornbeam are the species commonly chosen—or even holm oak for evergreen effect. An iron and wire framework is necessary to support what becomes a considerable weight on slender stems; the maintenance, especially in the early years, is laborsome, but pleaching, as this process is called, is a wonderful way of obtaining quick, controlled height.

Variations on this theme use the same trees to form arbors, garden houses and tunnels or to furnish formal pergolas. With the well-known laburnum tunnel at Barnsley House, Rosemary Verey set a fashion that has circled the temperate world (sadly, what many happy plagiarists failed to note is how such a feature fitted into the whole garden design, how Mrs. Verey underplanted with tulips and alliums and how much careful planning and work went into it). A recent extension to the genre is the use of willows. These have the advantage of ease of propagation and quick growth, but without continual pruning and interweaving the intended shape is soon lost. Such informality of material associates unfortunately with what

is essentially a formal requirement—a bit like wearing a kaftan to a black tie ball, amusing but not quite right.

The possibilities of trained trees are taken to the furthest extreme (leaving out bonsai, where only an oriental distillation of treeness remains) in the art of fruit growing. It goes back into the very beginning of gardening and in its evolution combines all man's expectation of trees as providers: for food, drink, timber, fuel and as objects of esthetic admiration. Citrus fruits (among which oranges are contenders for the famous golden apples of the Hesperides) move into the classical world from the sub-tropical climates so that eventually special buildings—orangeries—are invented to grow them ever farther north. Clipped into formal shapes and grown in huge containers (Versailles boxes with hinged sides to facilitate "potting" are the

ABOVE, LEFT AND RIGHT: Red-twigged lime (*Tilia platyphyllos* 'Rubra') is closely planted to form an avenue and pruned to create an informal "hedge on sticks." In spring, before shade develops, pheasant-eye and other narcissi enliven the scene; by midsummer, their dying foliage is mown away, and soon all is green again.

ultimate), they are stood out in summer on palace terraces throughout Europe.

Everyone could not aspire to such epitomes of luxury, but alternatives were possible, though not with the same wonderful plant (citruses have everything: glossy, aromatic evergreen leaves, scented flowers, ornamental edible fruit). Sadly, the range of hardy broad-leaved evergreens that can accept the formal role is small: except for sweet bay and phillyrea and box, all need some greenhouse protection in cold climates. However, pairs of clipped box trees at every other smart front door today continue the lineage (you can even get them in plastic that looks almost as good).

More productive has been the development of fruits hardy throughout Europe and much of North America. As they move north, success has to be worked at so that even apples and pears may be containerized like citruses. Garden design evolves around them. Walls are built, sometimes heated by back boilers and internal flues and with facilities for hanging frost-protective curtains. Fruits are trained against the walls and cover pergolas and tunnels, as well as growing in the open in ways that become an art form in itself: fans, cordons, espaliers, palmettes, and so forth.

So while the provision of fruit is the basic reason for such cultivations, the visual effect of the plants as full-scale trees or in some trained form was almost equally important. Today, the roles are rather dottily reversed—the convenience of fresh supermarket fruit from across the world can reduce a prodigious crop in the garden to an embarrassment. But the seasonal beauty of such trees—spring flower, summer foliage, autumn fruit and winter architecture—is still matchless, whether they are trained for formal effect or encouraged into normal tree shape.

Thus decisions have been made: species and cultivar chosen, shape— natural or controlled—determined, order placed or plant collected. What now? Well, the requirements for plant growth have already been made clear. What follows is to ensure as far as possible that they are made available to the new tree from the moment it is planted until it can fend for itself. The first weeks and months are vital. Soil preparation and care for the trees to be planted go hand in hand. Ideally, the site will be made ready before the plants arrive. Having labeled stakes

TOP LEFT: Flowers, like these fleeting cherry blossoms, and fruit are added bonuses to the attractions of fruit trees in the garden. RIGHT: The architectural form of old fruit trees gives interest and structure to the garden throughout the year.

available is a great help; they can be pushed in where each tree is planned to go and moved around if second thoughts prevail. Designing on paper is fine, but transferring it to the ground effectively is essential because this is a garden or landscape picture that will develop for decades.

It would be remarkable if ordered plants were delivered exactly on the morning when you are free to plant them or indeed when the weather is perfect: though the sooner the better, heavy rains on soggy clay soil or hard frosts demand the day be put off. Whenever possible, bare-root trees should be unpacked and their roots laid temporarily in a trench in a sheltered corner. Similarly, it is best to protect containerized plants by covering the roots with soil right up to the top of the pots. If for whatever reason dormant plants cannot be thus "heeled in," temporary storage in a cool but frost-free shed will suffice for a couple of weeks.

Moisture is essential. Should plants arrive dry at the root, stand them in water for a couple of hours before dealing with them; this is vitally important with summer planting. Before planting, make sure that not only the root ball but also the planting hole and the surrounding soil are fully moist.

Recovery here is based upon early renewal of the root system. Remember bare-root plants need to replace those roots lost when lifted, while the roots of containerized plants have to be able to move from the encircling tangle that can literally strangle the developing tree. Planting holes must be wide and deep enough to take the existing root growth with no constriction, even when the coiled roots from within containers are stretched out. Depth is critical: over-deep planting is one of the major causes of loss. It is usually enough to ensure that the original soil level, shown by the darker bark, is repeated, but heavy mulching in the nursery can make this line appear higher than it should be. The point at which major roots leave the trunk should be only just below the finished ground level. Some soil improvement is bound to be necessary. Break up any "pan" of subsoil and mix in a few buckets of well-rotted garden compost, leaf mold or purchased potting compost with a

A small courtyard garden shows the fully furnished effect provided by conifers—both clipped and in their natural forms—and other woody plants. Full tree growth occurs beyond the garden's walls.

handful of slow-release general fertilizer containing the nutrients necessary to encourage growth. The old adage of putting a one-dollar plant in a five-dollar hole is just as valid today, so long as it is suitably increased for inflation. Organic material soon decays: tread the plant in hard—but with due care for the roots—to reduce sinkage and a subsequently too-deep plant. On heavy clay soils, drainage may be a problem; adding grit and compost, though desirable, may merely develop a sump. Planting on a shallow mound of good soil above the prepared space will help. Space the bare roots octopus-like on the mound, cover them, and heel them in.

Here staking—though essential for all but seedling trees—is especially important. The availability of suitable stakes and tree ties at planting time is part of the "five-pound hole" account. It used to be thought necessary to take stakes to the height of the tree's head but it has been shown that—so long as the root ball is secure—some flexibility actually encourages growth. For standard trees, stakes a couple of feet above ground are sufficient: either knock the stake in before you fill the hole with soil, or insert it diagonally facing the prevailing wind. In either case, roots are undamaged. Obviously, you should take care to protect the tree stem against rubbing by the tree tie. Professionally planted large specimens must have equally professional staking.

You will need to be alert to the risk of subsequent damage. Animals, particularly, can cause a lot of harm, and if you are not vigilant, years of hope and care and much expense may be swept away in a season. The problems are compounded where suburbanization has moved into the countryside without the countryman's pragmatic attitude to damaging animals being understood or adopted. Of course deer and squirrels and rabbits and even voles are delightful furry creatures, but when their natural predators are gone and the Bambi, Nutkin and Thumper lobbies prevent reasonable culling, tree growing can become very difficult. This situation, so far at least, is most difficult in parts of North America. If only prevention is permitted, variations on the tree-guard pattern must be employed. Plastic tree guards can help up to three feet, until a couple of feet of snow gives rabbits and hares a leg up. And while that snow gathers around the trunk, its base is vulnerable to voles. Preventative netting or even traps may be necessary. As the tree emerges from its guard tube, then deer and squirrels lick their lips. In Britain, the deer problem is less from actual browsing than from antlers rubbing young bark away. Some form of tree guard is essential *before* the event, and early local knowledge is vital. All of which sounds somewhat depressing; but the thing is to be, like the boy scouts, prepared.

Parkland planting is especially vulnerable and here wooden rail or iron guards are essential to prevent stock damaging trees. Lower branches must be pruned off above the height of a stretching, browsing animal; only as the trees mature can the guards be removed. Then, with only thin secondary shoots within reach, the traditional flat browse line will develop. In the early years, growth is greatly helped if herbage within the guard is kept clear with weedkiller.

Once trees are planted, aftercare really is common sense; its main goal is to minimize the shock of transplanting and to encourage the plants to feel at home. With spring and container planting in summer, the major need is maintaining sufficient moisture at the root. The unfolding (or existing) foliage continues to transpire and will wilt and even desiccate if the roots cannot keep up with demand. Buckets of water in the evening or a trickle irrigation system are the obvious answer, combined with ways to reduce stress. In spots fully exposed to the sun, it will help to give some shade (this is when the wisdom of planting small becomes evident) by lightly tied horticultural fleece— an initial couple of weeks may make all the difference. The same system is also invaluable in the early years for protecting leaves that unfold unwisely early. *Cercidiphyllum japonicum* is notoriously careless and can get badly burned by frost; when a bit older, it will leaf out again without much problem, but at the start, such an additional shock may be just too much.

Transpiration is also increased by wind, and again, fleece or some other form of windbreak is wise; those sudden hot, windy days typical of the North American East Coast's sudden spring are always difficult for newly planted things. An evening spray will also help. Moisture is lost, too, from the soil surface, and a couple of inches'

mulch of some organic material, taking care not to raise the soil level at the stem, conserves moisture. Maintain the mulch to the diameter of the branch-spread for four or five years, as competition even from lawn grass has a noticeably depressive effect on young tree growth. Indeed, older lawn specimens growing poorly can often be revitalized by removing a canopy-wide patch of turf and replacing it with a soft organic mulch (but not those horrid big bark chips). When you renew the mulch, you should also apply a dressing of slow-release fertilizer of the sort you used when planting.

Unlike formally trained plants, trees that are to develop naturally need little pruning in subsequent years. You may need to take out a badly crossing branch or competing leader. With open-ground specimens, you may wish to remove lower branches up to a chosen height in a sequential fashion. In mixed planting, this gradually happens naturally. With such plantings, it is necessary to look critically at what is happening. Tree growth, which at first appears so slow, is strangely insidious, and it soon becomes apparent that you have planted too closely together (we all do) and that this specimen or that will have to be sacrificed for the proper development of the next. The earlier such dire decisions are made the less traumatic it is But before the chainsaw roars into action, it may be worth considering whether some plants could be moved with professional tree-spade help. With advance preparation and immediate replanting, large specimens may be worth conserving.

Trees in parkland, a glade in a wood. Summer light is reflected, refracted; shade moves around with the sun, and brilliance and darkness change places so that we are continually shown our spaces "in a new light."

which tree where?

In the Directory section of this book, tree genera are described in some detail and in most cases with enthusiasm, which is why they are there. Only one or two get a bit of a brush-off. It will be noted that most of the genera have several distinct species, often from very different parts of the world. I never cease to be amazed at how trees that virtually define the eastern North America tree scene—for example, liriodendron, nyssa, liquidambar and sassafras—have oriental kissing cousins. And in addition, there are a number of cultivars of these species that have been propagated from naturally occurring variants (purple leaves, vertical habit, etc.) or intentionally bred for particularly desirable characteristics—frost-hardiness, or flower or fruit size.

While common names are used conversationally in the general parts of the text because it is both unnecessary and pretentious always to refer to beech, for example, as *Fagus sylvatica*, there is no alternative to botanical names in the lists. These define exactly, universally, what plant is being referred to and when used in a nursery catalogue ensure that you are getting the plant you want. It would be maddening to find you had planted, say, *Acer pseudoplatanus* when you wanted *Platanus occidentalis*, just because both are commonly called "sycamore," albeit on different sides of the Atlantic.

Using botanical plant names is neither snobbish nor showing off; it's just sensible and universal. It's no big deal, anyway. Pronunciation need not be a concern, for correctness varies, depending on where one is. Every syllable has weight: thus *Daphne*, of course, has two and *Nerine* three. So the answer is to utter the names where needed loudly and with complete conviction. One doesn't need to be a Latinist to do that; just read names phonetically, for there are no dotty surprises that have to be learned as in English (cough through the bough, etc.). And if you really want to know more than everyone else has forgotten, consult Professor William Stearn's monumental *Botanical Latin*.

There is also reference throughout to climatic zones, as published by the United States Department of Agriculture. As a guide to what plants are hardy where, North

Americans are very conscious of these zones, and with reason. Climates on the North American continent vary from the frigid to the subtropical, and a glance at the map on page 198 shows that average annual minimum temperatures differ vastly. But it must be emphasized that these are agricultural macro-concerns based on isotherms, while most gardens are on a small scale in which helpful microclimates occur and can even be encouraged. Any winter weather forecast warns in tones of doom about today's wind-chill factor and how necessary it is to wrap up warmly. Keen gardeners are equally concerned to wrap up their plants metaphorically or even literally (in Japan the latter has developed into an art form in its own right) and much can be done.

The important thing is to take zone lines as valuable general guides but not as prescriptions; unfortunately, especially in North America, too many gardeners accept them as gospel and suffer from a complaint known as zonitis. This leads to an unquestioning belief in media pundits who are bound, for fear of their reputations, to substitute cowardice for caution.

In Britain, the mildish oceanic climate would show, if the same system were adopted, most of the country to lie within the 7–9 zone bands, which sounds wonderful. Not surprisingly, next to this, North America's continental climate is apt to be unfavorably compared. But this is a simplistic view: the vagaries of the British seasons, which must be compared with the near-certainties across the Atlantic, are a major concern. Problems are equally present. They are just different.

Following the above barb against populist punditry, it is rash to write rules here, but offering some suggestions is in order. While being conscious of zonal guidelines, one must observe, record and work within the potential and limitations of one's own space. Thus:

Young evergreens often benefit from a little protection in their first couple of winters. Here, a row of Austrian pines (*Pinus nigra*) are wrapped with burlap to provide protection from not only Ontario's minus 13 degrees F (−25°C) temperatures but also salt spray from traffic on the adjacent road.

1 Choose the right plant for the right place. Trees whose role is protective, giving wind shelter, must be utterly hardy and adapted, especially in coastal conditions, to that particular role. These are not the sites for one-off optimistic experimentation—that comes within the garden which is now protected.

2 Be conscious of katabatic effects: cold winds drifting downhill are caught in frost pockets, which exaggerate cold nights. Those traditional sloping walled gardens in Scotland often omitted the southern side, reduced its height or replaced it with railings to let the cold air flow away. Making a gap in a similarly sited hedge or taking out a tree or two to break a line has the same effect.

3 Good soil drainage is often just as important; plants whose roots sit wet over winter are more vulnerable to winter cold. Mulching around plants with known shallow root systems, such as rhododendrons and most of the *Ericaceae*, is a help. Magnolias and Japanese maples are equally appreciative.

4 It is always upsetting when newly planted trees get beaten up in their first winter, and if there is doubt as to their ability to withstand it, plant in spring, which gives a longer period for root establishment before they have to meet adverse conditions. Also, as plants seem to acquire a bit of extra hardiness with increasing maturity, added protection for the first winter or three is really worthwhile. A tepee of evergreen branches or a windscreen may make all the difference. The moment of its removal in spring is as important as its installation. A warm March in Britain may herald a frosty April and the situation must be watched, while in North America that sudden spring warmth can provoke growth inside that is dangerously soft if uncovered too late. No apology is offered for re-emphasizing these warnings and adding them to concerns about protection from rodents and deer: nothing is more maddening than to lose young trees when one could have done something about it. None of this, however, is meant to inhibit trial and experimentation. Few things are more pleasurable than proving the experts wrong, and success is wonderfully encouraging.

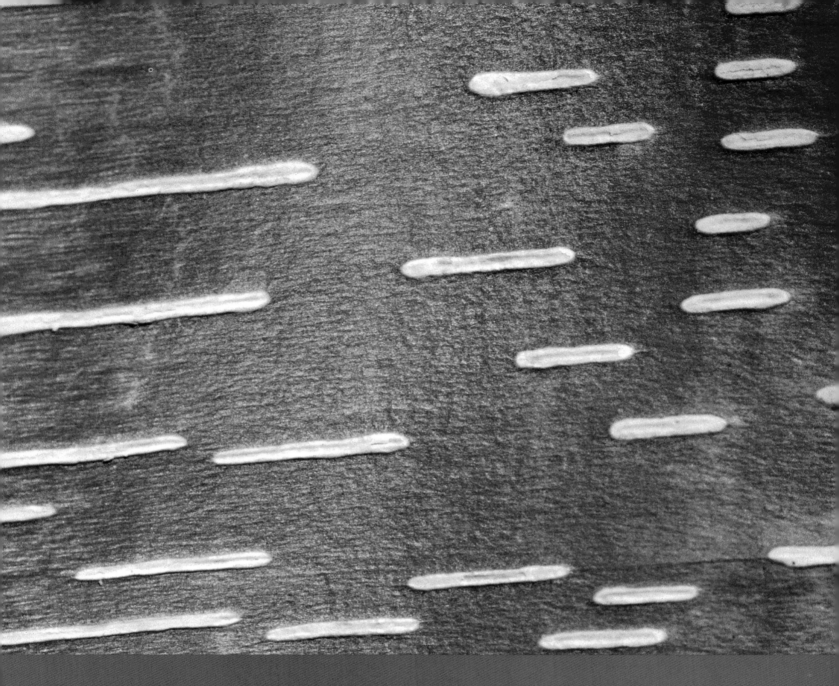

directory of broad-leaved trees

Fragrant sprays of Acacia dealbata *'Florist's Mimosa' now commonly appear in London.*

Acacia
Mimosa

There is a bright moment every winter when the first airy sprays of yellow mimosa appear in florist shops and cornerstores. For the sun-starved British, the sight and scent evokes the south of France; to the chilly East Coast of North America, it brings a breath of Californian warmth; for expatriate Australians, it means home and a whole range of indigenous wattles.

But in the milder parts of Britain, and particularly in London, where the micro-climate produces some almost frost-free years, great clouds of soft yellow are to be seen billowing up above garden walls in January and February. It's that same plant, *Acacia dealbata*, the silver wattle. In the wild in their native land, these are 100-footers (30 m), but in Britain half that height is likely to be the limit. Growth is rapid, up to 3 to 4 feet (90–125 cm) a year of feathery foliage. Flowering soon begins, within five years from seed, as sprays of soft yellow fuzz; no wonder it has received the AGM in Britain. Only when seed pods are produced does it become apparent that here is a member of the pea family, *Leguminosae*.

This is a zone 8 plant and a hard winter will cut it to the ground, but it will usually grow again from the base. Where *A. dealbata* seems safe enough, one is almost bound to try others. *A. baileyana* is especially beautiful; of naturally restrained growth with blue-gray foliage, it deserves every care.

These mimosas are happy in any normal garden soil; good drainage is always a plus when plants are at all tender. In limy soil they can look pale and yellowish—this is known as lime-induced chlorosis—and a dose of acidifying fertilizer will help.

Acer
Maple

With about 150 species from around the northern hemisphere, acers are some of the most valuable of garden trees. There is a maple for every size of space, from

Acer palmatum *'Atropurpureum' is of interest, whether in or out of leaf, throughout the year.*

parkland's broad spaces, where the sycamore (*Acer pseudoplatanus*, not the American sycamore, also known as plane) makes a superb specimen, to a handkerchief-sized roof garden, where, with some protection from wind and full sun, Japanese maples succeed wonderfully in containers. While not usually grown for their flowers, some varieties of *A. palmatum* and *A. japonicum* make quite a show in spring and later as the fruits develop. The common, easy-to-grow Norway maple (*A. platanoides*) is a splendid sight in spring, becoming a cloud of bitter yellow-green; individual flowers in heads of a couple of dozen are strangely like those of alpine saxifrages.

Some species, such as the American sugar and red maples (*A. saccharum* and *A. rubrum*), are renowned for autumn color, while others earn their keep with varying patterns of colored bark; a number of garden varieties have been selected for leaf colors, purple, golden or variegated.

A. campestre is the field maple of dry chalklands and limestone uplands common in southern England. No British native plant produces better golden autumn color. It will also grow perfectly well on non-alkaline soils and takes drought and city conditions with impunity, making a tidy little tree to 30 feet (9 m) or so high, although trees twice as tall as that

and more are recorded. 'Carnival' is a recent selection with clean green-and-white variegation. With less photosynthetic tissue, it is obviously going to be even slower to get to any height, but it will be attractive in small gardens while it does. The species is a zone 5 plant in North America where it is grown both as a specimen and as a useful tight-growing hedge. *A. capillipes* is alphabetically the first of a small group of lovely small orientals known as snake bark maples; grown in zone 6, these are known particularly for their green-and-white striped branches, though the trunks will lose the effect with age. Other snake barks include *A. davidii*, *A. forrestii*, *A. grosseri* var. *hersii* and *A. rufinerve*. It is not easy to distinguish these effectively in print. It is difficult even when visiting an arboretum, for a good specimen of any one of them is apt to seem *the* snake bark to fall for—until you see the next, looking just as fine. First love is notoriously fickle, and the situation is made more complicated by specialist nurseries offering further delicious-sounding selections. In addition to bark color, all have the virtue for smallish spaces of rapid early growth, an elegant showering habit and a top height around 40 feet (12 m). Autumn color is usually splendid, the tints varying with species and site.

In North America, these are all 5–6 zoners and enjoy moist, preferably low-lime soils, but all is not lost in colder areas because of the excellent native moosewood (*A. pensylvanicum*). Just as good in bark effect as the orientals, it grows as a small understory tree, often on north slopes, from Nova Scotia westward along the top of the Great Lakes, which indicates zone 3 acceptance and preference for cool soils. The cultivar 'Erythrocladum', which boasts bright pink young shoots throughout winter, is particularly fine. This was the first snake bark to reach British gardens and has been quite undeservedly overshadowed by its oriental

relations. *A.* x *conspicuum* 'Silver Vein' keeps its stripes on the trunk.

A. tataricum subsp. *ginnala*, native to Mongolia and north China and known as Amur maple, is renowned for its ability to flourish in areas with really cold winters—a zone 2 plant of real quality, making a twiggy little tree to 20 feet (6 m). The creamy-white flowers are noticeably fragrant in May, and autumn is celebrated, though fleetingly, with brilliant orange and red.

A. griseum is the paper bark maple, renowned for its mahogany bark, smooth at first then peeling off in curled flakes—irresistible to tree-strokers. This effect and

In autumn, the fingered leaves of Acer japonicum *'Aconitifolium' turn from green to pink to flame.*

the autumn colors of its trifoliate leaves give interest even when the plant is young (eventually a narrow 40 feet/12 m) or so is possible), but so often it seems to sit rather sullenly after planting with a mean couple of inches in annual extension growth. Planting when small in good soil and part shade will help it along. It often looks lonely; a little grove of three or five planted 15 feet (4.5 m) apart would make a wonderful legacy.

On the face of it, the Japanese maple (*A. palmatum*) is the ideal small garden tree, with an elegant habit, beautiful fingered foliage that often colors dramatically in autumn, and attractive fruit. But it must be admitted that many years will pass before the chairs can be set up underneath to take advantage of its gentle, dappled shade. Nonetheless, given a sheltered site and a good soil (the old gardening manual's "deep rich loam, well-drained yet retentive of moisture" would, if it existed, be ideal, while thin limestone soil is anathema), *A. palmatum* can put on 12 inches (30 cm) or so of growth a year. It shows from the start its esthetic potential; so many trees have to go through a gangling youth before reaching the elegance of maturity. Here is beauty day after day, from the beginning.

This species and the closely related *A. japonicum* were cultivated and cherished in oriental gardens long before they reached the West in the 19th century, and many variations in leaf form and color have been selected, propagated and named. The true species and the lovely dark-leaved cultivar *A. palmatum* 'Atropurpureum' the choice where a real tree, some 20 feet (6 m) in height, is required in the foreseeable future. The splendid cut-leaved types (known as the

Dissectum and Linearilobum Groups) are likely to remain as slowly increasing mushroom-shaped domes of foliage throughout the lives of their planters. But eventually, the canopy lifts up and a perfect bonsai-like specimen emerges 10 to 15 feet (3–4.5 m) high and as much across—a fine inheritance for anyone fortunate enough to take on an old garden in which it grows.

These plants are renowned for their autumn color in Britain; in North America, they are just as good, but the competition is greater, so it is worth realizing that the tints of the unfolding leaves in spring can be equally attractive.

Because of the reduction in green photosynthetic tissue, variegated-leaved types of *A. palmatum* are bound to be less robust and even slower in growth. They remain shrubs. Other cultivars offer special attributes. 'Ôsakazuki' is renowned for its fiery scarlet autumn coloring and 'Sango-kaku' (syn. 'Senkaki'), the coral bark maple, for its distinctly pink shoots, admirable for winter-garden effect. These both belong to the Palmatum Group with larger seven-lobed leaves. 'Bloodgood' with wine-red summer foliage and the golden 'Aureum' also belong here. More effective methods of propagation and new cultivars selected in the West and in Japan provide an increasingly wide range of lovely plants, and it makes sense to contact specialist nurseries and if possible visit gardens with good collections. Choice is a personal thing, but it helps to accept that one's own non-specialist garden is unlikely to provide the perfect conditions—wind shelter, light shade, a zone 5+ winter, maybe even a lathe house for further protection—so robustness of

habit should come high in the list of desiderata. After all, every Japanese maple is beautiful.

Norway maple (*A. platanoides*) is, as its name suggests, plane- (that is *Platanus*-) like, with big, glossy, sharply lobed leaves. The foliage is sufficiently striking to make it worth growing—it will grow anywhere —like a clump of hazel coppice; encourage it by cutting out a couple of the bigger stems each year. But as a proper tree, its March/April flowering, as mentioned above, makes it one of the joys of spring; its autumn color is clear yellow.

A. platanoides is native from northern Europe to the Caucasus and is now naturalized in North America, so it is not surprising that it has given rise to a number of useful cultivars, such as 'Goldsworth Purple' and 'Crimson King'. 'Royal Red' grows more quickly. All these are best, as with purple beech, planted in gardens, not out in the countryside. 'Columnare' and 'Crimson Sentry' make narrow spires, the latter with purple foliage. *A. p.* 'Drummondii' is happily known in North America as harlequin maple, which gives a good hint to the effect of its white-and-green leaves. This is one of the very best of medium-sized variegated trees, but watch out that all-green branches don't appear and become dominant: early removal is essential.

Sycamore (*A. pseudoplatanus*) is no exotic tree—its native range is probably central France eastward—and it has made itself completely at home in Britain (but as it is a zone 5-er, such ubiquity is not the case in North America), to the point that it can be a weed tree, seeding in all directions in all soils, rapidly shading out competitors and depressing ground flora with blankets of slow-to-rot fallen leaves. If cut down, it suckers from the base and starts again. But what is unacceptable aggression in most places becomes a virtue where conditions conspire against tree growth. Sycamore can be the first line of shelter against salt-laden winds on the coast; it will colonize industrial waste sites; it will give a bit of protection to remote farms on the most inhospitable hillsides. In gardens, however, only its harlequinesque forms 'Brilliantissimum' and 'Prince Handjery', with pink, white and green unfolding leaves—the effect gradually diminishing by early summer— are planted. These grafted plants are a bit lollipop-like when young, but as they mature and open out, the effect among other foliage is excellent, attaining no more than a third of the 100 feet (30 m) possible with the type. 'Worley' is rare but worth looking for; the leaves unfold primrose yellow and then darken to gold before turning green. It makes an elegant balanced tree 40 feet (12 m) high.

Most other big-leaved species are North American. *A. macrophyllum* certainly lives up to its name, with huge, deeply lobed leaves up to 12 inches (30 cm) across on equal-lengthed petioles. It is a plant of the West Coast from the north end of Vancouver Island down into Oregon, and it is sometimes called Oregon maple. Long sprays of yellow-green flowers hang among the crimped unfolding leaves. A tree for big spaces, it grows quickly to 50 feet (15 m) or so, reaching twice that in its moist forest home, where the bronze flaking trunk so noticeable in Britain is lost in a welter of epiphytic ferns and liverworts and mosses.

The East Coast maples seem to epitomize so much of early New England and Upper Canada life, as main contributors to the amazing fall color display, source of valuable commercial hardwoods and, in the case of sugar maple (*A. saccharum*), a vital food miraculously available at the very end of winter, like manna in the wilderness. Learned from the native peoples, the method of sugar extraction was published in 1684 by the Royal Society in London; a visit to a traditional sugaring-off site in the "bush" is still a moment in which to celebrate the turn of the seasons—as is the bacon, pancake and maple syrup breakfast served on the spot.

Native from the Ottawa valley down to the mountains of Georgia, *A. saccharum* can reach 100 feet (30 m) in height, growing in mixed forest or almost pure stands. Noble specimens growing alone are broad-headed, but narrower selections such as 'Endowment' and 'Columnare' (syn. 'Newton Sentry') are available. Others, such as 'Bonfire', 'Green Mountain' and 'Legacy', are chosen for their speed of growth and wider tolerance of environmental conditions in zones 4–8. All have spectacular autumn color. *A. saccharum*, of course, is the national emblem on Canada's flag.

In Britain, the sugar maple has had a bad press; in fact it can do well, and the newer North American cultivars should be tried. Here it rather resembles Norway maple but with orange to red autumn color. It will be necessary to turn to those Transactions of the Royal Society for directions in sugar extraction; sadly, the brilliant days and cold nights needed for fast sap-run are unlikely to occur, and we will still need to import maple syrup from across the ocean.

A. saccharinum is the silver maple, whose name becomes clear in a summer breeze when the long, swaying branches wave and the leaves flash their silver backs; in 'Silver Queen' this characteristic is even more noticeable. This cultivar also has a more dominant leader, giving a stronger framework to the tree. Eventually, *A. saccharinum* is a big tree and 100-footers (30 m) are not unknown, but its quick, elegant growth, early flowering and fine foliage make it useful for smaller spaces, even if it has to be taken out before maturity.

Closely related is the red maple (*A. rubrum*). This has a similar range to the sugar maple and extends farther north. Its redness includes the fuzz of flower clusters and its twigs, buds, leaf stalks and immature fruits; then, come fall, red maple closes the year in a burst of scarlet and orange. Many selections have been made, including the conical 'Scanlon' and narrower Scarlet Sentinel ('Scarsen'). Others have more certain autumn color, which is especially necessary in Britain: for example 'Embers', 'Red Sunset' and 'October Glory'. For smaller gardens, 'Schlesingeri', with good early leaf color, is ideal, seldom getting much above 25 feet (7.5 m).

Some North Americans may switch off at this point because their native *A. negundo*, the Manitoba maple, also known as the box elder or ash maple, has the sort of reputation that sycamore has in Britain. It is a "weed tree," a "dirty tree," and it is unlikely to appear in North American plant catalogues. Prophets and honor come to mind. However, the ash-like leaves of box elder, unique among maples, turn a good yellow in autumn, and the tufts of pale green flowers on male trees are attractive in early spring; the rapid growth and ability to accept zone 2 cold make it valuable in the prairie provinces of Canada as well as farther south.

In the garden, several cultivars are excellent for mixed plantings, having variously colored leaves. 'Kelly's Gold' and 'Auratum' are self-descriptive, as is 'Variegatum', to whose green and white 'Flamingo' adds pink overtones in the new growth. As always, such plants must be watched for reverting green branches. Manitoba maple is a plant of the wet banks of streams and rivers and is happiest in soils that do not dry out.

Aesculus
Buckeye

Known as buckeyes in parts of North America and horse chestnuts in Britain, this splendid group of trees is immediately recognizable. The commonest is also the finest and probably the most spectacular flowering tree for temperate, zone 4–8 planting. This is known in Britain as the conker tree (*Aesculus hippocastanum*). But even in Britain, while it retains its colloquial name, one fears its significance is rapidly declining into a sort of boring when-I-was-a-boy folklore. Autumn school terms no longer open with "conker" battles.

For historical record, it is necessary to describe the scene: two British schoolboys, each with a single horse chestnut, the bigger the better, which is threaded on to a string with a knot at the bottom, and held up and hit with the other; the boys take alternate turns until one chestnut shatters. That which stays whole is a "oner." It might go on game after game to become a miraculous "tenner." As in all children's games, rituals developed and methods of preparation were religiously followed. Just as James Bond's dry martini had to be "shaken not stirred," conkers might be drilled not skewered; they might be baked

Aesculus x carnea *offers a pink alternative to the usual white species of horse chestnut.*

or soaked in vinegar—both rather déclassé wiles and in fact no match for the perfect, fully ripe chestnut. Local knowledge recorded the trees with the biggest chestnuts; those that usually had a single nut in each prickly case—doubles are unattractively one-sided; and those that dropped the first perfect fruits without having to be knocked down with sticks. By half term, it was all over, the trees

started to color, the heavy-fingered leaves began to fall on the shattered nutshell litter, and the boys moved on to something else.

With leaf fall, the horse chestnut's full majestic skeleton becomes visible. Mature trees in open sites have lower branches that sweep almost to the ground and then turn slightly up again, showing off the fat, sticky buds, shiny as chestnuts themselves.

By mid-winter the terminal buds have next May's incipient flower spike inside, gift-wrapped in white fur like that of a hyacinth within its bulb. Cut branches brought indoors unfurl their leaves elegantly; though the flowers abort, they make a splendid background to early spring bulb arrangements. Then, come true spring, the great fingered leaves begin to appear, and flower spikes nearly 12 inches (30 cm) high extend on every branch tip. From a distance, the effect might well be the inspiration for Elton John's famous "Candle in the Wind." Close up, it will be seen that each long-styled flower is exotically marked with red spots.

Reaching over 100 feet (30 m) in height, this is obviously not a tree for small spaces, but in parkland or in the corner of a field there is hardly anything better. Growth is encouragingly rapid in the early years. *A. h.* 'Baumannii' is a double-flowered and therefore fruitless cultivar suitable for those who wish to avoid the mess, and the pleasure, of a chestnut crop.

Though this wonderful tree is recorded in cultivation since the 16th century, its origins were long unknown. It is in fact from the mountainsides and rocky gorges of northern Greece and Albania. Coming from this fierce continental climate, it is as suitable throughout Europe as for eastern North America. Unfortunately, in North America, in company with some of the native buckeyes, it is prone to disfiguring leaf blotch in midsummer. It succeeds better in the north—even, in sheltered sites, to zone 3.

The red horse chestnut (*A.* x *carnea*), has the small American *A. pavia* for its other parent. Magnificent in flower, it is not quite the size of the common chestnut.

A. x *c.* 'Briotii' has deep red flowers, while in 'Plantierensis' the flowers are soft pink.Like the lovely Indian horse chestnut (*A. indica*), they belong in large gardens and parks. *A. indica* has more elegantly fingered leaves, pink-flushed when young with pale pink flower spikes often over 12 inches (30 cm) in length, at their best in late June and into July. 'Sydney Pearce' is a fine selection from the Royal Botanic Gardens, Kew, where Mr. Pearce was curator of the arboretum.

Eastern North America offers several fine buckeyes (the smooth brown and white seeds provide this name). *A. glabra* has dullish horn-yellow flowers but can be more decorative in autumn; 'October Red' is a cultivar of fairly dependable leaf color. *A. flava* offers brighter yellow flowers on a bigger tree. It reaches 100 feet (30 m) in moist valley bottoms in its native Georgia and Tennessee and approaches that in southern Europe; less in Britain.

Specialist nurseries offer a further dozen interesting species and hybrids. All *Aesculus* species resent soils that dry out in summer: leaves brown early and growth

Tree of heaven (Ailanthus altissima).

is slowed. The smaller North American species are naturally mixed woodland plants and accept some shade from adjacent trees.

Ailanthus altissima
Tree of heaven

If ever a tree deserves praise in our concrete jungle cityscapes, it is this. It softens and clothes those dismal New York freeways that lead to JFK airport; it adds a touch of natural beauty to nasty back alleys in downtown Toronto. But, of course, its very prodigality makes it suspect. It is native to north China and was introduced to Europe by the mid-18th century, and its common name is Chinese-inspired: to them it is a tree that meets the sky. We should be grateful that it makes the attempt.

In fact 80 to 100 feet (25–30 m) is the usual mature height in the West. It has a fine gray-fissured trunk and on female plants, reddish fruit keys—like those of an extremely productive ash—make quite a show in late summer. The green male flower heads smell somewhat fetid and ideally are best avoided; unfortunately, known-sex plants are seldom sold. But the stinking season is short.

The fruiting resemblance to especially lush ash trees (though there is no botanical relationship) continues to the foliage—long, pinnate leaves. On adult trees, these are around 18 inches (45 cm) in length; they may be twice that on young, vigorously growing plants, and even more if trees are regularly coppiced and fed hard. Here, as with paulownia, there is a dramatic foliage display.

Clearly, ailanthus, with its bone hardiness and willingness to grow in the roughest places, is not the conventional choice for sophisticated gardens. But its

Albizia julibrissin *is a pink mimosa lookalike that tolerates hot, dry conditions, so it is worth trying in a city courtyard garden.*

ability to provide quick, elegant height should not be underestimated, even in small areas. It is easily grown and almost as easily removed when more desirable species need the space both above and below ground. Then the commoner that has acted as nurse can be thanked and pensioned off.

Albizia julibrissin
Silk tree, pink siris

Whereas in North America well-behaved gardeners are apt to believe the pundits unquestioningly and accept the published restrictions of the climatic zone in which they live, most Brits continually dice with death. Not their own, of course, but that of plants regarded as doubtfully hardy, which they are determined (to try) to grow.

This is very good news for the nurserymen always ready to supply another. It also pushes out the borders of knowledge, and most surprising and encouraging results can be achieved. But it is not necessarily winter cold that is the determinant.

Albizia is a lovely, mimosa-like tree that grows 30 feet (9 m) high, coming from Iran and eastward, where a fierce winter and searing summer ensure that young wood matures wonderfully. Thus it adapts well to the southeastern United States and up to New York City and beyond. I have even seen it on the Canadian north shore of Lake Ontario, but doing better in Fort Worth. This indicates its tolerance range. It quickly makes a wide, flat-topped tree of open effect with its delicate doubly

pinnate leaves, which it is both late to produce and late to lose. In between there is a show of pink flowers, all stamen fuzz. Sadly, where it does best in North America it is susceptible to debilitating wilt disease. In Europe, it is probably a plant for the more definite climate of the south, but it is now a serious contender for the role of a single tree in warm London gardens where its rapid growth and near-instant height combine conveniently with thin shade. The exotic floral display is a bonus.

Alnus
Alder

Creeks and streams in northern England and Scotland are often lined with dark-leaved alders. On bare branches in late

Alders are fine waterside trees. Here, Alnus cordata *hangs out its spring catkins.*

winter, the sprays of little cone-like fruit from last year are joined by swelling catkins ready to shed their pollen to pollinate the next—always an attractive harbinger of the burgeoning new year.

The ability of alders' roots to "fix" atmospheric nitrogen, rather as legumes do, helps them to succeed even in poor, ill-drained soils, and this obliging characteristic is exploited by gardeners; there are not many trees so accommodating. While the common alder (*Alnus glutinosa*) is admirable in the wild—a narrow, often multi-stemmed tree, sometimes approaching 100 feet (30 m) in height— its cultivars and some of its relations are better garden plants.

Several have finely cut leaves: *A. g.* 'Imperialis' and *A. incana* 'Laciniata' both offer a light showering effect in summer. Others have golden leaves. *A.g.* 'Aurea' is a first-class tree, and even better is the gray alder's variant, *A. incana* 'Aurea', which offers distinct attractions season by season. The gold-to-orange young branches against a blue winter sky make a fine picture, and by April they are swinging with orange-red catkins. The downy leaves unfold in a soft yellow, which they maintain throughout summer. Altogether a lovely plant for moist spots without fierce winds; leaf petioles seem to be easily half-broken and the resulting hanging dead leaves are disfiguring.

From Corsica and southern Italy comes Italian alder (*A. cordata*), but it is still happy in zones 5–8. It prefers the usual alder habitat but will also succeed in dryer, even chalky, soils. It is a robust pyramidal tree, with lustrous leaves that are rather pear-like (not pear-shaped). Its 3-inch-long (8 cm) catkins and sprays of upward-facing woody fruit look good in early spring. This is an excellent street tree, even in northern cities.

Amelanchier
Serviceberry, snowy mespilus

One of the joys of spring in the Great Lakes area of North America is the way in which the woodlands suddenly wake from

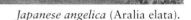

Serviceberry (Amelanchier), *awash with spring blossom.*

Japanese angelica (Aralia elata).

a winter that had seemed interminable. First bloodroot and hepaticas, then trilliums and dogtooth violets star the ground, rushing on with their life cycle before the tree canopy closes above them. And on woodland edges, often where woodland meets water, appears an ethereal cloud of white. In a week or two it is gone, petals blown, downy foliage unfolding around the remains. This is an amelanchier, one of three or four small tree species that offer a sequence of pleasures as the year moves on. In only a couple of months after that April display, delicious red-purple fruit weigh down the slender branches, from which come the complaining cries of greedy American

robins. The fall is marked by a kaleidoscope of yellow, orange and dusky red, and soon the bare gray-striped trunks stand out against the snow. Botanical nomenclature is confusing and nurseries' lists are equally so. *Amelanchier arborea*, *A. canadensis*, *A. laevis* and *A. lamarckii* are the ones to choose from where description definitely states "large shrub or small tree." A number of selected clones also exist and are worth consideration.

The elegant outline and general effect of amelanchier make it seem a perfect choice for a small garden specimen tree, but gardeners have to learn, as always, from a plant's natural habitat. Amelanchiers lead a colonial life and they need a bit of

midsummer shade; that woodland edge, ideally seen across a pond for twice the effect, is where they belong in zones 4–8.

Aralia
Angelica tree, devil's walking stick

"Exotic effect" and "tropical appearance" are just two of the almost inevitable clichéd phrases used to describe these extraordinary plants. In winter, they are just a sketchy skeleton of upward-pointing branches irregularly armed with short spines. While single-trunked plants are sometimes seen, aralias' propensity to sucker (especially if roots are wounded) usually provides for multi-stemmed specimens. This is to be encouraged:

three or five trunks (they are never more than a few inches in diameter) of varying heights provide an interesting silhouette, 20 to 30 feet (6–9m) in height.

Leafing is late, but once it begins one thinks it will never stop: from terminal and widely spaced secondary buds enormous compound leaves unfold. Eventually, the dominant leaf rosette might be 10 feet (3 m) across, and from its center in late summer emerges a cloud of creamy white flowers, to be succeeded by sprays of elderberry-like fruit. Exotic effect indeed.

The fruit of the strawberry tree (Arbutus unedo).

Aralia elata is the Japanese angelica tree and A. *chinensis* its very similar mainland cousin—some botanists have suggested they are in fact the same plant. Certainly they are very similar. The former has produced a couple of handsome variegated cultivars whose leaves are splashed with white ('Variegata' syn. 'Albomarginata') or yellow ('Aureovariegata'). Reduced photosynthetic tissue results, of course, in less vigorous plants, and these seldom attain more than half the size of the green originals. Since they have to be propagated by grafting onto the stocks of the type, any suckers will "revert" to green. Expensive to buy, slow to make a specimen, these cultivars are still dramatic additions to a critical half-shady spot in the garden.

In addition, the southeastern United States have their own native species, A. *spinosa*. Though shorter than the orientals, it is very similar, flowering and fruiting somewhat earlier; as its name suggests, it is more formidably armed. Thus the descriptive local names of Hercules' club and devil's walking stick.

All three species succeed in zones 4–8/9, but the American really needs a hotter summer than northern Britain can provide. Here, too, the oriental species may flower too late to set fruit. But the foliage effect is still magnificent, either against the sky or from above on a steeply sloping site.

Arbutus
Strawberry tree

Broad-leaved evergreen trees are not a feature of temperate floras—nor, therefore, of temperate gardens. Our climatic pattern militates against big plants maintaining a transpiring leaf canopy throughout cold winter months (conifers have evolved special adaptations to deal with such difficulties). So we expect our trees to lose their leaves in autumn and enjoy the utterly changed appearance that follows, just as we anticipate with joy foliage renewal in spring. It is a part of our cultural—and not just horticultural heritage. For this reason, bringing examples into the garden of the few species that prove the rule needs careful thought; their year-round presence can be dangerously dominant. (See also *Eucalyptus, Ilex, Magnolia grandiflora, Quercus, Trochodendron*.)

Arbutus is a strangely distributed genus. The traditional strawberry tree, *A. unedo*, grows wild in southwest Ireland and trickles down through the Mediterranean littoral and some of the islands, where in Greece and Crete it meets *A. andrachne*. They interbreed, and the more robust hybrid *A.* x *andrachnoides* occurs. The latter pair make lovely specimens of architectural outline with smooth pink-red bark. Sprays of white urn-shaped flowers are followed by orange-red berries.

A. unedo can reach or even exceed a height of 20 to 30 feet (6–9 m), but in a typical gardener's generation, it is likely to remain a big solid bush, dangling its extraordinary orange "strawberries" in autumn just as the next season's flowers begin to open. *Unedo*, incidentally, means "I can eat one," because, though the berries look delicious, their appearance is misleading; that one is more than enough. Another claim to fame is that, unusual in its *Ericaceae* family, it does not insist upon lime-free soil.

The noble madrona of western North America is *A. menziesii*. It is a plant of the coast, sometimes leaning out over the water of British Columbia's sea

lochs. If only the bunches of crimson fruit were as lusciously edible as they look, it would be the ideal tree: dark, glossy evergreen leaves, almost white beneath so that they flash in the wind; an elegant open habit; cinnamon to red bark of the trunk and branches smooth and polished; relatively rapid growth to

The Chilean Azara microphylla.

100 feet (30 m) in the wild (in cultivation, half that is good); sprays of white flowers in May. There is not much more one could ask of an ornamental tree, and so it is surprising that it is not grown more often.

A. menziesii has a reputation for frost-tenderness, but fine specimens exist on the east side of Britain, including a famous one at Crathes Castle in Aberdeenshire, a spot not noted for balmy breezes. Perhaps the stock one usually comes across has been propagated from the southern end of its range, which is well down into California.

None of these trees is suited for the rough and readiness of mixed tree woodland; their strangely sophisticated

character suits and enhances architectural settings close to buildings or against terrace walls, and any important site, in reasonable shelter, where an eye-catching tree is required.

Azara microphylla

If the essence of tree-ness is size and bulk, this elegant Chilean fails the test. If, however, it is the ability to develop a crown of branches above a single stem, it joins the throng. So often in the small garden scene there is a need for a bit of height without weight, without the risk of excessive shade being cast. This is especially the case in city gardens, which are often little more than courtyards, where any conventional tree would soon outgrow its position.

Azara is a South American genus of evergreen shrubs, rather mimosa-like in flower. Only *A. microphylla* is much seen and, while not spectacular in flower, it has real year-round charm. A good specimen will be of 15 feet (4.5 m), with sprays of tiny leaves, rather like those of the common hedging plant *Lonicera nitida*.

By Christmas, the pinhead-sized flower buds can be seen swelling on the underside of the leaf sprays. A hard winter may knock them off, even if the plant itself is not damaged very much. But in most years on a mild February day, where they grow there will be drifts of vanilla scent that can only come from azara. And sure enough, turn over the sprays and there are rows of little yellow fuzzy flowers casting that scent upon the winter air. This is a zone 8+ plant, happy in a sheltered spot throughout most of Britain and in West Coast North America. It certainly should be tried more often, as should the delightful

The distinctive shaggy bark of the river birch (Betula nigra).

interchangeable. North American insect pests, for example, find exotic species easy game—presumably natives have developed a certain resistance to the equally native birch borers and leaf miners. In most cases, therefore, and especially in North America, it is wise to make one's choice from those species known to be reasonably immune. But then not all birches are "silver": all species have the ability to shed strips of bark horizontally and often vertically, exposing new layers and new colors beneath; these may be cream, pink, buff or brown, sometimes shining, sometimes mat.

Beauty of bark is not the only virtue of birches. There is rapidity of growth: a 12-inch-high (30 cm) seedling may reach 20 feet (6 m) in 10 years, yet without any feeling of imbalance. They offer a lightness of branch pattern, often clear yellow autumn color and an elegant winter silhouette. Birches can make admirable lawn specimens as single-stemmed trees, especially when grown in a multi-stemmed form. As the trunks' colors and textures are the prime reason for growing birches, it makes obvious sense to grow one that is multi-stemmed, though this is done far more in North America than Britain, where good three- or five-stemmed specimens are much less commonly available. One way of circumventing the search is to plant several small plants, not all the same size, in one well-prepared hole. Clever early staking can produce an interesting shape at maturity. Such plants are admirable at mediating that area in larger spaces where lawn meets woodland, by linking the vertical with the horizontal.

Silver birch in Britain means *Betula pendula*; in North America, this species is generally known as European white birch.

variegated form, whose leaves are bordered with cream and whose whole effect is airy and charming. It is obviously slower and ultimately smaller than the type, but what a perfect small tree for a smart courtyard. Any well-drained soil will do.

Betula
Birch

Everyone wants a silver birch. But which one? There are white-barked birches from North America, from Europe and from the Orient. All are lovely, but in cultivation terms they are not necessarily

It has a huge distribution in the wild, being the archetypal woody plant of hilly northern regions throughout Europe and into Asia. Thus it will take with impunity almost all the vagaries of Old World climate, making thin, elegant trees of up to 100 feet (30 m), though half that is more typical. Any observation of a bit of natural birch wood will exhibit considerable variation in form, with individual plants being noticeably more pendulous and others showing whiter bark. Particularly fine cultivars have been selected and named.

B. *pendula* 'Dalecarlica' is one of these. Known as Swedish birch, it is recorded from the mid-18th century and renowned for its shower of weeping branch ends and almost fingered leaves. A most beautiful plant, *B.p.* 'Tristis' has a similar habit on a tall, narrow tree with entire leaves. But the pendulous habit is not always synonymous with elegance. Young's weeping birch (*B. p.* 'Youngii'), so often recommended as *the* silver birch for small gardens, is nothing of the kind. It is incapable of producing leading shoots, so it has to be grafted on to a high standard stock from which Mr. Young's growth falls, hiding any silver trunk. The resultant mushroom is admirable as a refuge for small children playing hide and seek but lacks all the grace of common silver birch that grown-ups want.

Two other variants have their uses: *B. p.* 'Fastigiata', as a stiffly upright form, is obviously a botanical oxymoron. 'Obelisk' may also be available, and both are useful to frame a gate or point a vista. Very different is the purple-leaved birch (*B.p.* 'Purpurea'). It can look rather heavy but lights up well with variegated shrubs such as golden elder.

Paper birches (Betula papyrifera) *have spectacular fall foliage and winter-white trunks.*

On the whole, with its combination of virtues, this native is the best silver birch for general use in European gardens. But, inevitably, we are apt to lust after exotic species, which the Orient is very ready to supply. For brilliance of bark, none surpasses *B. jacquemontii* from the western Himalayas; it has a rich creaminess in its color, emphasized by dark lenticel lines. The ground beneath it can be strewn with shreds of shed bark. Growth is upright, with large lustrous leaves that turn a golden yellow in autumn. It should be noted that nomenclatural confusion is apt to dog this plant; authorities now relegate it to a geographic subspecies of *B. utilis*. For most of us, it is better not to worry about such niceties but just look to reputable nurseries offering names of selections that have been given the British AGM, such as 'Doorenbos' or 'Silver Shadow', where other worthwhile species can also be found. *B. ermanii*, for example, from Russia's Pacific rim, is renowned for its beautiful peeling bark, which, though predominantly white, has pink and cream shading. As a multi-stemmed tree it is particularly attractive. Stock has been propagated from the famous specimen at Grayswood Hill in Surrey whose name it takes, and this, with its AGM attached, is worth searching out.

As mentioned above, these Old World and oriental birches, though happy enough in North America in the lower climatic zones, are mostly vulnerable to borers. There is one exception. This is 'Whitespire', a vegetatively propagated form of the Japanese white birch (*B. mandshurica* var. *japonica*), which becomes a good medium-sized tree in the Midwest states (it originated at the University of Wisconsin). Otherwise, North American gardeners should stick with the considerable range of North American birches.

The paper birch (*B. papyrifera*) does for the North American high latitudes what *B. pendula* does for Europe. It has a rather heavier outline, with bigger leaves, and its famously white trunk takes the color higher into the canopy. Splendid multi-stemmed plants are seen in East Coast gardens way up into Labrador. Zone 6 is probably a sensible limit to the south. Any birch that is not

flourishing is more likely to be badly attacked by borers and leaf miners than healthy specimens, and spraying is both an effort and environmentally undesirable. The paper birch commonly exceeds 50 feet (15 m) in the wild and, like most birches, looks well long before maturity. As well as offering fine bark, it has a clear butter-yellow fall color that is outstanding.

The other worthwhile North American birches are a great contrast. The yellow birch (*B. lutea*) and *B. lenta* both have polished brown bark and good autumn color and again exceed 50 feet (15 m) in height. The former seems more able to accept British conditions, as does the lovely river birch (*B. nigra*). Its natural habitat is along streams and rivers in the

A young Betula pendula *'Tristis' hanging with spring catkins.*

southeastern United States. This tree typically branches into three or more trunks low down, which of course helps to show off more of the flaking dark-cinnamon bark. Mature trees are splendidly statuesque. Moist soil is more necessary in North America, with its hotter summers. We should celebrate its ability to thrive in land that stands waterlogged after spring floods. 'Heritage' is a valuable cultivar with pinkish-white bark and is by far the best near-silver birch in such sites.

As is obvious, many birches are from poor soils and situations—the snow-bent *B. jacquemontii* (or *B. utilis*) on 8,000-foot (2,500 m) Kashmir mountainsides are a sight to behold; in cultivation, therefore, they will accept pretty poor conditions. But the mere fact of being away from the home for which they are environmentally programed adds further stress. We may expect birches to be a part of a planned plant association, the light shade they provide being perfect for rhododendrons. But in shallow soil the tree, naturally dominant above ground, will be equally so below, soaking up available moisture like a sponge to the visible detriment of everything beneath. Where deeper rooting is possible, good mulching around the shrubs will permit that desirable layered effect of well-furnished garden space.

Triads of European hornbeam (Carpinus betulus) *are here planted for formal effect.*

Carpinus betulus
European hornbeam

Because it is such an accommodating plant, hornbeam is much more commonly seen clipped into near-anonymity as a hedge. Used thus it can easily be confused with beech, especially as, like beech, it holds on to its dead leaves over winter. Similarly, this phenomenon is a mixed blessing: the advantage of full-russet furnishing from November to March offering interest and better wind shelter than most deciduous hedges is set against the tedium of dry leaves blowing around the spring garden when you thought you had finished sweeping in November.

Two types of hornbeam offer formal vertical shapes ideal for avenues or planting in pairs to frame a view or guard a gate, even without the use of shears. *Carpinus betulus* 'Columnaris' makes a small narrow tree; relatively slow-growing, it is suitable for small gardens. More frequently seen is *C. b.* 'Fastigiata' and this is ostensibly the better choice. However, it has an unfortunate anthropomorphic growth habit, being enviably slim in its fast youth but soon moving into an ever-increasing middle-aged spread. A planted pair can meet only too soon. Single specimens with their sky-reaching branches provide distinctive silhouettes in open-garden or parkland positions. They are rather cypress-like, without that evergreen heaviness.

Where space permits, the normal tree develops noble proportions, growing up to 100 feet (30 m) high with an elegantly layered branch pattern. The oval corrugated leaves turn clear yellow in autumn. Growing wild throughout Europe and into Asia Minor, in Britain it is very much a plant of the heavy clay soils of the Sussex Weald, which gives an indication of its ability to flourish where beech would fail. The bract-fringed fruit clusters remain attractive for much of the summer.

Eastern North America is home to another admirable hornbeam. *C. caroliniana* (in spite of its name, it continues into Canada) is also known as blue beech. It is an elegant, open-branched small tree with a steel-smooth, gunmetal-gray fluted trunk. Also happy on heavy soils, it will tolerate considerable shade from high-woodland canopy.

The other half-dozen hornbeams from the Orient are seldom seen, but a small group of closely related trees—*Ostrya* spp.—occasionally stray from esoteric arboreta and deserve to be more widely planted. *O. virginiana*, known as ironwood in North America, has especially good autumn color and holds on to its typically hop-like fruit clusters into winter. A southern European relation is *O. carpinifolia*. It is really very similar to *O. virginiana*—the diagnostic lack of glands on the twigs has little effect on the gardener's choice, which is best made geographically. Plant the native.

Foliage of shagbark hickory (Carya ovata) *starts to respond to October's shorter days and cooler nights.*

Carya
Hickory

Pecan pie is as American as the star-spangled banner. How wonderful it would be to have one's own supply of these delicious nuts, which come from *Carya illinoinensis*. If one can give it deep, rich soil and broad acres in a moist river valley in the southern states, it is not particularly difficult. Britons need not think about pecans—except by post—and even Americans out of the favored areas where it is native should be aware of its rather sophisticated needs. If the fruit doesn't ripen, the tree isn't worth its space and, as with so many southern species, autumn color is not a feature.

This does not rule out other caryas. They are related to walnuts, with similar olive-green pinnate leaves, usually of two-or-three-pairs-and-a-terminal leaflet pattern. The half-dozen species commonly grown are all from eastern North America, happy in low winter temperatures but demanding the sort of summer wood-ripening that Britain conventionally fails to provide. Nonetheless, smart arboreta south of, say, St. Albans will want to try one or two of the following. If members of a tree genus provide juicy fruit or worthwhile nuts, it seems obscurantist not to plant those known to be edible as a first choice. Thus the shagbark hickory (*C. ovata*) is distinctive for its exfoliating gray bark curling like the caps of judge's wig toadstools. It has dark golden autumn color and this and its close relation shell bark hickory (*C. laciniosa*) are often seen glowing on October woodlot edges from Quebec down to Georgia; residents need to beat squirrels to the small nuts. Though they appear on the thin alkaline soil of the Niagara escarpment in cultivation, a deep

rich loam will encourage good early growth. All hickories resent root disturbance and should be planted young with really effective protection—from rabbits above ground and voles at the collar. Otherwise, one's time is wasted.

Castanea
Chestnut

It's a happy coincidence that pecan, North America's most celebrated endemic nut tree, should here abut that of Europe, sweet chestnut (though some might claim the title for walnut). *Castanea sativa* is also known as the Spanish chestnut,

southwest Europe being the epicenter of its range, which spreads both northward and along the Mediterranean littoral into Asia Minor. Its delicious fruits never fail to make their seasonal mark, brazier-roasted on the streets of Paris and London, stuffed into millions of Christmas turkeys and turned into luxury sweetmeats such as marrons glacés. Perhaps in the hope that such treats would be available in their colonized Britain, the Romans introduced the tree to these islands 2,000 years ago. As a tree, it succeeds right up into northern Scotland but not, unfortunately, as a

The creamy catkins and corrugated foliage of the Spanish chestnut (Castanea sativa).

Indian bean (Catalpa bignonioides) *produces frilly flowers and long seed pods.*

source of chestnuts. Even in southern England, many trees fail to produce worthwhile fruit.

On the grandest scale, sweet chestnut is one of the most magnificent trees we can grow. Its long, shiny corrugated leaves turn gold to bronze before dropping to lie among the silk-lined prickly fruit cases, split open by their fall. In southern Europe, the fall of the fruit coincides with a prodigal effusion of edible fungi that brings whole families out to garner yet another part of nature's bounty. Britons are apt to be more wary and merely enjoy the esthetics of the scene. Documented trees in 17th-century parkland can be over 100 feet (30 m) high with utterly distinctive spirally ridged bark —trees that are spectacular in July when splashed with cream-white flower spikes. On dry acid soils, owners of large lots should plant sweet chestnuts on behalf of posterity. Less grandiloquently, sweet chestnuts make excellent quick-growing screens or nurse plants to protect other things, and they can be pruned to the ground as often as necessary. Such coppicing was once a vital part of the Sussex economy for hop poles, fencing and trug baskets. The wood is prized in southern Europe, and traditional Provençal furniture and floorboards are often of chestnut.

In smaller spaces, though not small gardens, one of the French cultivars famed for regular fruit production might be planted; such selections usually produce one, therefore big, nut per case, and cultivars such as 'Marron de Lyon' begin producing nuts as teenagers. Unproductive but handsome as foliage trees are variegated and cut-leaved variants 'Albomarginata' and 'Aspleniifolia'.

These plants are not for the continental climate of eastern North America, where a wonderful native equivalent existed before being almost eradicated by fungal disease.

It was hoped that the Chinese sweet chestnut (*C. mollissima*), which is immune to the blight and does well in zones 4–9, would become an alternative, but its fetid-smelling early summer flowers rather put it out of the running as a garden tree.

Catalpa
Indian bean

Mark Catesby's *Natural History of Carolina, Florida and the Bahama Islands* (1730–47), with its splendid engravings, brought some of the most graphic accounts of southeastern American flora and fauna to mid-18th-century London. Often they were elegantly shown with associated birds and insects. It all seemed amazingly tropical (after all, Louisiana is 1,500 miles/2,400 km to the south), and one of the most powerful images is of the Indian bean (*Catalpa bignonioides*). In Britain, it retains its exotic image, with its wide spread of velvety dessert-plate-sized leaves, summer heads of delicate flowers and clusters of long brown "beans." For this reason, these trees are not plants for woodland, nor really for the countryside. In Britain, at least, they are townies and, suitably, some of the best specimens to be seen are in Palace Yard, Westminster— you can't get more central than that. Acceptance of hot, dry summers and atmospheric pollution follows.

Catesby's catalpa is native to the southern states of Georgia, Florida and Louisiana. Where it flowers well the display is splendid. Individual flowers are often described as "foxglove-like," but this fails to indicate the frilled outline and the exotic purple and gold honey-guide markings—the effect in July is more like bunches of aerial nemesias. Typically, mature trees are as wide as high, up to

40 feet (12 m) in both directions. June flowers seen on a tree of taller, narrower outline are usually of an otherwise almost identical species, *C. speciosa*. This has a more northerly distribution in the wild, into Illinois, and hence is noticeably more frost-resistant, certainly down to zone 4. Both are remarkably tolerant of soil type, so long as drainage is good.

The oriental catalpas are not often grown, but a cross between the Chinese *C. ovata* and the Indian bean is making a claim to be the best for general planting in Britain. This is *C.* x *erubescens*, which quickly makes a big tree and flowers at an early age. It has a cultivar known as 'Purpurea', with chocolate-colored young leaves, while the Indian bean itself has the splendid golden-leaved *C.b.* 'Aurea'. This makes a smaller tree than the type, and, as any floral effect is diminished by the leaf color, little is lost when it is grown purely for foliage effect. Standards cut back in winter produce striking lollipop heads for summer display of truly exotic effect.

Cercidiphyllum japonicum
Katsura

Plants that offer their leaves as the major attraction are bound to be winners over the flower-power lot. Floral display is likely to be sadly fleeting, and even the pleasures of anticipation, on the better-to-travel-hopefully-than-to-arrive principle, can be blighted for a whole year by a single late-night frost. The argument ought to extend to the fact of evergreen foliage being tops because of its omnipresence, but that is exactly its trouble: like the poor and plastic roses, it is always with us. All of which considerations make *Cercidiphyllum japonicum* a three-season star; only winter is without its lovely foliage. It is one of the best garden trees for a great swath of the temperate world. The only surprise is that it remains uncommon in spite of its being perfectly easy to grow in any normal soil, acid or limy. Only summer-dry spots and irrevocable frost pockets are to be avoided. Winter cold is not a worry: there

The leaves of the katsura (Cercidiphyllum japonicum) *resemble golden coins as they unfold.*

The Judas tree (Cercis siliquastrum) *needs perfect drainage and good summer sun.*

are fine trees in eastern Germany and all down the East Coast of North America. It likes a continental climate.

The name *Cercidiphyllum* is fully descriptive, meaning "having leaves like *Cercis,*" but that is only helpful if you know what *Cercis,* the Judas tree, is like, and that is not common either. The leaves of *C. japonicum* are like rounded hearts, and they unfold softly pink along slender branchlets before developing fresh green sprays that are maintained throughout summer. Then with the first hint of frost,

the show begins. Individual leaves become tinged pink and darken to ruby; others turn clear yellow. In different years, presumably in response to a varying sequence of climatic change, the overall display can be gold or it can be red. Then they fall, producing wafts of aromatic scent like that of ginger treacle pudding.

C. japonicum is commonly known as katsura, the original non-Linnaean Japanese name. When young, it is bushy and twiggy and the decision has to be made whether to train it up

conventionally on a single trunk. For garden effect and perhaps to emphasize its oriental origin, an irregular two-or three-stemmed specimen is best. It associates wonderfully with waterside planting and enjoys the moisture.

Cercis
Redbud, Judas tree
One of the joys of a Mediterranean holiday in spring is the inevitable association, seen in gardens, public places and even roadsides, of wisteria and Lady Banks'

rose tumbling through olive branches. Nearby, sometimes a part of the tangle, are the startling rosy-lilac clouds of the Judas tree (*Cercis siliquastrum*.) Here are two exotics and two natives, wonderfully combined. Farther north it is difficult to arrange the necessary wood-ripening for these plants in an open-garden site. The climbers need warm walls and selective pruning, while the cercis needs a little cosseting. But in the case of the cercis, it's worth the effort, and its eventual rugged appearance on a low trunk makes it a slowly developing living sculpture, ideal in sunny town gardens and courtyards; 25 feet (7.5 m) in height and width is a fine tree in captivity.

The bright clusters of pea-flowers (followed by purplish pods) occur conventionally on well-ripened shoots from the previous year, but they also appear back on spurs from wood that is older and extend even to the trunk itself, as if the wood cannot bear to give up its productive youth. And all this before the leaves unfurl—a unique sight in early June. Good treatment given at the start to a strong young plant will encourage early trunk development. In Britain, the traditionally drier southeast seems to show the best specimens—there is a great crawling creature (the naturally low, often self-propping branches are said to demonstrate their shame as being the tree on which Judas hanged himself) in Cambridge University Botanic Garden, but noticeable climate change brings most areas into play.

Eastern North American gardeners are likely to miss out on such southern Europeans that cannot take their winters. But in simple visual terms, flowering redbud, *C. canadensis*, a kissing cousin

Autumn gold leaves of the American yellow wood (Cladrastis lutea).

native from Massachusetts to Mexico, is almost identical—it has the same brilliant spring display, the distinctive foliage, the brave shape (though without the excessive Judas-myth hang-up), the black bark, the rustling pea-pods. Easy to please, it succeeds on heavy alkaline clay in Ontario to acid sands in the South. Although a wilding, the redbud is fully sophisticated enough to furnish the smartest town garden: perhaps the lovely white-flowered form is even more so.

A recent addition to the couple of flower-color-variant cultivars is 'Forest Pansy', which has splendid soft reddish purple foliage in the early part of the year, though the effect pales as the summer advances. This is also worth cultivating in Europe as a unique foliage plant. *C. canadensis*, however, seldom performs well and is best left at home.

Cladrastis lutea
American yellow wood

This is one of the most beautiful of hardy trees. Though a native of North Carolina

The tiered branches and white-and-green foliage of Cornus controversa.

white laburnum and think how the world would queue up for that. Trails of brown pea-pods follow.

In North America, the need for summer shade of conservatories and picture windows, which otherwise heat up unacceptably, encourages tree planting close to buildings. Not only does this help visually to link house with garden: the canopy demonstrably reduces energy use in air-conditioning. Yellow wood, leafing late and deeply rooting, is an ideal tree for this role. There is, however, a point to watch out for: the somewhat upright branches develop narrow, potentially weak crutches, which are a hazard in exposed situations. Damage from a late-winter ice storm just as sap begins to move often results in prodigious wound "bleeding," though once tidied up no ill effects are apparent. But preventative bolt-and-wire stays are worth considering, as is occasional surgery to reduce weight of the canopy before damage occurs. Such a lovely tree deserves every care.

Cornus
Dogwood

The common shrubby, suckering dogwoods with red and yellow bark are among the brightest of winter garden ornaments. But the genus extends far beyond these and offers several beautiful small trees from southern Europe, the Orient and both sides of North America. Go to the Carolinas in late April to see the eastern flowering dogwood at its best. There, in every garden, around every building and against every classical pillared portico and pediment are clouds of dogwood, white on white. The effect is magical. There, *Cornus florida* is a plant of such ubiquity that it would appear

and Kentucky, it is happy in zones 4–8. Early growth is rapid and self-sown seedlings often appear, soon making a tree 30 feet (9 m)high; twice that is possible. Bark is smoothly gray and beech-like, and the typical pinnate leaves of a legume are a distinctively clear pea-pod green. There is a marvelous annual moment as they silkily unfurl, creating a haze-like effect. Leaf fall is a golden glow.

In European gardens where summers may fail to ripen the wood, this may be the sum total of yellow wood's virtues, and it is quite enough to make it worth planting. However, at home in North America, just before that haze-gray stage and joining with it, the tree becomes a cascade of flowers: long panicles of creamy pea-flowers whose warm scent is carried on the wind. Picture a tall, elegant unable to fail, but we always need to remember that care with site, soil, planting and aftercare are essential in the inevitably artificial conditions of the garden. Knowledge of natural habitat, too, is always valuable. Pests and diseases are much less of a problem when plants are growing well. Here then is a naturally wild woodland-edge plant enjoying some shade and a soil that does not dry out erratically; 20 feet (6 m) high and as much across is usual. With a natural distribution from Ontario (just) down into Mexico, hardiness obviously relates to the origin of any given stock, and cultivars can be taken as being of garden worthiness through much of its range. Among the best are 'Cherokee Princess', 'Cloud Nine' and 'Pluribracteata' with double flowers. 'Cherokee Chief' is an exciting red cultivar, but it doesn't outshine the ethereal beauty of the others. Pink cultivars can seem altogether too sweet and sickly.

This spectacular spring display—the "flowers" actually being composed of four petaloid bracts with a cluster of true flowers making a yellow button at the crossing—is just one of the tree's virtues. In good years, there is also a conspicuous crop of shining red fruit followed by purple and red autumn leaf color. And when that is done, the gray netted bark is attractive throughout winter, especially seen against snow. Altogether this is a wonderful plant. Sadly, a fungal disease known as anthracnose has become rife in North America, particularly affecting plants under stress.

Across the continent is C. *nuttallii*, another woodland-edge plant, from British Columbia southward. This is the Pacific dogwood, a splendid tree up to 100 feet (30 m) high in the wild, with creamy-white

Large bracts surround the little flower clusters of Cornus kousa *var.* chinensis.

"flowers" close to 6 inches (15 cm) across. It needs the moist mildness of the maritime west—rashly, it carries immature flower heads from autumn till they open in spring —and is well worth trying more often in Britain in moist, deep woodland soil. Less choosy is a famous hybrid between these two American species, itself of American origin, 'Eddie's White Wonder'. It fully deserves its AGM status in Britain, being

easier in Europe, as well as in its homeland, than either of its parents.

Except in real Eastern dogwood country, the most reliable of all flowering dogwoods on both sides of the Atlantic is C. *kousa* var. *chinensis*. At 20-to-30 feet (6–9 m) high, it is one of the great small garden trees. It flowers in June; the showy bracts, white gradually turning toward pink, are narrower and more pointed than the Americans are and line the upper sides of near-horizontal branches like icing on a cake. The fruits, too, are very distinctive: pink arbutus-like berries and much more pleasant to the taste. Good, long-lasting autumn tints, pink and red, complete the season. This is a plant for any but the cruelest of hot limy soils; full sun or part shade are equally acceptable.

An exciting new hybrid group called C. x *rutgersensis* has been introduced from Rutgers University in New Jersey. These promise to combine the virtues of C. *florida* and C. *kousa*, so will be valuable on both sides of the Atlantic. Specialist nursery lists should be scoured.

While petaloid bracts produce the display of these flowering dogwoods, with the cornelian cherry (C. *mas*), that central button of true flowers is the conspicuous part. These crowd the leafless twiggy branches with yellow in February and March, after the witch hazels and before the forsythias, making a brave early spring show. Unfortunately, they smell like old fish boxes and are no use for cut decorations indoors. In some years, there is a good autumn crop of red oval "cherries," which make an unusual preserve, good with cold meats.

C. *mas* has to be encouraged to develop a decent trunk but can reach 30 feet (9 m) or so. Gold and white variegated forms are available, useful as border shrubs but slow to attain tree form. Growing in zones 3–8 and in any soil, this is one of the easiest of plants, though, as always, good initial treatment pays dividends.

Two other dogwoods are well worth consideration. Here it is foliage and form that earn them their keep. C. *controversa* from Japan and China is distinctive in its regular horizontal branching habit,

The fine, flaking bark of Turkish hazel (Corylus colurna).

making a fine tiered tree, ending up rather flat-topped and 40 feet (12 m) high. This is even more spectacular in a good specimen of its white-variegated form, which can be truly dramatic. Too often, however, young plants are unwilling to develop a good central leader to carry the horizontal branchwork; you need to choose a good strong specimen and give it the best possible start.

Similar but smaller in all its parts is the North American C. *alternifolia*. An undemonstrative little tree of quiet beauty—layered branches, flat heads of little white flowers whose pink stems and blue fruits continue the interest— this is ideal to link garden sophistication

with natural growth. It seeds around happily in the Great Lakes area. The charming variegated 'Argentea' seldom attains tree status even in the eyes of the most optimistic.

Corylus
Hazel

It is not usual to think of the European hazel *Corylus avellana* as an ornamental garden plant, or as a tree—prophets again not without honor except in their own country—but it does have much going for it. In Britain, hazel was traditionally coppiced on a dozen-or-so-years rotation under oak standards and the 20-foot-high (6 m) wood provided woven fencing, sheep hurdles, stakes and sticks for

The narrow evergreen leaves and scarlet fruit of Cotoneaster salicifolius.

supporting peas in the kitchen garden—nothing was wasted. A percentage of plants was thus cut to the ground each year so that a crop was always ready for next winter's work as the others built up. The oaks needed a century or more before being felled. In visual terms, hazel makes a perfect intercession between garden and woodland (particularly fine against the grace of silver birches); a few plants are more sensibly encouraged to carry five or seven stems, with the biggest being taken out every or every other year. The resultant open vase shape permits the February primrose-yellow lambs'-tail catkins to hang out to best effect. There may even be a crop of hazel nuts if the local squirrel population is somehow foiled.

In really small spaces where the impression of trees without their height is required, the extraordinary contorted hazel, *C. avellana* 'Contorta', is a good choice. Planted in a raised bed to give a bit of early presence, it soon provides a remarkable focal point of twisted branches, twisted catkins and twisted leaves. Selective pruning will produce a sort of bonsai form 10 feet (4 m) high: any straight growths must be expunged at the base. Such sucker growths are from the ordinary hazel stock on which 'Contorta' is often grafted; plants propagated on their own roots from layers are obviously best.

Closely related is filbert (*C. maxima*), with its longer nuts within fringed husks. It has a remarkable dark, purple-leaved

form, heavy in the mass but effective against pale variegated leaves of, say, *Acer platanoides* 'Drummondii'.

By comparison with these somewhat twiggy plants, the Turkish hazel (*C. colurna*) is a major tree. Given space, it makes a superb triangular silhouette; it has a strong corrugated trunk, low branches almost to the ground and thick foliage. Typical purplish hazel catkins (male flowers) appear in spring and then in autumn, there are clusters of nuts enclosed in husks like bristly sea anemones. Coming from Asia Minor, this tree is well adapted to a continental climate and does as well in eastern North America (zones 4–8) as in Britain. Any decently drained soil will encourage a 30-foot (9 m) tree in as many years. Twice that may well be reached—a marvelous plant for parkland on both sides of the Atlantic.

Cotoneaster

These plants have become so much a part of our gardens that they haven't, even in a century and more, developed a common name. Cotoneasters they remain, regardless of pronunciation. There are dozens of species, from tiny ground-hugging mats to the robust shrubs that, with suitable pruning, can bring the following into our category of garden trees. These are all Himalayans, happy in any well-drained soil in zones 5–8. In mild areas or mild winters, most can behave as evergreens or certainly keep their leaves into the New Year: equally, they can be deciduous. All have a decent show of white flower clusters in May and June (often irresistible to newly emerged queen wasps), but it is the brilliant show of fruits that makes them so valuable in the garden, with a display that can last for months.

C. frigidus is the biggest; round-headed trees of 30 feet (9 m) or so are not unknown, carrying huge crops of large berries. It is rather a coarse plant. Its virtues, however, combined with the greater elegance of species such as *C. henryanus* and *C. salicifolius*, have given us a number of splendid hybrids capable of making wide-spreading showering trees up to 20 feet (6 m) in height, laden with fruit. They are splendid as lawn specimens or used in open positions among trees.

'Cornubia', usually listed under *C. × watereri* but sometimes considered as a cultivar of *C. frigidus*, has won all the horticultural Oscars: AM, AGM and FCC. *C. frigidus* 'Saint Monica' is as good, with the additional charm that many of its leaves turn red as they fall. Color variants are the optimistically self-descriptive *C. × watereri* 'Pink Champagne' and *C. salicifolius* 'Exburenis', with yellow fruits that become pink-tinged. These are left much longer by the hungriest flocks of winter migrant birds before going the way of all winter berries.

Crataegus
Hawthorn

Here is another big genus in the rose family (*Rosaceae*), closely related to the preceding cotoneasters and equally renowned for fine fruiting. One obvious difference is that the thorns fully deserve the title; pruning can be a hazardous occupation and fallen hedge clippings are fierce enough to puncture a car tire. No wonder the common European hawthorn has been the ultimate animal-proof hedging plant since the Middle Ages. Unclipped, it is also a very beautiful plant. So, too, are several native American

species, which compensate for the lack of big cotoneasters in cold areas.

Because it is such a frequent plant in Britain and much of Europe, where uncut hedges foam with scented may blossom ("Ne'er cast a clout till may be out" may well refer to this plant rather than the calendar month), may, or hawthorn, is apt not to be considered a legitimate garden tree. We are always seduced by the exotic.

But as countryside is pushed ever farther away, repatriation of some of its best-loved plants becomes entirely logical. *C. laevigata* (syn. *C. oxyacantha*) and the almost identical *C. monogyna* are the two common European species. All soon make a rather contorted little tree up to 20 feet (6 m) high with branches crossing in all directions, to the despair of conventional gardeners. It is probably best to accept this

This hawthorn cultivar, Crataegus laevigata *'Rosea Flore Pleno', has double flowers.*

as typical, but it is vital to remove the wickedly armed shoots that may emerge from the gnarled trunk below head height. In late May, the tree is lost in a cloud of snow-white, and then in September the fruits, or haws, start to color. After leaf fall, the full display becomes evident, lit up by the low winter sun. Pink and red ('Paul's Scarlet') double-flowered forms are available—spectacular in May but usually lacking fruit. Known in North America as English hawthorn, it is apt to be a martyr to a disfiguring leaf spot. In turn, the splendid American species seem to lack some of their sparkle in a European maritime climate.

C. *crus-galli* is the cockspur thorn. It makes a tightly branched tree 20 to 30 feet (6–7 m) in height and as much across. The huge shining thorns can be 3 inches (7 cm) long. Typical white flowers, glossy leaves, leaves that color well in fall and a brilliant berry display lasting into the New Year make this a plant for most—if not all—seasons, happiest in the lower zones of the 3–7 range.

Washington thorn (C. *phaenopyrum*) is one of the most distinctive of the genus. Glossy vine-shaped leaves that color well in fall, a creamy white flower display and fine crops of dark red fruit hold on almost till Easter.

The potential of other North American species continues to be exploited by plant breeders trying to extend the range, and a number of new cultivars are appearing in reputable nursery catalogues. C. x *mordenensis* 'Snowbird', C. *punctata* 'Ohio Pioneer' and C. *viridis* 'Winter King' are just three; all combine the usual hawthorn virtues in various measure.

One distinctive oriental thorn well worth European attention is C. *orientalis* (syn. C. *laciniata*). The name refers to the deeply indented leaves, which have gray undersides that flash in the wind. The usual white flowers produce marble-sized, coral-to-yellow-red fruit that last well. This is a sophisticated little tree, admirable as a lawn specimen backed by a dark conifer.

All hawthorns are remarkably tolerant of poor soils, easy to please and wonderfully responsive to good early care.

Davidia involucrata
Handkerchief tree

Here is a plant of great mystique. The story of plant collector Ernest "Chinese" Wilson trekking through the Chinese Himalayas in search of the single specimen reported to him and, amazingly, finding it has passed into botanical folklore. Not least because, poor man, when he got

The "handkerchiefs" of Davidia involucrata—*long fluttering bracts.*

there, only a stump remained, local villagers having cut it down for firewood. The story improves: other trees were found, seeds collected, and this splendid tree was introduced to Western gardens just a hundred years ago. Trees from early collections are in every major garden and arboretum, now 60 feet (18 m) high and looking superficially like a large-leaved lime tree or linden. Except, of course,

The oleaster (Elaeagnus angustifolia) *is one of the best small gray-leaved trees.*

when in flower in June; then *Davidia involucrata* fully lives up to its common name. True flowers are rather like those of a flowering dogwood, pressed together into an inch-wide "button," but what attracts the pollinators is the unequal pair of huge, white papery bracts fluttering in the breeze. The bigger can be up to 8 inches (20 cm) in length, and when they fall, the ground is covered with white.

Davidia is pretty frost-hardy (zones 5–7) and grows quickly in any decent soil. But it is slow to produce its first handkerchiefs —that takes up to 20 years—and it will be perhaps another 10 before the proud planter can look up into the branches and enjoy the spectacle that Wilson went so far to see.

Elaeagnus angustifolia
Oleaster, Russian olive

Trees, we feel—unless it is autumn color time—are green. We live in a green world but not one that is monochromatic: green is a single short word for a vast range of visual sensations. Not only does every green leaf have its own specific tint, but this is modified or emphasized by its shape and texture; downiness or polish absorbs or reflects light; length and strength of petiole determines whether the leaf hangs stiffly or flutters in the wind. Green is not just green.

Yet in the ornamental garden, contrast in foliage is a part of the considered design. Gray leaves are apt to be a feature of hotter, drier lands, adaptations to shrug off sunlight or to protect pores from excessive moisture loss with tight-packed hairs. There are surprising exceptions to this sort of ecological presumption: why, one wonders, are silver poplar and white willow plants of moist soils? The fact that

The lizard-like bark of Eucalyptus pauciflora.

they are makes them acceptable in the wider countryside beyond the garden where their Mediterranean near-look-alikes seem out of context.

These do have considerable value, especially to evoke an image of the warm south. Olive is the classic evergray, and while everyone knows it is not a plant for permanence in much of Britain (a notable exception would be the famous old tree in the Chelsea Physic Garden upon which fruit actually ripens), numbers are imported annually for smart London gardens. But then London's microclimate is becoming markedly milder.

A very similar effect can be achieved without the risk by the oleaster or Russian olive, the biggest of several species of *Elaeagnus* with distinctive gray foliage. Suitably pruned to a single trunk and then prevented from developing too thick a head of branches, this provides a lovely semi-weeping tree 20 feet (6 m) or more high. Leaves are long and willow-like and the silvery effect extends to the young shoots, the outside of the floral tubes and then to the small olive-like fruit. The scent on a hot June evening can be quite intoxicating. It is said that in Persia, men locked up their women when the trees were in flower to avoid such dangerous proclivities.

Coming from continental eastern Asia, this is an extremely hardy plant, accepting zones 2–7 and virtually any soil. In North America's equally continental climate the overall silvery effect is especially marked, and it is dramatic sited against dark evergreens.

In the same context another Asiatic (and seaside European) is worth consideration. This is the sea buckthorn (*Hippophae rhamnoides*). Just as silver-gray as *Elaeagnus angustifolia*, if rather stiff in habit, it has the advantage of brilliant orange berries that persist throughout winter. But it is uncomfortably spiny, and a group is necessary to ensure pollination. For a rougher spot in poor soil.

Eucalyptus
Gum tree

Gum trees spell Australia as much as koala bears and Sydney Opera House, so there is some conceptual difficulty in integrating them into the northern hemisphere garden scene. They exude exoticism, as their leaves give off aromatic oils. Evergreen (or more often evergray) foliage, frequently changing shape as a plant moves from the juvenile state to adulthood; distinct, somewhat skeletal, branch patterns; spectacular marbled bark; a fuzz of bee-busy white flowers (perhaps it's just as well that the red-flowered species lack hardiness)—all combine to make a very definite statement that, like marriage, is not to be embarked upon wantonly or lightly.

Of the 500 or so species in the wild, which include trees taller even than the giant redwoods, only a dozen or so eucalyptus are reliably hardy in Britain and similarly in West Coast North

America (California, of course, has its own rules). This is based upon their provenance; seed collected in Tasmania and high altitudes of, especially, New South Wales is likely to be genetically more frost-tolerant. But, as always, cold winds and poor soil drainage are more often killers than simply low temperatures. Some species seem to develop added hardiness with age, but this can only be worked at and waited for, as gums must be planted when young if good roots are to develop to support the rapid top growth. Spring planting is best. It is

essential that a plant is not permitted to rush upwards in the first couple of years, for it is bound to blow over in the third and no amount of staking will hold it afterward. Thin young plants are best cut back to 12 to 24 inches (30–60 cm) in the second spring, the resultant growth being carefully selected for the future. While a single trunk usually develops, fine effects can be obtained from a plant pruned to develop a three-to-five multi-stemmed clump (a harsh winter may do the job for you), rather as for silver birch, thus capitalizing upon gum's ability to regrow

from a "stool." These can be selectively replaced as they exceed the required height. The snow gums *E. pauciflora* and *E. p.* subsp. *niphophila* are especially effective grown like this. Wonderful snakeskin bark, sickle-shaped gray leaves and relatively restrained growth to 30 feet (9 m) make these much better small garden gums than the taller and commoner *E. gunnii*. They associate well with buildings, especially when their shivering leaf shadows are thrown onto a color-washed wall.

In general, species with an open habit and smallish leaves, these and others such as silver mountain gum (*E. pulverulenta*) and *E. coccifera*, as well as *E. gunnii*, are the most satisfactory, providing form without too much weight and, in northern winters, evergreen shade.

In larger landscapes, though not perhaps into the full countryside, these showering gray shapes can make a fine effect against the dark formality of conifers.

Eucryphia

There are not a lot of southern hemisphere trees which are fully safe in northern gardens—our inhabited latitudes are much closer to the pole—but such is their beauty that we are bound to try. South Africa offers nothing, but Chile and Australasia, sharing a number of genera, are more productive. The eucryphias are one such genus, mainly tall, tight evergreens with a splendid display of shining, white scented flowers in late summer and autumn. In their homes, several are renowned bee plants and eucryphia honey is famous.

From Chile, *Eucryphia glutinosa* is the one exception to the evergreen rule, and the fact that it does not hold on to its leaves makes it the hardiest of the genus.

Eucryphia x nymansensis *'Nymansay' is perhaps the best late-summer flowering tree.*

Beautiful in foliage, flower and autumn color, it seldom really takes on tree status. However, its virtues are wonderfully combined with *E. cordifolia* in the hybrid *E. x nymansensis* 'Nymansay', producing an upright quick-growing tree, rather like a smaller evergreen Dawyck beech. In August and September, good specimens become columns of white, each flower like a white hypericum, every cup of petals holding a boss of pink-flushed stamens. While a bad British winter will beat it up, browning or even partially defoliating it, healthy plants generally recover and are fully worth the risk. A bit of woodland protection is a help but not essential.

Fagus
Beech

There must be many contenders for Housman's Shropshire lad's "loveliest of trees." He chose wild cherry (*Prunus avium*) for that blissful spring moment when the branches are "hung with snow." But what then? European beech (*Fagus sylvatica*) must be way up the list of anyone's choice of top arboreal beauties for the length of its attractions, in spite of the fact that the floral show is nothing much. Male flowers are little hanging mops of stamens, whose pollen the wind blows on to the stigmas of equally insignificant female flowers. These become hard and nut-like, clanging in late-cutting lawn-mower blades and holding two or three seeds in secondary sharp-edged shells, pleasantly edible but hard work to reach.

The beauty of beech lies in an almost perfect combination of smooth, shining foliage elegantly borne, a well-balanced branch pattern and the smoothest silvery gray bark. Leaves unfold from the long sharp buds as the palest shimmering green,

The golden weeping beech (Fagus sylvatica *'Aurea Pendula') is an elegant, narrow tree.*

the canopy gradually filling in so that summer shade in a beech wood prevents almost any understory, emphasizing the church-pillar effect of the stone-gray trunks. Autumn goes golden, first on the branches and then on the ground where the leaves resist decay for weeks.

This is a major tree that grows quickly and 100-footers (30 m) are frequent, with a spread to match, though surprisingly it lives to no great age—a couple of centuries or so and then decline sets in. Such a size, it would seem, precludes use in small spaces, but this need not be so. A specimen that it is planned to replace offers much throughout its youth, but a wiser choice would be one of the narrow forms. The Dawyck beech has the form of Lombardy

poplar and looks superb framing a vista or, with more space, in a small group.

Beech has produced more variants than perhaps any other deciduous tree, with close to 50 being offered by nurseries. There are fern-leaved cultivars such as 'Aspleniifolia'; splendid weeping beeches include 'Pendula'. There is the golden foliage of 'Zlatia', and 'Tricolor' is variegated with pink edging; popular purple and copper beeches are ubiquitous, and it is even possible to find combinations of variants. 'Aurea Pendula' describes itself, while 'Rohan Obelisk' is a narrow, purple, fern-leaved tree.

It must be emphasized that these amazing cultivars are sophisticated garden trees not to be taken out into the countryside, where nothing should try to upstage the native tree. The caveat applies especially to the purple beeches; they are wonderful trees but hugely dominant in the landscape.

Drawing the line only at full coastal exposure, beech accepts all situations and soils, hilltops and deep valleys, limestone and acid sands, though it resents drought. It easily shrugs off the vagaries of British weather, and it is happy in zone 5 in North America. It also makes an admirable hedge; the late shoot growth caused by clipping holds on to the dead leaves throughout winter, creating a warm, furnished appearance. This is only to be regretted when they eventually drop and blow about in March and April winds.

America's own beech, *F. grandifolia*, is a similar and beautiful native tree from north of Lakes Ontario and Erie and on southward. The leaves are larger and less toothed than *F. sylvatica* and it suckers profusely, so that a mature tree appears to grow in a developing grove. Though less amenable to cultivation than its European cousin, it should always be preferred for countryside planting. It is not happy as a town tree, nor in an oceanic climate; nor particularly are the half-dozen oriental species occasionally seen in arboreta.

Fraxinus
Ash

There are about 60 species of *Fraxinus* strewn around the northern hemisphere, mainly medium- to large-sized trees. Apart from specialist botanical collections or arboreta, few are seen and, indeed, they are not particularly ornamental. But there are exceptions. In Europe, *Fraxinus excelsior* is rather demeaningly known as the common

The dramatic branch cascade of weeping ash (Fraxinus excelsior 'Pendula') *in winter.*

ash; certainly it is very often seen, happy on most soils and often in inhospitable places. An old gnarled ash tree and a sycamore or two are the frequent companions of small hillside farms in the north of England and in Scotland. A well-grown mature specimen is a noble sight, and a replacement should always be in the pipeline and given plenty of space. Wherever there are existing trees, seedlings are frequent and it may be enough to permit several to grow before selecting the best for shape and position. Straight ash timber remains valuable for handles of implements and other wood

turning; it is also wonderful firewood, burning fiercely even when green.

For the closer garden scene, *F.e.* 'Jaspidea' is more suitable and can be kept in check for the beauty of its yellow winter wood, against which the typical black buds stand out.

Victorian gardens in Britain invariably had a weeping ash or two on the lawn, and one often remains in old vicarage gardens—a weeping ash is a period piece that makes a splendid silhouette, especially when it has been grafted high and trained up. Without help, it is a living arbor ideal for children's games.

Mount Etna broom (Genista aetnensis) *offers a fountain of golden flowers in June.*

A couple of American species do well in Britain—the white ash (*F. americana*) and the green (*F. pennsylvanica*). The white ash makes splendid timber, but neither develops the brilliant fall colors that make them such worthwhile landscape trees in their homes. The white ash exceeds 50 feet (15 m) in height and, in good soil, is happy in zones 3–9. It takes on its most brilliant fall red at the northern end of its range, and selections such as Autumn Purple ('Junginger') are available that emphasize the fact.

There are also cultivars of the green ash that have particular virtues: *F. pensylvanica* 'Summit' and *F.p.* 'Patmore' are both more regular in their branching pattern, making very tidy trees, and have the advantage of not producing fruit. Green ash is tolerant of exposure and poor soils.

All these conventional ash trees are grown for their stately size and ability to take the harshest conditions, while maintaining elegant pinnate leaves and a fine outline. But like most of our forest trees, they are wind-pollinated and thus have no need of insect-attracting flowers. Against this general rule, there is a small group of insect-pollinated "flowering ash trees." From southern Europe eastward comes the manna ash (*F. ornus*); it makes a distinctive round-headed, heavily leaved tree that in June becomes a cloud of creamy white. Deep breaths drawn close to it will identify a slightly fetid scent, rather like that of privet (to which, surprisingly, the ashes are related), but not enough to disqualify it in big gardens.

Genista aetnenis
Mount Etna broom

Here is the ideal plant where height is required without any weight and with almost no shade being cast. This would seem to be an impossibility, but *Genista aetnenis* is a tree in spite of itself. Coming from the arid hillsides of Sardinia and Sicily and specifically the high black lava slopes of Mount Etna (where in fact it looks pretty ratty), it has learned to survive on very little. To that end—and to avoid excessive transpiration where there is not much to transpire—it has virtually dispensed with leaves, with the gaseous exchange occurring instead through the stomata on the green branches. Once a good central stem is trained up, it makes a lovely showering screen of branches, especially in late June and July when all are lost in a mass of yellow pea-flowers, 15 to 20 feet (4.5–6 m) high.

Obviously, since it comes from such a habitat—the ultimate in Mediterranean maquis—the most important aspect of cultivation for this tree is perfect drainage at the root. Given this, and provided it is given the sunniest spot available, on most soils, Mount Etna broom is amazingly tolerant of the normal vagaries of the British climate, though it does not enjoy the high rainfall of the northwest. It is the perfect plant for a warm courtyard or deck and can even be placed on the south side, safe in the knowledge that little sun will be lost to people or plants in its lea. It is also one of the few small trees that can be happily incorporated into herbaceous plantings, and it can become a major player in midsummer associations of blues and yellows.

Gleditsia triacanthos var. inermis
Thornless honey locust

Although this excellent American tree (a thornless form of the type) can reach a height of 70 feet (20 m)—and indeed is superb when it does—it has the advantage of developing a maturity of form when young and hence is also suitable for small spaces, from which it can be removed

The thornless honey locust (Gleditsia triacanthos *var.* inermis) *succeeds in city spaces.*

when it outgrows its spot. Also, with its delicate ferny foliage, only the lightest of shade is cast from the spreading crown of branches. Flowers are inconspicuous, with separate male and female spikes; much more apparent are the distinctive long twisted seed pods. They are seldom set in Britain in sufficient quantities to matter but fruit heavily in North America, where the concept of a "dirty tree" becomes a bit obsessional. Unproductive selections include 'Moraine' and 'Shademaster'.

Typical foliage is a fresh, bright green turning bright gold (even in Europe) in autumn. 'Sunburst' has become a favorite small garden tree for its early yellow leafing becoming green by midsummer.

A form of dense shrubby habit, 'Elegantissima' is sometimes used in formal situations, in parterre beds or lining a walk. When suitably grafted onto a stem of the type, pretty lollipops are produced. Staking is essential and needs to be as elegantly contrived as the plant it supports or else the whole effect is lost.

Gymnocladus dioica
Kentucky coffee tree

On a vastly bigger scale, gymnocladus plays the same surprising game as aralia. A summer canopy of huge doubly pinnate leaves up to 36 inches (90 cm) long by 24 inches (60 cm) across is shed in autumn—first the leaflets and only eventually the central midrib—leaving a gaunt, rough-barked skeleton that catches and holds wind-blown snow wonderfully.

The foliage is distinctively verdigris green in color throughout summer (but without much autumn excitement) and effectively hides the spikes of greenish flowers and the developing pods. These, after leaf fall, hang black and stiff—up to

The Kentucky coffee tree (Gymnocladus dioica).

The snowdrop tree, or silverbell (Halesia).

10 inches (25 cm) long—on the end of the twigs. As gymnocladus is monoecious — that is, with separate male and female trees—it is possible to choose fruitless named clones such as 'Espresso' and 'Stately Manor'. But why would one?

As gymnocladus is a rather rare North American native with a New York State to Tennessee distribution, a zone range of 4–8 is acceptable, as are most soils; 60 to 70 feet (18–20 m) in height and almost as much across are possible. It is a tree for hotter summers than Britain can generally provide, but it is certainly worth planting in the south at least, even if it won't reach its North American potential. There is nothing remotely like it.

Halesia
Snowdrop tree, silverbell

It is difficult to know why the North American silverbells (or snowdrop trees in Britain) are not seen more often. On the face of it, this is a tree in which every prospect pleases: small to medium in size, with a light, open habit, producing clouds of white or pink bell-like flowers in May and interesting winged fruit in autumn—everything combines to make what should be an irresistible choice. Perhaps the competition from cherries and crabs, more outgoing in their spring glory, tends to overshadow the quieter beauty of halesia. Perhaps they are a little more choosy in their needs.

The two or three species—about which there has been much botanical discussion over the years—are all native to those species-rich streamsides and moist valleys of inland Georgia and Virginia, and they seem to keep these conditions very much in mind. Winter cold is not a problem (zones 5–8 or so), but a cool, rich root run, especially in the early years, encourages the development of a good branch framework.

Halesia tetraptera is a recent name that lumps *H. carolina* and *H. monticola* together. Where catalogues still list them separately, the latter, known as mountain silverbell, is the one to choose. It is likely to be a bigger, stronger plant, with larger flowers as well.

Starry flowers of Hoheria sexstylosa.

The fluttering leaves of Idesia polycarpa.

Hoheria

Here is a small genus of delightful New Zealand plants to which more attention should be given. In big gardens, as seen wonderfully effectively in Ireland, they appear as very big shrubs (but then everything there is apt to appear larger than life); in smaller spaces their tree status is clear. Obviously, with such an origin, these are plants for mild conditions: they generally do well on the western side of the British Isles and from Oregon southward in North America.

The effect of a hoheria is that of a particularly elegant mock orange with white showers of wide, open scented flowers in July or August, quickly building up to a small tree of 20 feet (6 m) or so. *Hoheria lyallii*, with its gray-backed leaves, should perhaps be the first choice ; *H. glabrata* is similar—and there is some confusion in nurseries between the two. Both are deciduous.

A fine hybrid between *H. glabrata* and *H. sexstylosa* originated in a garden in Anglesey whose name it bears, *H.* 'Glory of Amlwch' (the w is pronounced as u). It makes a slender tree of narrow leaves, evergreen in mild gardens or mild winters, covered in flowers in August.

Any decent garden soil seems to suit these accommodating plants. They are,

perhaps, not long-lived, but that is not necessarily a disadvantage; there are so many good plants clamoring for our attention and space in our gardens, and small trees don't have to live for ever.

Idesia polycarpa

This is an unusual and interesting Chinese tree that, even if it never gets to flower and fruit, is worth consideration for its foliage alone. The leaves are heart-shaped on long pinkish petioles and flutter from the near horizontal branches. Ultimately, it reaches 50 to 60 feet (15–18 m) in height, and, its habit being rather sparse, it provides only gentle shade.

The greenish flowers in long spikes make little show; this comes with the autumn display of trails of brilliant red berries, dramatic when seen against a blue sky. Unfortunately, as it is monoecious, both male and female trees are necessary for fruit, and as available plants are likely to have been grown from seed, there is no way of knowing until a plant flowers (and this may be after 20 years or so) which sexes are being grown. Just as well, therefore, that foliage alone earns its place. Vegetative propagation from known trees is possible, but such stock, grown from cuttings, is not often available. All of which sounds something of a hassle, but the effort is well rewarded; fine trees, fruiting heavily, can be seen at, for example, the Royal Botanic Gardens at Kew in Surrey, and Wave Hill in New York City in very different climates and conditions.

Ilex
Holly

In British and western European gardens, holly is apt to be a very specific term; it refers to the wonderful wild holly, *Ilex aquifolium*, found wild from Scotland in the north throughout continental Europe and on into western Asia. A plant of folklore and of literature, it permeates both Christian and pre-Christian cultures. That it is laden with symbolism should not be surprising; no other wild plant demonstrates so graphically, with its glittering evergreen leaves and brilliant winter berries, the hope of life's renewal from one year to the next.

Holly has been cultivated since early times, so it is not surprising that variants have been observed and propagated offering variegated leaves, gold or ivory, thornless or excessively armed leaves,

upright and weeping forms. But the wild type is remarkable enough. It can make a tall tree well in excess of 50 feet (15 m) in height, thin and open in mixed woodland but with a relatively narrow shape, furnished to the ground. Where there is no competition, it makes a great pillar of shining leaves. It is interesting to note how the leaves are extremely prickly on the

lowest branches and become less so, presumably as they grow beyond the reach of browsing animals, near the top.

The old belief that a well-berried holly in autumn presages a hard winter has no validity. What produces such a crop is effective pollination of the little white scented flowers in June, with good weather that then encourages pollinating

Variegated weeping holly (Ilex aquifolium *'Argentea Marginata Pendula'*).

A well-berried wild holly tree: a perfect evocation of the Christmas season.

unpruned screen or a trimmed hedge, holly offers good protection to a garden in its lea.

Among the best of the named varieties, 'J.C. van Tol' fruits well and has almost spineless leaves, and 'Green Pillar' lives up to its name. Of variegated types, 'Golden van Tol' is excellent; so, as foliage plants, are 'Golden Queen' and 'Silver Queen'. The catch is that both are male in spite of their names. Therefore (as long as there are male plants around), it makes sense to combine the advantages of colored leaf and berry on the same plant. 'Golden King' and 'Silver Sentinel' do just that. Sexual confusion on all sides.

European holly (*I. aquifolium*) is an oceanic plant, so is not suited to most of eastern North America. Fortunately, the New World has some good native hollies of its own that are fully adapted to the continental climate—they don't travel well to Europe or compete with its holly.

I. opaca is the one specifically known as American holly: it is native from Massachusetts down to Florida and inland to Missouri. The huge number of selections available are apt to be rather local, and it is important to choose cultivars known to succeed in one's own area. Ultimately, though slow-growing, it makes a fine cone-shaped tree to 50 feet (15 m) in height. Foliage and fruit lack luster but any broadleaf evergreen existence is worth celebration in the East Coast winter scene. Similar shape and texture but more of a shine come from cultivars of *I.* x *attenuata* (*I. cassine* x *I. opaca*): these are happier in the South, as names such as 'Savannah' and 'East Palatka' suggest. North American hollies flourish, but enjoy some shelter from drying winds, in zones 6–8.

insects, and the certain presence of male and female plants. Obviously only the latter bear berries. Again, the length of the display depends upon weather: a long, mild autumn offers birds more food, and a rush on holly berries, often just before we hope to harvest Christmas branches, is avoided. (Yellow berries always hang on longer.)

With good soil preparation and preferably late-September planting, one can confound holly's reputation for slow growth: over 12 inches (30 cm) a year is easily reached. Whether used as a tall,

There are numerous Asiatic hollies, varying from small box-like shrubs to big broad-leaved trees. Few of the latter are seen outside specialist collections—a loss to the rest of us—but one is highly distinctive and worth pursuing. *I. pedunculosa*, which comes from China and Japan, accepts zone 5–7 conditions in North America where it is becoming more valued. Eventually a small tree 20 to 30 feet (6–9 m) in height, it is strangely unholly-like. The leaves are glossy and unarmed, rather like those of arboreal ivy; even more unusually, the berries hang on long stalks, so very different from the usual clustered effect.

Juglans
Walnut

Although there are several fine oriental walnuts with long, pinnate leaves, they are seldom seen and even less likely to be available. Thus there are just two species frequently grown, one from each side of the Atlantic. The common walnut (*Juglans regia*) is an Old World tree, cultivated since gardening began and hardy enough to grow well and fruit in Scotland and in North America, succeeding down to zone 4. But it prefers warmer climates, and commercial walnut production occurs in France, in other parts of southern Europe and in California. In Australia, the old French cultivar 'Franquette' is becoming popular; this is a late-flowering form with nuts of particularly good flavor. It is worth emphasizing that the flavor of fresh, newly fallen nuts is of an entirely different order than that of the usual dried-out Christmas offerings.

Although walnuts can make large trees—heights of up to 100 feet (30 m) are known—*J. regia* remains suitable for

This walnut (Juglans regia *'Mayette'*) *produces good crops at an early age.*

relatively small gardens, where normally any prospect of a tree this size would appear ridiculous. It leafs late and drops its foliage early, branching is open, and as a result, the effect is never heavy. And if it does outgrow its space, it recovers well from branch-pruning. Eventually there is always the happy thought that the wood is valuable. Deep, rich soil encourages strong early growth. Although seedlings are likely to make good trees, it is wise to choose a cultivar that offers good crops of nuts. These include other French selections such as 'Mayette' and 'Parisienne' as well as

'Buccaneer' and 'Broadview', all becoming more available from the trade.

J. nigra is the black walnut of eastern and central North America. It is a most impressive tree, often with a straight trunk, bare of branches for 20 to 30 feet (6–9 m) and supporting a great head of pinnate aromatic leaves. The green fruits are almost spherical and drop in huge quantities over a long period; unfortunately, the inner nut cases are extremely hard and it is difficult to extract the flesh. It does well in Europe but is more a plant for parkland than normal gardens. It has a not entirely undeserved reputation for discouraging, by a root exudation, competing plant growth beneath its canopy. Fortunately, the frequently heard statement that "nothing grows" under a black walnut is exaggerated. It seems to vary, but members of the rose family (*Rosaceae*) seem particularly susceptible to the upas-like blight and should be avoided. The decomposing outer cases stain anything they touch, so evergreen ground cover beneath black walnuts is best avoided; herbaceous plants and deciduous shrubs on the other hand can start each season anew.

Kalopanax septemlobus (syn. *K. pictus*)

This is the only member of the ivy family (*Araliaceae*) that is a really hardy tree. In arboretum collections, that would be sufficient reason to grow it, but in fact it is sufficiently distinct to earn its place in less elevated circles. It is native to Japan, Korea and the Russian far east.

Kalopanax is rather gaunt in youth with its thick prickly branches but attains if not grace then undoubted presence with age,

Leaves of Kalopanax septemlobus.

attaining over 50 feet (15 m) in height. The leaves have a noticeably tropical appearance in the temperate landscape, somewhat maple-like but evocative of fatsia or the true castor oil plant, ricinus. Indeed, one collection was named *Kalopanax ricinifolius*. Leaf size—often well beyond 12 inches (30 cm) across— and depth of the lobes varies greatly; those on offer such as *K. septemlobus* var. *magnificus* and *K. s.* var. *maximowiczii* are worth seeking out.

It flowers better in North America's continental climate than in softer, milder Britain. In good years, it is covered with angelica-like heads of cream florets in July.

Any decent soil suits, in zones 4–7.

Koelreuteria paniculata
Goldenrain tree

From China, Korea and Japan comes this splendidly distinct tree. Though it may reach 30 to 40 feet (9–12 m) in height, its beauties are displayed at an early age, and hence it is happily suited to quite

Seed pods of Koelreuteria paniculata.

small spaces. It has been grown in Britain since the 1760s, but individual trees are typically not very long-lived. Early growth from seed-grown stock is rapid, soon building up a head of elegant divided leaves and sometimes even flowering in five years or so. As the tree develops, the display is spectacular in July with great airy sprays of golden star-shaped flowers. These are followed, rather improbably, by large, inflated lantern-like seed pods that make their own show, first green, then gold, then brown with rattling seeds inside. Self-sown seedlings sometimes appear.

In Britain, goldenrain does best in the warmer counties where there is also a bonus of good yellow autumn color. In North America, where fall expectations are higher, this aspect is not considered particularly noteworthy. There, in zones 5–8, goldenrain is happily accepting of hot, dry spots without becoming bedraggled before the summer is out. Eventually trees become wide-spreading and quite statuesque in branch pattern. It is surprising that this has not become a much commoner tree; it deserves attention in gardens large and small.

Laburnum
Goldenchain

There was a time when, in England at least, laburnum was considered a rather down-market little tree. It had been overplanted along 1930s town bypasses and in too many suburban front gardens, and familiarity bred its inevitable contempt. What shattered that foolish image as much as anything was the photograph in virtually every gardening book of Rosemary Verey's Barnsley House laburnum tunnel underplanted with alliums, where the golden chains of scented pea-flowers swung down to join the onion's purple globes. It has been copied a thousand times.

While planting thus as for a close avenue and then training the branches over metal arches is a charming conceit, as a small free-standing tree, laburnum is still one of the sights of early June. *Laburnum anagyroides* is the common laburnum, starting the show in late May, but as the flower racemes are rather short, it lacks the swaying grace of its close cousin the Scotch laburnum (*L. alpinum*), with its chains 12 inches (30 cm) long.

Hybrids between the two are grouped under the name of *L. x watereri*, and in the cultivar 'Vossii' the flower racemes can be up to 24 inches (60 cm) long. A well-furnished plant blowing in the wind is an amazing sight.

Laburnums are commonly sold as standards on a 6-foot (1.8 m) stem, but the effect can be dangerously lollipop-like. A much more elegant effect comes with two or three stems spreading from the base and leaning out over a path or a terrace wall.

Flowering is frequently followed by heavy crops of green "pea-pods," and it is worth noting that these are very poisonous; babies in strollers, it is sensibly suggested, should not be left in laburnum's gentle shade when it is in fruit.

The so-called purple laburnum (x *Laburnocytisus* 'Adamii') is an extraordinary graft hybrid, or chimera, between common laburnum and *Cytisus purpureus*. In flower, it dottily displays branches of pure laburnum, pure purple broom and a strange brownish combination of the two all at the same time. If not a thing of beauty, it is certainly a conversational joy forever; nothing could be more strange.

In North America, laburnums grow well enough in zones 5–7, but flower-set tends to be erratic at the warmer end of the range.

Laburnum, especially when well grown, is one of the finest sights of the June garden.

This Chinese privet (Ligustrum lucidum) *makes an admirable evergreen in a warm spot.*

Ligustrum lucidum

As broad-leaved evergreen trees are not a common feature in temperate gardens, this fine Chinese privet is to be welcomed. It succeeds best and is certainly more floriferous in warm spots. In Britain, beautifully balanced trees, 30 to 40 feet (9–12 m) high, flourish in town environments, enjoying protection from buildings and seemingly immune to air pollution. See it at its best in North America, in Georgia and Alabama, where it also fruits prodigiously.

The flower sprays start to appear in spring and gradually develop throughout summer. The buds open at last in September, ivory-white and sweetly scented. This is a plant of continual interest. Several variegated forms have appeared, of which the best is 'Tricolor', whose rather narrow leaves have white edges, pink-flushed when young. As with all plants whose photosynthetic leaf area is reduced, this is less vigorous than the fully green parent.

Liquidambar styraciflua
Sweet gum

Liquidambar is one of the most evocative names in the plant lexicon. It refers, in fact, to the aromatic resin produced by *Liquidambar orientalis*, a species seldom if ever seen in cultivation. But the name seems equally apt for the famed fall color of the American *L. styraciflua*, though amber is just one of the tints that may be produced; shades of red, purple, bronze and yellow occur and develop on different trees over a long period in autumn.

Native from New York southward and inland to Illinois, sweet gum is a striking tree in summer as well, with lustrous almost star-shaped leaves, rather maple-like, over 2½ annual inches (6 cm) across. No big tree—it will attain close to 100 feet (30 m) in height and half that across—is capable of such dramatic fall color. In oceanic Britain, the display is apt to be erratic, and cultivars that generally perform well should be sought out. *L. styraciflua* 'Lane Roberts' is one such.

In its home, although there is little likelihood of the display failing, selections such as 'Burgundy' and 'Festival' have been made. But there is a downside—the prodigious production of the hard, spiny fruits, 1 inch (2.5 cm) or so across, that litter the ground for several months from

The autumn display of Liquidambar styraciflua.　　　　*The tulip tree, or tulip poplar* (Liriodendron tulipifera).

September on. This is seldom a problem in Britain where, again, a milder, moister climate inhibits flowering and fruiting of east North American plants.

Liriodendron tulipifera
Tulip tree

The tulip tree was one of the first big North American trees to be grown in Britain. Bishop Compton had it at Fulham Palace in the 1680s, and he was not the first. Certainly it is one of the most distinctive of all trees for foliage, the leaves being of a unique shape rather like (if there were such a thing) a sort of truncated violin. Held on slender stalks, they move in the slightest wind. In southern England, trees have exceeded 100 feet (30 m) in height but almost twice

that is reached in its happiest homeland. Though tulip trees are wild from Massachusetts and Ontario (just), down to Florida, it is in the rich river valleys of the Carolinas and Georgia that the tree shows its full potential, quickly making a tall, straight tree with a regular branch pattern that provides another name: tulip poplar.

The tulip tree is obviously capable of taking its place in major landscapes with a fine foliage effect throughout summer that turns clear butter-yellow in the autumn. In spite of its name (which is apt to be misappropriated by some magnolias) it is not a colorful flowering tree. The flowers are indeed tulip-like and individually very beautiful, strangely painted orange, yellow and green, but they blend so easily into the mass of foliage that their effect is muted.

One may wait 25 years before they appear anyway. Following leaf fall, the narrow cone-like fruits are more noticeable.

Accepting that one's space cannot take an adult tulip tree, it is perfectly possible to enjoy the foliage, rather exaggeratedly large in the early years, in its own right. If height but not width is required, *L. t.* 'Fastigiatum' is available, and for slower growth the brilliant yellow and green-leaved 'Aureomarginatum' can be chosen. This is unlikely to get huge; indeed it can be difficult to establish and to get to develop a decent leader. But it is worth every effort.

Winter cold is not a problem, zones 4–9 being acceptable, but lush summer growth especially in youth is easily damaged in exposed positions.

Chilean myrtle (Luma apiculata) *has superb cinnamon-stick bark.*

Luma apiculata

In moist, mild zone 9 gardens of Cornwall and Devon and also in Ireland and western Scotland, this marvelous South American tree-myrtle is one of the most consistently attractive sights gardens can show. Young plants are charming, small-leaved evergreens, slightly box-like (as is the timber from big specimens). In August and into September, the creamy white flower-fuzzes dot the branches, followed in good years by purple fruits, pleasantly sweet to the taste.

But it is essential that it is happy enough to grow quickly toward and attain tree status (half the 60 foot/18 m height seen in its Chilean and Argentinean temperate forest home is to be celebrated), because as the lower branches are shed, the superb bark is seen. This is clear cinnamon-colored and bits flake off to show warm cream patches beneath. Competition with other trees will cause it to reach for the light, and there will be more bark for one's

money. With open-lawn specimens, encouraging pruning will be needed to expose the bark.

Luma apiculata can be tried in western Britain and the mild West Coast of the United States, where moisture and acid soil suitably combine. Pretty variegated-leaved forms typically remain disappointingly bushy: it's the tree we want.

Magnolia

It is not just latent puritanism which suggests that brilliantly showy exotic flowering trees are out of place in our northern landscapes. The native plants don't welcome them and the light is not strong enough to compete, so it is perhaps as well that so many of them just don't do. Or is that sour grapes? For when there is a tree or group of trees that does make a floral show, we rush toward it with glad cries. Never more so than with magnolias. But then every prospect pleases; it is never coarse, never ill-mannered, but poised,

considered, balanced. In a word, beautiful. All of which is perfectly true much of the time in most places; what is vital, of course, is that the right plant is chosen for the right place. This is the case with all garden trees, but somehow with magnolias, the stakes are higher, just as the rewards are greater.

There are difficulties. Late frosts can play havoc with early flowering types to the point at which, even if the plants grow well, one must decide whether floral success one year in three or four is sufficient return on the investment, not just of initial cost and garden space but of worry and mental exhaustion. A tree full of hope one week becoming a mass of tattered brown Kleenex the next may be just too much to bear yet again. It comes back again to suitable choice of which magnolias to grow; nothing can be guaranteed, but risks can be reduced.

The commonest magnolias on both sides of the Atlantic are the results of a cross first made in France early in the 19th century between two Asiatic species, *Magnolia denudata* and *M. liliiflora*. Named *M. x soulangeana* after its breeder, this is the classic magnolia with narrow tulip-shaped flowers, 4 to 5 inches (10–12 cm) high, standing on leafless branches in April and May. Typically white flushed with purple at the base, richly fruit-salad-scented, they open wide (hence the American name saucer magnolia) before falling petal by waxen petal just as the plants' leaves unfold. The best forms include 'Lennei', 'Rustica Rubra' (a rich purplish rose color) and 'Brozzonii', with huge late flowers.

Because *M. x soulangeana* grows easily, flowers early in life (as such plants from cuttings or grafts usually do) and is always available, it is apt to be the one everybody plants. There it is, 5 feet (1.5 m) high in a little London front garden with a dozen or two flowers showing heartening color in March. In April, trees 30 feet (9 m) high foam with blossoms in front of classical columns in Washington D.C. A month later still, equal in size and perfection, they provide annual astonishment in southern Ontario. How they love a continental climate that is certain when spring is irrevocably sprung. In much of countryside Britain, the utterly frost-hardy buds, safe in their silvery fur coats, are tempted into unwary opening: today's balminess, tonight's frost. Every wile to reduce the problem—light tree canopy above, avoidance of early-morning sun, west-wall protection—is worth trying. They will all help. As will, in the early years, rushing out with horticultural fleece and clothes pegs, but one soon tires, muttering about its "having to take its chance."

All of which is even more compounded with the great tree magnolias of the Himalayas. In famous Cornish gardens, we make our genuflections before breathtaking plants of *M. campbellii*, 40 feet (12 m) high with its 12-inch-wide (30 cm) pink and white water-lily flowers adrift against a blue sky. This in February or March and after 30 or 40 years: one needs a suitable climate, plenty of space and a reasonable expectation of a long life or primogeniture under control, a combination given to few.

The closely related *M mollicomata* (perhaps just a geographical variant) may well open its first deep pink flowers in a dozen years from seed. Plant a four-year-old and one is nearly there, though for

The striking branch pattern of a mature Magnolia x soulangeana *in winter.*

some time there is a feeling that the huge flower size is out of scale on a relatively small plant.

This last thought is emphasized—though happily easily discounted by pride of success—with the new generation of hybrid tree magnolias. Purists will say they lack that certain something of the great species; but they have yet to reach full maturity, and meanwhile, they extend the possibility of such plants into the garden of everybody who needs a small-sized tree. The search for "instant *campbellii*s" in North America, Europe and New Zealand has produced superb plants that flower later in the season or do so over a length of time, which ensures that some miss the frost every year. Vegetatively propagated, they flower when young—often in three or four years—growth is vigorous and upright branching trees develop in a decade or so. In limited space, they can be limbed up like any other young tree to encourage a single trunk. With magnolias,

this is best done in August when the sap run has slowed down. These wonderful plants are available from specialist nurseries (look in the RHS *Plant Finder* or in North America in *Andersen's Source List*). Swallow quickly any stingy considerations of cost and think of the joys to come: 'Star Wars', 'David Clulow', 'Galaxy' and 'Pegasus' are names to seek.

The sheer extravagance of these big-flowered magnolias should not blind us to other groups in this marvelous genus. More elegant in small gardens and in early age are plants derived from *M. kobus* and the star magnolia (*M. stellata*). The pure white *M.* x *loebneri* 'Merrill' and pink 'Leonard Messel' have been around for half a century, the latter renowned for the fact that its open flowers accept two or three degrees of frost without turning to mush. Newer cultivars of this type with huge quantities of small flowers, small leaves and an elegant twiggy branch pattern (those with *M. salicifolia* in them have lemon-scented bark) include 'Marillyn' and *M. s.* 'Wada's Memory'.

North American gardeners will be very familiar with the native cucumber tree, *M. acuminata*, which makes a fine foliage tree in the landscape. With its rather strange pewter-green blossoms, it does not have much floral impact, but its hardiness offers a valuable constituent. Indeed, a breeding program at Brooklyn Botanic Garden has developed a unique group of magnolias with deep cream or yellow flowers. 'Elizabeth' is still the favorite, easy and quick to grow and flower, hardy and late enough to miss spring frosts (even in Scotland, I find), yet just soon enough to make its main show before the leaves unfold. Some lime in the soil, which the *campbellii* lot abhor, is no worry. It may well reach 50 feet (15 m) or so in height but hasn't yet had time.

The United States provides more marvelous magnolias. *M. grandiflora* is one of the noblest evergreen trees from any flora anywhere in the world. When perfectly suited, at home in the southern States or around the Italian Lakes, it develops into pyramids 80 feet (25m) high, clothed to the ground with glossy, suede-backed leaves. Great creamy white scented flowers lie along the branches. Not a plant for everyone. But one or two modern North American cultivars offer smaller size, youthful flowering and greater hardiness; 'Edith Bogue' is even suggested for zone 4. In a very sheltered spot, no doubt.

A final group of magnolias are also North American. They don't make much of a floral show, though the individual, rather spidery flowers, heavily scented, are always of interest. But they are almost lost against the spectacular leaves. *M. macrophylla* is the doyen. Coming from Ohio down to Florida and hence happy in zones 5–8, it makes a tree 40 feet (12 m) high and as much across, with individual leaves 24 inches (60 cm) or more in length, flashing white beneath. If this seems altogether too large a scale, the related *M. tripetala* is easier to accommodate and possibly to grow. This is known as the umbrella tree, which reflects the way the paddle-like leaves radiate out from the branch ends. The red fruit clusters, rather cone-like, often make a good autumn show.

Magnolia campbellii, *perhaps the most beautiful in its genus but slow to reach flowering size.*

Malus
Apple

There is evidence that apples were cultivated in Asia Minor over 8,000 years ago, gradually spreading westward with developing civilizations. No doubt for most of this time our modern separation of "eating" and "cooking" apples from "crab" apples was unknown; indeed it is only over the past few hundred years that gardeners' selection of distinct forms has moved from the tiniest trickle to the current flood. Today, therefore, we are likely to consider the culinary fruits as entirely different entities from their "ornamental" cousins and separate them in different parts of the garden. But all belong to the same genus, *Malus*, and merely vary in the desirable attributes for which they have been collected in the wild (there are *Malus* species from all over the northern hemisphere), found by chance or consciously bred in cultivation. Joseph Addison's famous lines in the *Spectator* of 1712 have already been quoted, and we must agree that the beauty of an apple tree in flower is unsurpassed. That unique pink-and-whiteness has made "apple-blossom" a description and a color in its own right. When laden with ripening fruit or when, in winter, showing off the elegance of effective pruning, such trees can fully earn their place in the garden scene well beyond the flowering period.

Though apple trees are no more difficult to grow than any other small tree, there are interesting complications. Fruit trees are usually grown as a union of two plants—the named variety is grafted or budded on to a rootstock. The chosen rootstock determines (though moderated somewhat by soil and situation) the ultimate size of the tree. Rootstocks vary from the very dwarfing— ideal for little formally trained trees—to the very vigorous, which will produce big orchard-furnishing trees. There are garden roles for both and for the variants in between. A second concern is genetic. While most culinary apples (*M. domestica*) are diploid (with two complete sets of chromosomes in each body cell), a few popular varieties such as 'Blenheim Orange' and 'Bramley's

Malus domestica *cultivars are worth growing for their blossom alone.*

Seedling' are triploid, with 51 chromosomes. Triploids are poor pollinators and all apples show some amount of self-incompatibility. Thus any choice must take two factors into account, the chromosome group and the flowering period of the variety it is hoped to grow. An apple tree may flower prodigiously but set hardly a fruit. In fact, however, the possible pairings are many, and any book on fruit culture or good nursery catalogue will offer advice on this. Often, too, plants in neighboring gardens will fortuitously do the job. In addition, many crab apples make good pollinators for culinary types; there is, of course, no effect upon fruit produced—'Cox' will still be 'Cox'. Only if trees were grown from the seeds would unpredictable offspring occur. Which is why some sort of grafting method is used to ensure the known, named and desirable line.

Reference to specialist books on growing fruit may just be intimidating, with rootstock numbers, pollination charts, pruning instructions, pest avoidance and disease control, but it should not be. Such books (a splendid example is the RHS *The Fruit Garden Displayed*) are counsels of perfection and rightly so. However, in the context of garden trees, any apple, plum or pear can be grown as an ornamental flowering tree, with any crop a bonus. And a treat. Choose a couple of favorite varieties that are compatible, or plant a single "family tree" where three or four compatible varieties are grafted onto one rootstock.

If the making of crab apple jelly is a much-loved autumn ritual, then a couple of cultivars are essential. *M.* 'John Downie' carries huge crops of almost pear-shaped red and gold fruit, perfect harvest festival material. The challenge is whether to pick them and lose the display or keep that and miss the jelly. Planting *M. pumila* 'Dartmouth' as well, with its less showy, purplish apples is perhaps the answer. Both have a fine white floral display.

These crab apples seem to be less bother,

but since they are derived from apple species, albeit different ones, the situation is not vastly changed; it's just that less is expected of them. Nonetheless, some are among the most spectacular flowering trees we can grow, especially in the colder zones of 3–4. Much breeding and selection has been done in North America to cater to this need, and literally hundreds of cultivars have been named. More appear each year. But they do not displace some of the original species and some early cultivars that are still among the best.

Of the former, *M. hupehensis* is the first choice: Ernest Wilson (he of davidia fame) thought it the best flowering tree he ever introduced. This was in 1900, and now there are fine plants 40 feet (12 m) or so high that annually demonstrate his confidence. The tree becomes a great white cloud of flower in late April as the pink buds open up. Autumn displays of little green-yellow, flushed red fruits can be almost as spectacular, and in America especially they are joined by fine leaf color. The Japanese flowering crab *M. floribunda* is just as floriferous, rather smaller in size. Its branch pattern can become a bit of a mess and needs occasional thinning. The fruits, on long stalks, look like small yellow cherries. These two are the classic flowering crab apples used with other species and their hybrids to produce the vast range of modern crabs.

In general one wants effective flowering and fruit that lasts well on a tree which develops a reasonable shape (few hybrid crabs are remarkable here) and texture for winter effect when nothing else is happening. Well-known cultivars include *M.* x *zumi* 'Golden Hornet', 'Harvest Gold', *M.* x *robusta* 'Red Sentinel', 'White

Malus hupehensis, *the finest oriental flowering tree introduced by Ernest "Chinese" Wilson.*

Angel' and *M.* 'Winter Gold'. *M.* x *schiedeckeri* 'Red Jade' and Weeping Candied Apple ('Weepcanzam') have, as the latter suggests, a pendulous habit. By contrast, vertical branch pattern and a narrow silhouette offer plants for formal pairing or for further avenue effects. *M. tschonoskii*, a fine Japanese tree with spectacular autumn color, *M. baccata* 'Columnaris', a zone 2 plant, and *M.* 'Van Eseltine' with double pink flowers 2 inches (5 cm) wide, are good examples.

'Van Eseltine' is about as dark in flower color as I am willing to go. The *M.* x *purpurea* group, though often admirable for their floral fortnight, tend to move into a dark foliage phase for the whole of summer, and this can look unhappily heavy in the garden scene.

Mespilus germanica
Common medlar

Plants are affected by fashion, and the current interest in this little tree is clearly

Medlar fruit (Mespilus germanica) *are only edible once they have become over-ripe.*

influenced by the restoration of old gardens or new developments of "traditional" design. Certainly medlar has been in cultivation since early times; it is included in Charlemagne's fruit list of AD 800 and is referred to in 13th-century records of the garden of Westminster Abbey. And of all hardy fruits, it has probably changed the least over the centuries, still only edible when half-rotten. Pleasant enough but pretty pointless. Mrs. Beeton, Victorian England's most renowned home economist, offers a recipe for medlar jelly to be eaten with cold meat.

But as a small, gnarled tree in the garden it is more distinctive. Long, ridged leaves among which pink-flushed flowers 1½ inches (4 cm) wide are irregularly strewn; in autumn, the mature (one can hardly say ripe) fruits are like small brown golf balls as the foliage, in good years, takes on brilliant russet tints.

A wide-headed small tree, it reaches heights up to 20 feet (6 m). 'Dutch', dating from the 17th century, and 'Large Russian' have bigger flowers and fruit than the type but are said to be less flavorsome—not a comparison often to be made.

Morus
Mulberry

Mulberry is not just a tree, it is also a color: that rich, purplish magenta with which the fruit so irrevocably stains the clothes of anyone unwise enough to take a late summer picnic under its branches. The great tree at the Glyndebourne opera house in Sussex must have provided enormous employment to dry cleaners over the years: white dinner jackets especially never recover. But with the warning comes an even stronger recommendation to plant the black mulberry (*Morus nigra*). It has been cultivated since time immemorial in Asia Minor, where it probably originated, and throughout Europe. It is said the Romans brought it to Britain, and it has even been postulated that trees from that time survived into the Middle Ages and the rebirth of gardening, and that their offspring exist today.

Because of this reputation, black mulberry is inevitably considered a plant of old gardens, and it is assumed that all large trees—it can reach up to 40 feet (12 m) in height, with great spread—are equally venerable. This is not so: rather like old English sheep dogs, they take on an aura of age in early middle life. Nor is their reputation for slow growth justified: vigorous young shoots of a couple of feet a year are not unusual. It may certainly be a dozen years or so before much fruit appears, and then gradually, the tree will settle down to develop the typical gnarled trunk and branch pattern. As trees age, the weight of branches and leaf canopy can often be too much and a limb may crash down; those important to the shape of the specimen may be propped or wired, while others might be reduced in winter when danger of "bleeding" is least.

Black mulberry looks particularly well in association with buildings, but because of falling fruit it should be sited carefully. The fruit itself, like large loganberries, is delicious when fully ripe and makes wonderful preserves, ice creams and puddings. Leafing is late and leaf fall early, so shade is only cast in full summer, when it is appreciated.

There are named forms—'Chelsea', 'Wellington' and 'King James'—ostensibly propagated from significant trees, but in fact they vary little if at all from the rest. King James, if we are to believe the stories attached to all the old trees that he supposedly planted, must have spent his life doing little else. He did, of course, attempt to establish a British silk industry, but his advisors chose the wrong mulberry.

Black mulberry is considered a zone 5 plant—low winter temperatures are not a problem. And it definitely needs summer heat (this makes north of England fruiting erratic, though the plant grows well enough in well-drained soil). So it is surprising that it is almost entirely the white mulberry (*M. alba*), from China, and the native red mulberry (*M. rubra*) that are grown in North America.

M. alba is the tree on which silkworms feed and which has been grown in the Orient for thousands of years. Though about the same size, it is less statuesque than the black mulberry, and its fruits, pale pink to reddish when ripe, are rather insipid. More often seen in gardens are weeping cultivars top-grafted on to a standard of the type plant—these include 'Urbana', 'Chaparral' or simply 'Pendula'. Indeed they have become something of a cliché in suburban front yards that have been "landscaped." These domes of foliage 10 to 15 feet (3–4.5 m) high can look at home lining a formal walk or as an entrance-gate pair.

Heavy limbs of black mulberry (Morus nigra) *are supported here with a circle of stakes.*

Several southern beeches (Nothofagus) *make distinctive trees throughout the British Isles.*

North America's wild red mulberry (*M. rubra*) is a looser, more open tree, especially when grown in or on the edge of woodland. It is not a first choice for garden ornament, but its copious fruiting over a long period makes it well worth adding to plantings devised to attract wildlife. Native from Massachusetts down to Florida and Texas, this is a zone 5 plant, and is happy in any reasonably moist situation.

Nothofagus
Southern beech

Just as there are true beeches that circle the northern hemisphere—Europe, the Orient and North America—so, south of the equator, the southern beeches circumscribe the globe. A number come from New Guinea, but those of interest to temperate gardens are native to southern South America and New Zealand. Unlike species of *Fagus*, which are all deciduous (holding onto dead leaves in a beech hedge doesn't count), several of the best of these are elegant evergreens. None are happy on the thin limestone downland soils that the European beech accepts so readily in southern England and France; this may be associated with the need of nothofagus for high humidity and plenty of moisture at the root as much as an acid soil.

Thus it is not surprising that nothofagus grows best in western Britain—a National Collection is at Crarae on the shore of Loch Fyne in Argyll. But indicating that the soft maritime climate is not essential for all, trees can be seen doing splendidly at Dawyck, in the hills southwest of Edinburgh, in very chilly conditions.

Nothofagus antarctica spreads right down to Tierra del Fuego and so is highly frost-resistant. It quickly reaches 40 feet (12 m) or so, with a thin habit made up of elegant horizontal sprays of little leaves. It often takes on an irregular leaning habit that foresters abhor but which can be welcome in the garden scene.

N. obliqua is known as the roble beech. Its bigger leaves are rather like those of hornbeam, and it quickly attains forest-tree status even on thin, sandy soils. Needing more summer warmth, it seems to be the best southern beech for England's eastern counties. The fresh green of opening leaves appears earlier than on most British natives; autumn tints are often good. The roble can grow very fast—shoots 3 or 4 feet (90 cm–1.25m) long occur, which is positively eucalyptus speed. As with the gums, it can blow and break at the crown, but what a splendid tree to nurse other plants in the early years.

The evergreen species are likely to be less frost-tolerant, but two, the Chilean *N. dombeyi* and *N. solanderi* from New Zealand and its mountain form *N.s.* var. *cliffortioides*, make good trees over much of Britain—the usual requirements being met. All are unusual in the sprays of small leaves, which prevent such robust evergreens from heaviness. These are wonderful plants for positions of importance but where winter shade from a tree 50 feet (15 m) high is acceptable.

Nyssa sylvatica
Tupelo

If gardeners in eastern North America lament that they cannot grow southern hemisphere trees, they are fully compensated by members of their own flora that are so much happier at home.

Nowhere is this more true than with those species renowned for fall color; nowhere else is the tupelo so spectacular.

Nyssa grows wild from Maine and southern Ontario down to Florida and Texas (which incorporates zones 4–9), sometimes on the edge of swamps,

Tupelo (Nyssa sylvatica) *can be one of the most brilliant components of the fall scene.*

sometimes on dry soils. In cultivation it is difficult to transplant and should be started young in rich, moist, acid soil with good protection from predators. The first slow decade can be wasted overnight by deer at the head and voles at the base. Good trees eventually reach 40 feet (12 m) or so in height and half that across.

The glossy oval leaves seem to anticipate autumn as on no other tree. Before summer is out a few start to take on brilliant colors, and by mid-October trees are aflame with yellow, orange and scarlet. A group of five or six trees will exhibit a whole palette range of fiery shades.

In Britain, the warmer southeast offers the best sites for these trees to color well, as demonstrated by the dozens of amazing century-old trees at Sheffield Park in Sussex. At such gardens the whole row of RHS awards it has received—AM, FCC and AGM—can be seen to be justified. For nyssa at home, across the Atlantic, medals are unnecessary. It's all so obvious.

Oxydendrum arboreum
Sourwood

Anyone who grows *Pieris japonica* but wishes it five times the size should have a go at sourwood. The pieris analogy is a bit tentative because the plant is deciduous and the look-alike effect is only when it is in flower in midsummer. Then every branch ends in sprays of typical white urn-shaped flowers. By the time those at the tips open, earlier flowers have set similar little green-white fruits, so the display goes on for many weeks. Then, come September, this splendid North American starts to celebrate its homeland's fall, turning yellow, scarlet and maroon. The leaves fall, leaving those dry fruit sprays to hold the filigree of hoar frost or snow.

Sourwood is a plant for several seasons, but it is not always easy to grow. It should be planted when young in good rhododendron-approved conditions: moist, acid, leafy soil. Full sun is needed in Britain if autumn color is to be encouraged. At home, ideally in zones 6–8 —adding one at each end, if everything else pleases—it will still perform in half shade or under light tree canopy. A narrow 20-foot (6m) tree is a fine specimen, usually clothed to the ground.

Fruit clusters and turning leaves of Oxydendrum arboreum *continue to show into winter.*

Parrotia persica
Persian ironwood

By comparison with eastern North America, where the certainty of dramatic fall leaf display is as inevitable as Thanksgiving Day, which follows soon after, British gardeners have to work at it. The choice of the right cultivar (they are invariably called 'October Glory' or some such) of the right species of the right genus can still be brought to naught or nearly so by the imponderables of soil, situation and microclimate. Or just, as we say, clutching at any straw however conventional, it's been very wet this year. Or not.

Fortunately, there are a few winners, five-star performers that never fail. Parrotia is one of these. Of course, it varies from year to year in the British variable climate, and from place to place, but its constancy is such that only one "selected form," other than a strange, pendulous one, seems to have been propagated in over 150 years of cultivation in Europe and in zones 4–8 in North America. This is the rarely available 'Vanessa', claimed as being even better than the type.

Although tall trees, 50 feet (15 m) high and more, are known, their height is generally less; parrotia has a tendency to thrust out strong, almost horizontal branches and some care with training and pruning is necessary in the early years if a clear trunk is required. Often, however, one is happy with the natural effect, especially if it is planted at the top of a bank. Progress is slow to begin with, even on good soils; fortunately it will accept almost anything and gradually get away. Lime is not a problem.

Lustrous summer foliage starts to color in September and moves branch by branch

Parrotia persica *can be relied on to color well over several weeks every year.*

to gold, red and bronze as the autumn progresses. Then, when leaf fall is complete, the flaking bark of trunk and main branches is seen, marbled like London plane. This is lost on the domed *Parrotia persica* 'Pendula', as with Young's weeping birch.

Parrotia is related to the witch hazels and rather takes over from their midwinter

flower. In late February or March, black buds erupt into little scarlet fireworks of stamen clusters. There are bright petals, but the distant haze of red and close-up detail offer an annual pleasure.

Trivia: the name commemorates a Herr Parrot, known for the first recorded ascent in 1829 of Mount Ararat. Noah, it will be recalled, went by water, earlier.

Paulownia tomentosa
Princess tree

In flower, this is one of the loveliest trees of any climatic zone, with its splendid spikes of scented lavender-blue foxgloves in May on leafless branches. Good specimens provide an entirely unique effect in temperate gardens. Jacaranda is sadly out of the range of this book, but royal paulownia or princess tree, as it is sometimes called, at least gives a flavor of it. Ideally—not easy with a tree 40 to 50 feet (12–15 m) high—it needs to be seen from above, as the color is apt to be lost against a blue spring sky. In towns such views are available from upper windows, as lucky residents of top-floor apartments in Paris, where it is used as a boulevard tree, know to their pleasure. Careful country siting against a conifer background will help, and in Britain, this is also desirable to give a bit of winter protection to the furry flower buds that, rather unwisely, stand fully formed on the branch ends throughout winter. Constant cold is not a problem, as zone 5-ish acceptance in North America indicates, but periods of cold-mild-cold spell death to next May's display.

Once flowering is over, woody beaked seed capsules develop, turning from green to brown, holding them over winter after the thousands of little winged seeds are shed. In southeastern North America self-sown seedlings are apt to appear only too frequently, and this imperial interloper from China has gone wild.

Summer effect is somewhat that of a lush catalpa (to which some botanists ally it) and when young, the soft felted leaves can be enormous. To obtain a well-formed tree it is important that early growth is really robust; a typical garden-center potted plant, having been planted in a well-manured hole, is best cut to the ground the following spring and the most robust new shoot selected as the tree-trunk-to-be. This process, plus liberal mulching, is sometimes pursued annually to realize a truly tropical scene of paired leaves 24 inches wide (60 cm) on stout 10-foot (3 m)

Spikes of lavender foxglove flowers of Paulownia tomentosa *decorate the tree in May.*

shoots. If space permits, a half-dozen or so plants could be grouped together for a truly extraordinary scene.

A couple of similar species from China, *Paulownia fargesii* and *P. fortunei*, are reputed to be more suited to an oceanic climate and are available (see *Andersen's Source List*) from one or two specialist nurseries. The general effect is similar, but the flowers are creamy yellow inside and the lavender trumpets held more loosely on the branch ends.

Phellodendron amurense
Amur cork tree

Both the botanical and the vernacular names of this Asiatic tree seem to hint at rare arboricultural riches, but in Britain at least these are not entirely fulfilled. For this tree and its relations (described below) really need the late, definite spring and hot summers of eastern North America.

Phellodendron (cork tree is a direct translation) in leaf is another tree of heaven/ash look-alike, with long, pinnate leaves. Heads of yellow-green flowers are followed by green-changing-to-black berries. These are noticeably aromatic, as are the crushed leaves, typical of its family, *Rutaceae*, which includes all the citruses and such diverse oil-scented plants as choisya and dictamnus. *Phellodendron* has good yellow autumn color; the eponymous corky bark is only on mature trees. With rapid growth to 40 feet (12 m), widely spreading, it accepts zone 4 winters.

Rather similar is one of its oriental cousins offering midsummer flowering and conspicuous fruit. But even generic nomenclature is confusing: this tree is now formally placed in the genus *Tetradium*, though many nursery catalogues that understandably hold to older names still used by their customers are likely to list *Evodia* or *Euodia*. Both were valid until recent years. Thus one must look for *Tetradium* (or *Evodia*) *daniellii* (or *hupehense*), which might be enough to put anyone off the whole idea. But that, in the Great Lakes or Boston areas, for instance, with their ideal climate, would be a mistake. There are very few really hardy trees to offer a midsummer show—and *T. daniellii* follows on splendidly there from *Syringa reticulata* in July and August with its flat heads of white flowers. It makes a fine backdrop then to massed herbaceous flowers and repeats the compliment later when its red to purple fruits echo the colors of New England asters (Michaelmas daisies). In North America, it seems happy on any soil, succeeding even on heavy alkaline clay; in Britain lighter, well-drained spots in full sun are essential to encourage wood ripening and thus the likelihood of good flower and fruit. It has the potential therefore as a good city tree.

Photinia

It's not just rhododendrons and azaleas that limestone-soil gardeners are apt to lust after. The range of calcifuges goes on and on, and either one moves house (and

Pinnate leaves of Phellodendron amurense *turn a clear gold in autumn.*

garden) or comes to terms with it and concentrates on those lovely things that actually prefer the lime, like most of the Mediterranean maquis plants. Not much comfort for climates that won't grow rosemary. But occasionally there are entirely different plants that offer a similar attribute. Think enviously of the scarlet shuttlecock new growths of *Pieris forrestii*. Then think alternatively of evergreen photinias.

Here is a group of oriental hawthorn relatives, so with hawthornish white flowers and red fruit but noted particularly for their bright bronze young growth. Making a proper small tree, 30 feet (9 m) or more, is *Photinia serrulata* (syn. *P. serratifolia*). It can be spectacular when the shining young leaves coincide with the flowers—a splendid spring picture. But as with pieris, those young leaves are frost-tender, so it's a plant for the west of both continents.

Several fine new hybrids such as *P.* x *fraseri* 'Red Robin' (quite up to pieris brightness) and *P.* x *f.* 'Robusta' are now readily available and show potential to reach beyond the current front-garden-shrub use to small specimen tree. These evergreens are all zone 8 plants.

Quite different and safe down to zone 4 is the deciduous *P. villosa*. It has good flower, excellent and persistent fruit—justifying its common name of Christmas berry—and fine autumn leaf color; it can be pruned up to small tree shape and looks well as a lawn specimen. Sadly, however, this one is not a plant for lime.

Platanus
Plane tree, sycamore

There seems to be a peculiar affinity in London between the formal elegance of

late Georgian architecture and the branch pattern of tall plane trees, through which it is so often seen. Indeed, in great patrician enclaves such as Berkeley Square and Mecklenburg Square the effect seems positively symbiotic in its balance of size and proportion. It is hardly surprising that this tree, happily surviving amidst 18th- and 19th-century coal smoke from myriad chimneys, became the street tree, as long as generous Georgian

Photinia serrulata *has long evergreen leaves and wide-headed late spring flowers.*

proportions prevailed. It was bound to be called the London plane.

But it is equally fine in the country, where with space its full potential can be achieved and appreciated. Trees of well over 100 feet (30 m) in height exist throughout the south of England and in France, with vast trunk girths of 20 feet (6 m) or so. In the north, they are less exuberant. A good specimen will maintain a central trunk to the very top with a canopy of surprising delicacy; sometimes lower branches are pendulous. The maple-like leaves can be 12 inches (30 cm) or so across and when they fall, the fruit clusters are seen to hang like so many Christmas-tree decorations until they break up in the spring. Across the seasons the cream flaking bark of trunk and branches is immediately diagnostic and always attractive.

This paragon is *Platanus* x *hispanica* (syn. *P.* x *acerifolia*), a putative hybrid of 17th-century origin that is now grown throughout the temperate world. In good soil, early growth is rapid and a true tree feeling soon appears. Obviously, space is needed—the London plane is a wonderful parkland tree—but in the country as in the town there is a rightness in association with buildings. Two disadvantages should be mentioned: the shedding of fine bristly hairs from unfolding leaves and from the ripe fruit has been linked to attacks of hay fever. This is more noticeable in hot, dry climates. There, by way of recompense, plane-tree anthracnose, a fungal disease that causes a dieback of shoots early in moist seasons in the north, is uncommon. Fortunately, where it occurs, regrowth usually takes place with little damage being done.

Flaking marbled bark of the London plane (Platanus x hispanica).

A number of cultivars exist. 'Augustine Henry' is widely praised for its especially fine architecture and prominent bark but is not readily available. 'Suttneri' is also uncommon but does appear in the *Andersen's Source List*; it has distinctive variegated leaves and therefore less vigorous growth. In America, where *P.* x *hispanica* is a zone 5–8 or so tree, selections include 'Bloodgood', 'Liberty' and 'Columbia' and these are spreading into European nurseries.

But North America has its own *Platanus occidentalis*. Known locally as buttonwood and sycamore, it is one of

Poplar trees (Populus *spp.*) *are a favorite host of semi-parasitic mistletoe.*

Populus
Poplar

Although they may be seen around the world, certain trees seem to hold fast to their nationality: oaks are English, gums are Oz and, in spite of those spire-like Italian ones, poplars are French. They are evocative equally mile after mile along straight Napoleonic roads or spreading widely and laden with mistletoe in soft meadows of the Loire valley. They make a clear and splendid statement. Where suited, they are the fastest-growing woody plants in temperate climates, and it is this that has made some poplars the inevitable choice to "screen" unsightly buildings. Invariably, however, a line of Lombardy poplars immediately catches the eye and proclaims that there is something nasty half-seen just behind, which does a disservice to a fine tree, as well more often than not failing in the aim. There are better ways.

Clearly, poplars, with their rapid growth and aggressively searching roots, are not trees for small gardens or confined spaces. Indeed, on clay soils their powers of water abstraction are such that serious damage has been caused to buildings within 50 yards (46 m) or so. The only small garden exception is *Populus* x *jackii* 'Aurora' (syn. *P.* x *candicans* 'Aurora'), which is usually cut back annually to obtain the maximum of its young, pink-flushed, creamy white leaves. The effect can be of an amazingly floriferous davidia. But because it is common, it doesn't get a good press: planted against dark conifers or purple-leaved shrubs and regularly renewed, 'Aurora' well earns her keep.

Striking foliage occurs with other poplars. *P. alba* has the most brilliantly white effect of any hardy tree, and on poor soil and wind-blown sand dunes, where it

the London plane's parents and has a huge natural range from New England to Florida and from Ontario down the Mississippi. In its chosen riverine gravelly soils, it is a splendid tree in cultivation, but it is more easily stressed than the hybrid. The same can be said of the other parent, *P. orientalis*, native to southeast Europe, where its elegant fingered foliage is such a feature along summer-dry waterways. Enormous old trees are especially noteworthy in village squares on the Pelion coast of Greece where, with a fusion of great smooth trunks, they look like copulating brontosauruses. To be visited, perhaps, rather than grown.

takes extreme exposure, it is a marvel, suckering, leaning, surviving. Rather smarter is 'Richardii', where the white-backed leaves have golden tops, living silver-gilt. Lovely narrow cultivars of the white poplar include *P. a.* f. *pyramidalis* (syn. *P. a.* 'Bolleana') and 'Raket' (Rocket), both available in North America, while

Populus candicans 'Aurora', despised by some, can look like the famous handkerchief tree.

'Balsam Spire' in Britain boasts an AGM.

Less spectacularly white is the gray poplar, *P.* x *canescens*, but it makes a better specimen tree, quickly reaching a large size. The 5-inch-long (12 cm) red catkins in February are noteworthy.

Remarkable in another way are the aspens, the European *P. tremula* and its North American cousin *P. tremuloides* (a zone 1 tree), when their quivering foliage moves in the slightest breeze with the continuous sound of softly falling water. The gray catkins in late winter are attractive, as is the smooth yellow-green bark of the American aspen. As suckering trees, multi-stemmed clumps are easily contrived and look superb.

Trees with scented leaves are not a common feature of British or North American gardens; true, a number are aromatic when crushed in the hand, but several big North American poplars, also called cottonwoods, cast out their delicious scent naturally with their unfolding leaves. These are the balsam poplars. *P. balsamifera* is self-descriptive. *P. trichocarpa* is equally fragrant and does better in Britain, especially a cultivar collected on Mount Baker in Washington State called 'Fritzi Pauley', which is said to be canker-resistant. It is this ugly disease that militates against some poplars, and their susceptibility must be assessed. Nonetheless, no other deciduous trees make their mark so quickly in the larger landscape. Whether it is a group (not a line) of Lombardies or other cultivars of the black poplar such as *P. nigra* 'Robusta', the cottonwoods or the aspens, all provide almost "instant trees" without the expense and doubt of semi-mature specimens of more fashionable trees.

And, of course, there should always be a celebration of plants such as these that happily accept the lower climatic zones.

Prunus
Cherry

> Loveliest of trees, the cherry now
> Is hung with bloom along the bough,
> And stands about the woodland ride
> Wearing white for Easter tide.

Housman's verse from "A Shropshire Lad," agonizingly regretting the evanescence of youth, is also a paean to an English spring and its passing. But if Brits, nostalgia-soaked as always, worry about the speed of spring, how much more is it lamented in North America where they assert (against all the evidence) that there is no spring at all: that winter rushes from winter straight into summer. Certainly in southern Ontario, for instance, the early April snowbanks can be suddenly shocked by sauna-like zephyrs from the south and everything bursts into life. Though the warmth retreats again. It's hardly worth bothering with daffodils and spring blossom, cry the pessimists—it doesn't last.

But that is exactly the point: the joy of spring and what it brings to the garden is the sudden celebration of annual renewal, that winter is defeated yet again. Lasting comes later with busy lizzies and petunias, of which we can get heartily sick.

Spelling spring at ground level are the Mediterranean bulbs, snowdrops, daffodils, scillas and tulips. Above, more than anything, it's the Japanese cherries, and in Japan and China the spring cult and near-worship of flowering cherries developed centuries before such plants came to the West.

There are several oriental *Prunus* species and their cultivars that we commonly lump together as Japanese cherries. The range is enormous, and one needs to take note not only of what one would like in one's garden but what is known to do well in the conditions on offer. Climatically happy throughout western Europe and northwest North America, in the East, they are zone 5–8 plants. Flower is not the only consideration. Size, shape, summer effect and autumn leaf color all come into the equation.

For many, cherry blossoms are the very epitome of spring. Choosing a range of species can extend the season over many weeks.

The great white cherry (Prunus 'Taihaku') *is spectacular, its white flowers contrasting with its unfolding bronze leaves.*

The earliest to flower for sheltered European gardens is the Japanese apricot (*Prunus mume*) and its double-flowered cultivars, pink or white and delightfully scented, are especially valuable. March is their usual moment, but seasonal variation may make it a month on either side.

P. x *subhirtella* is particularly renowned for its cultivar 'Autumnalis'. After the narrow, elegant leaves drop, the twiggy branches are seen to be packed with flower buds, some already showing color; a warm autumn can provide an unseasonal cloud of pink and white. But all eggs are not in that basket: mild spells throughout winter and on into April offer sprays of starry flowers. Spring-flowering *P. pendula* 'Pendula Rosea' is one of the most charming weeping trees for small gardens. Also with *subhirtella* blood is the wonderful Yoshino cherry (*P.* x *yedoensis*). This can reach 40 to 50 feet (12–15 m) in height and becomes covered in flower in April: cherry festivals are built around it. 'Ivensii' and 'Shidare-yoshino' are weeping cultivars, equally beautiful.

The large-flowered Japanese cherries are of mixed parentage and are generally now known as *Prunus* Sato-zakura Group, Japanese for "domestic cherries," each with a Western or oriental cultivar name. White or pink, single or double flowers with green or bronze unfolding foliage, on wide-branching, weeping or sky-reaching cultivars—the variation is enormous, to which is added early or late flowering habit. Thus you pays your penny and you takes your choice. Some are so popular, such as 'Kanzan', with its unfailing show of big, double, purplish pink flowers, as to have become something of a suburban cliché. But if the usual standard form is avoided and it is grown as a bush, the vase shape starting at ground level is excellent; a group of three is a revelation. Naturally

The flower spikes of Prunus padus '*Watereri*' *can be 9 inches (22 cm) long.*

Many of the group have respectable, if not spectacular, fall color but another oriental, *P. sargentii*, is renowned for it, in addition to its soft pink spring display. 'Rancho' is a fine American selection, narrower in habit, bigger in flower and spectacular in fall color. Even better for spring display is its hybrid, with *P.* x *subhirtella*, 'Accolade,' which in Britain has been given all the RHS awards, as measure of its merit. It succeeds wonderfully in southern Ontario. Sargent's cherry also has shining chestnut bark, and this attribute is sufficiently noteworthy to provide reason for planting both *P. serrula* and the Manchurian cherry (*P. maackii*). The former makes an elegant little tree with willow-like leaves.

Apart from the last pair, all the cherries so far extolled are more or less sophisticated garden trees; Housman's lines refer to a very different tree, the gean, or wild cherry, of English woodland edges (*P. avium*). Native throughout Europe and into Asia (and parent of most sweet cherries), it can reach heights of 100 feet (30 m), covered in white flowers at the end of April—the poet's "Easter tide" would have to be as late as it can get. Truly spectacular is its double-flowered cultivar, 'Plena'. Later flowering still is the bird cherry (*P. padus*), unusual in that its flowers are carried in drooping spikes, which in the cultivar 'Watereri' can be 8 to 10 inches (20–25 cm) long. This is a very hardy zone 3 tree, up to 50 feet (15 m) in height, extending in its natural range all across the Old World northern hemisphere from Britain to Japan. These and other wild or nearly wild Europeans are garden edge or parkland trees, contributing with their fruit (doubles excepted) to the feeding of wild creatures. It also has a very

those varieties with a pendent or horizontal branch pattern need training up on a stem. 'Taihaku', the "great white cherry," is a magnificent example. It makes a real tree, 30 feet (9 m) high and as much across, covered in large white flowers glistening against the unfolding bronze-red foliage. 'Ukon', too, must be mentioned as one of a

small group with pale, buff-primrose flowers, giving a very different vision. It's a lovely mid-season plant.

The Sato-zakura cherries are not, in terms of tree generations, long-lived trees. But 50 years (though usually less in North America) is a pretty good payback, and it will see most of its planters out.

important horticultural role as the common stock upon which most flowering cherries are grafted. Thus its speed of growth, ease of cultivation and acceptance of almost any soil becomes a part of the more exotic form that is grafted upon it. *P. sargentii*, for example, is much more difficult on its own roots and is invariably offered as a grafted plant.

North America has its own splendid cherries filling a similar environmental niche, and these are well worth planting, where they don't already exist. *P. serotina* is the rum cherry—the fruits are used to flavor liqueurs—with a huge 3–9 zone range from Nova Scotia to Florida and into the Dakotas and Texas. It is probably the biggest cherry of all, exceeding 100 feet (30 m) in height in the Virginian Alleghenies. It has bird cherry-like flower spikes followed by black fruit. A smaller but similar species is the choke cherry (*P. virginiana*), effective down to zone 2. The green foliage of its cultivars 'Schubert' and 'Canada Red' become purple as the season advances, with good autumn color to follow.

Purple foliage is also a feature of cultivars of the European cherry plum (*P. cerasifera*), such as 'Pissardii' and *P. x blireana*. It can be seen as rather heavy in midsummer, but the delicate pink blossom very early in spring is charming. In North America, these are more commonly West Coast trees, 20 feet (6 m) or so in height. 'Newport Thundercloud' is a recent, self-explanatory cultivar for zone 5 and above.

So far, the emphasis has been upon the purely ornamental aspects of various *Prunus* species and their hybrids and cultivars. But it must be remembered that others are, with the related apples and pears, the most important fruit of

Catkins of the Caucasian wingnut (Pterocarya fraxinifolia) *in early summer.*

temperate climates—sweet cherries, peaches, apricots and plums; almond, too, is a prunus. Obviously, flower must precede the fruit crop and often these Prunus grown for fruit rival the beauty of the "flowering prunus" trees. So why not plant these? Problems exist. Large crops of fruit can be an embarrassment: wasps will home in on ripening plums, as will small boys from next door. On the other hand,

the birds will almost certainly beat you to the cherries—no glut there. Peaches fall victim to disfiguring leaf curl (as do those *P. persica* cultivars grown for flower). But surely the possibility of growing one's own fruit is entirely desirable (a ripe peach warm from the branch is unrivaled) if it is taken as a serendipitous bonus rather than to be fought for with sprayer and pruning saw. No special pruning regimes are essential, and soils and cultivations are no different from the rest of the group. Again, the choice is open and enormously wide.

Quite extraordinarily different are two evergreen cherries, the cherry laurel (*P. laurocerasus*) and Portugal laurel (*P. lusitanica*). Inevitably, because they are so accepting of shears and secateurs and of being generally disfigured, these are seldom seen as mature trees. Cherry laurel with its lustrous leaves, up to 12 inches (30 cm) long in the cultivar 'Latifolia', and sprays of white flowers in April can be splendid, as an open-ground specimen 20 feet (6 m) or so in height. In light woodland, where it is perfectly happy in the drip of trees above, it provides excellent low-level furnishing and wind protection for choicer things. This is a zone 7 plant from Turkey and around the Black Sea, while *P. lusitanica*, as its name suggests, is from Spain and Portugal. It is perhaps even more ornamental and certainly hardier, and its long sprays of hawthorn-scented flowers make quite a show in June. Little dark purple cherries follow. Portugal laurel is wonderfully adaptable: trained up as a tree, it makes a 30-foot-high (9 m) specimen; tightly clipped, it will sit in front-door-flanking barrels to replace the bays that were killed by frost last winter and look just as good.

Pterocarya
Wingnut

As smaller gardens became the norm, nurserymen and plant breeders are continually on the search for compact, or fastigiate, trees suitable for restricted spaces. But bigger planting opportunities do exist, and fortunately there are trees to fill them—and to fill them quickly.

The Caucasian wingnut (*Pterocarya*

The domestic pear (Pyrus communis).

fraxinifolia) is a spectacular 100-foot-high (30-m) relation of walnut, to which the long, pinnate leaves are similar. In the deep, rich soil it needs, growth is prodigious, and its hybrid with a Chinese species is even more so. This chance coupling, which occurred at the Arnold Arboretum, is *P. x rehderiana*. The Arnold hybrid grows better there than either of its parents and is clearly the choice for North America. Moreover, it is recorded that at Kew a young tree reached 52 feet (16 m) in height and was nearly 6 feet (1.8 m) in trunk girth after only 17 years. In addition to the foliage, the 18-inch-long (45-cm) catkins on which the little nuts develop are noteworthy from midsummer.

The wingnuts generally develop a low branching habit with a propensity to sucker from the root so that, without

attention, a whole grove builds up. They are superb beside water.

Pyrus
Pear

One of Samuel Palmer's best-loved watercolors shows a tall, contorted pear tree in full flower under the inevitable moon. Such trees can still be seen at the bottom of Victorian town gardens, often neglected and unconsidered but still producing their exquisite Palmeresque vision every spring. Culinary pears are seldom grafted today on such vigorous stocks, but perry pears (*P. communis*) would do the job; old varieties such as 'Taynton Squash' and 'Yellow Huffcap' are still available, admirable for farmyard gardens.

Purely as an ornamental, *P. calleryana* has had a much better press. The North American selections 'Bradford', 'Chanticleer' and 'Capitol' have been planted in North America in enormous numbers as street trees over the past few decades. A respectable spring display of white flowers, fine glossy leaves all summer through and splendid fall color (though less so in oceanic Britain) adds up to a very desirable zone 5 plant. And with speed of growth—'Chanticleer' has attained 35 feet (10.5 m) in fifteen years—and catalogue descriptions proclaiming "a maintenance-free tree," its ubiquity is no surprise. Inevitably, one is apt not to want the plant that everyone else has got and is outside on the street as well; however, one can keep ahead of the crowd by choosing the latest cultivars such as 'Aristocrat' and 'Red Spire'.

On both sides of the Atlantic, fashion had also leaned heavily upon *P. salicifolia* 'Pendula' and its similar cultivar 'Silver

Cascade'. This is the willow-leaved pear, whose branches weep to the ground producing a dome of gray-white narrow leaves (indeed a "silver cascade") enhanced in spring by faintly pink-tipped white flowers. This small tree, often used as a lawn specimen, is probably better sited as part of a large foliage association. A pair used to act as "supporters" at a gate or viewing point must be given space to develop; each will get as wide as high.

A fine tree-sized pear, white-flowered as always, is *P. ussuriensis* from the Russian far east: hardier than the Bradfords, the selection called 'Prairie Gem' is safe to zone 3 in North America.

Quercus
Oak

The range of oaks is enormous—some 530 species are strewn around the northern hemisphere (and a few even cross the equator in the mountains of the Malayan archipelago)—but except in botanic garden collections, relatively few are commonly cultivated. In the wild, there are oaks that seem to define the culture of their native homelands—the Mediterranean cork oak and ilex, darkly evergreen; the spreading Scarlett O'Hara and Rhett Butler live oaks of Carolina and Georgia; the brilliant white and red oaks of the Eastern seaboard; the European oaks of Sherwood Forest and Windsor Great Park, all Robin Hood, Falstaff and hearts of oak. Their presence, their economic value in lumber and acorns entwines folklore, literature and music from the days of the Druids to modern times.

They are, of course, in most cases, big garden or parkland trees that count their span in centuries and for that reason are apt, in our culture of instant gratification,

Long-stalked acorns identify Quercus robur, *the common oak of ancient English parkland.*

to be neglected in favor of the more transient. But this is a mistake; where space is available and posterity as secure as may be, oaks should be planted. This emphasis, wonderful though the exotics are, should initially be upon the natives. Not only for themselves but for the hosts of interrelated organisms, plant and animal, that have developed symbiotic relationships within the trees' world of roots, trunks and enveloping branches.

In Britain, there are only two natives, the so-called common oak (*Quercus robur*) and the durmast, or sessile, oak

Regardless of its name, Quercus rubra *usually provides a golden contribution to the autumn scene.*

Surprisingly, some acorns from this clone do produce the narrow plant, but others widen out. It is best therefore to choose a selected cultivar of certain habit. *Q. r.* f. *f.* 'Koster' in Britain and 'Skyrocket' in America are generally available. Spires 50 feet (15 m) high are common and quite quickly attained, splendid in a group of three or five or so and using little space. Another desirable variant is 'Concordia', whose initial bright yellow leaves gradually turn green as summer wears on. Such cultivars are not for real countryside.

Several southern European oaks make splendid large garden or parkland trees in Britain. The chestnut-leaved oak (*Q. castaneifolia*) is vigorous in growth and distinctive in its leaves, which have corrugated bluish tops and backs; rather similar is the sawtooth oak (*Q. acutissima*) from Japan. It is hardier, too, more commonly seen in North America (zones 5–8), where its early leafing and late yellow to bronze fall color is noteworthy. Its acorns are held in bristly cups like aerial sea anemones.

The Turkey oak (*Q. cerris*) makes an enormous tree—100-footers (30 m) are strewn around southern England—and it grows quickly even on poor dry soils. For a lawn specimen, the variegated cultivar 'Argenteovariegata' is well worth considering and is obviously much less vigorous. Against all the rules, there is a splendid specimen at Inverewe, way up in Easter Ross, northwest Scotland. But the fact that this is on a latitude parallel with Moscow still doesn't mean it is a plant for most of eastern North America. Nor, sadly, is the Hungarian oak (*Q. frainetto*), which is one of the very best exotic oaks in Britain, soon reaching an impressive size even on limestone soils.

(*Q. petraea*). Planting for succession determines the species, which will ideally be of local stock, but if choice is open, durmast oak is the better tree. It makes a straighter trunk, going higher into the canopy with more regular branches, and is happy on all soils except the heaviest clay.

Its fastigiate cultivar 'Columna' is rare, and therefore we have to turn to the common oak (which also more commonly produces variants) for easily available 'Lombardy poplar' oaks. The original *Q. robur* f. *fastigiata* occurred in a German forest, and grafts were taken in the 1780s.

Vastly different from all the trees mentioned so far is that epitome of the Mediterranean littoral, the holm oak (*Q. ilex*). Cultivated in Britain since the 16th century, there it is the biggest of all broad-leaved evergreens. Not, then, a plant for small gardens it would seem, but it accepts clipping into topiary shapes and can even be used as an evergreen hedge-on-sticks,

pleached as for hornbeam. Ilex, especially blowing silver in a wind, starts looking strangely like an olive and has confused many hopeful gardeners. But it gradually builds up into great mounds of dark leaves. In May and June, there is the annual exchange: old leaves drop and litter the garden unforgivably, but above, the trees temporarily take on the silver of youth.

The wide-branching common oak (Quercus robur) *is still an important timber tree.*

From North American oaks, it is fall color that we expect. There, from the still enormous natural stands, parts of Canada and the northeastern United States completely change color in October (take a plane from Toronto to Boston and experience a red planet).

Of these spectacular trees, the scarlet oak (*Q. coccinea*) comes up to every expectation with a full month of color when truly happy. But it's difficult to transplant and to get established, and apparently fine specimens, bought at inordinate cost, are likely to just sit and quietly die back. If there is any doubt of likely stress (edge of climatic acceptance—which is ostensibly zones 4–8, poor drainage, exposure), better move on to another species. The red oak (*Q. rubra*) is a generally easier option, if not quite so brilliant a performer. Happy on most soils, growth is rapid in youth, with leaves 12 inches (30 cm) long ; the adult round-headed outline begins to show early in life.

A direct translation from the botanical Latin would encourage us to believe that the pin oak (*Q. palustris*) needs wet feet; not so, but like the European durmast oak, it will take a wide range of soils, including moist spots. It is the easiest of the red oaks to establish, grows quickly when young and builds up into a fine tree. An open-ground specimen develops a highly distinctive form: having grown a good, clean trunk for a few years, it then hides it with a skirt of low, lawn-sweeping branches. The effect is splendid but constrains its use. Selections without this habit include 'Crownright' and 'Sovereign', enabling the pin oak to be a fine avenue or even a street tree.

These red oaks are eastern North American trees *par excellence*, epitomizing its amazing tree flora, and their successful cultivation is a vital part of that area's heritage. In Britain, they generally grow well and are distinctive in their large-lobed leaves, rapid growth and, often, good autumn color (*Q. coccinea* 'Splendens' is most likely to perform well, keeping its leaves until Christmas). In short, they are splendid exotics in the British scene but do not replace the natives—they do a very different job.

The red oaks by no means exhaust the array of North American *Quercus* species; indeed there are Western species, such as the evergreen encina (*Q. agrifolia*), that fill an ecological niche in that Mediterranean climate similar to that of the ilex in southern Europe. And in the East, further white and black oaks contribute to the forest scene. The classic white oak (*Q. alba*) has good fall color and is frost-hardy to zone 3 but again is difficult to move, and members of this group are not happy Europeans.

While this book rather inevitably emphasizes the ability (or not) of plants to accept the cold winters of the lower climatic zones, it must be remembered that such acceptance usually means they cannot take the other end of the scale. So it is good to recommend the willow oak (*Q. phellos*), which thrives in the warm southeast of the United States. Particularly elegant in youth, with its unique narrow leaves, it can, like almost all the oaks referred to here, attain serious tree status of 100 feet (30 m) or so.

Because of the hoped-for permanence—far beyond our own span—of oaks that we plant, care with planting and origin of stock cannot be too strongly emphasized. The typical behavior of germinating acorns is to send down a strong tap root, which ensures

The Hungarian oak (Quercus frainetto) *is a fast-growing species from southeastern Europe.*

health and strength for all time. Nursery-propagated plants are unlikely to maintain this primary root, and transplanting can be a problem, especially with the North American species (*Q. robur* is more amenable, which is why the English oak, especially in its narrow forms, is often seen in zone 5+ in America). In an ideal world one would plant acorns in situ and watch for germination, encouraging them to grow where they began. That's what happens in nature. Even in our less than perfect environment it is still wise to plant small, young, open-ground plants, two or three years old. It is amazing how they catch up and overtake big expensive "specimens."

Rhododendron *'Loderi Sir Edmund' is one of many rhododendrons that attain tree status.*

—all are here, though not necessarily on the same plant.

While North America has a few wildlings (mainly deciduous "azaleas") and Europe a couple, the epicenter of rhododendron diversity lies all along the Himalayan chain. There they occupy every ecological niche from deep lowland valleys to mountainsides far above the tree line. In the wet, warm temperate forests of Sikkim and Bhutan, the 60-foot (18 m) *R. arboreum* fully lives up to that name, as *R. grande* and *R. sinogrande* do theirs. These last two species and others from western China make 30-foot-high (9m) trees with huge paddle-shaped leaves up to 24 inches (60 cm) in length and half that across.

But it is not essential to travel to the Himalayas to see these amazing plants. Over the past century or so, famous woodland gardens in southern and western Britain have competed not only among themselves but also with the Orient itself to grow them ever more successfully. There the mild winters and frost-free springs with high rainfall, even in summer, provide, with open woodland shelter, the necessary conditions; the results in and out of flower are a revelation. Parts of Oregon and Washington state are just as welcoming to the genus. These are not plants for small gardens, even in favored areas, as their scale is just too dominant.

Nonetheless, there are a few small-tree-sized rhododendrons that, with the usual cultivational requirements, are less frost-tender and whose every prospect pleases.

R. thomsonii is one of these, introduced to Britain as long ago as 1849. If it did nothing else, it would be worth growing for its rounded blue-green leaves and smooth trunks, purplish or orange in

Rhododendron

In North America, *Rhododendron maximum* is sometimes called the great laurel or rosebay, and deciduous kinds of *Rhododendron* are known to us all as azaleas. Otherwise, the hundreds of species and thousands of hybrids are just, simply, rhododendron. Seen throughout the gardening world wherever a suitable climate and an acid soil combine (and in containers or under glass where they don't), this extraordinarily diverse genus offers 6-inch (15 cm) shrublets, 60-foot (18 m) trees and everything in between. Fine foliage, spectacular flowers, fragrance, good bark, aromatic leaves color, just asking to be stroked. In late April, loose heads of blood-red bells adorn each branch end, and when these fall (waxy and firm enough to color the ground for days afterwards), the bitter-green calyces and developing seed capsules are also eye-catching. Then come shuttlecocks of smooth new leaves. Not surprisingly, this paragon has been used extensively in breeding.

Sometimes hybrids combine the best of both parents, as with the famous R. Loderi Group (*R. fortunei* x *R. griffithianum*) and its cultivars. Eventually 20 to 30 feet high (6–9 m), it can be encouraged to form a multi-stemmed tree with silk-smooth bark and long handsome leaves. Flowers are like trusses of arboreal Madonna lilies, equally scented and varying from pure white to cream and pink, usually with a flash of green within each trumpet. Further color comes as the new shoots and leaves push out from unfolding reflexed shrimp-pink bracts. Given a bit of shelter, this magnificent plant is safe throughout Britain but very much a northern West Coast plant in North America, as are most of the Himalayan species. There is, however, no reason why the native *R. maximum* cannot be encouraged in East Coast woodland gardens to take on small tree status. The white to pinkish purple flower heads appear in May and June; there are cultivars hardy to zone 4 and a height of 20 feet (6 m) is entirely possible. The new hybrids continually being introduced from Europe, North America and now New Zealand and Australia should be perused for our needs. Those tight little, right little rows of *R. yakusimanum* dwarves are not all that rhododendrons offer the 21st century.

Stag's-horn sumach (Rhus typhina) *is a suckering small tree from eastern North America.*

Rhus
Sumach

Just occasionally it is possible to avoid the lament that eastern North American natives, renowned for their fall color, are just not reliable in those bits of Europe without a similar continental climate. This is so with the sumachs. They are so common in their homes as to be rather unconsidered, and they perform in Britain too, even in wet western Scotland.

Typical is the stag's-horn sumach (*Rhus typhina*), which, suckering in all directions, can make great swaths along country roadsides from Quebec down to Georgia. In such situations, it is seldom much above 10 feet (3 m) high, but in gardens or at semi-cultivated woodland edges, suckering can be controlled and a multi-stemmed tree or small grove twice that can be expected. Plants are separately sexed, the male having broad spikes of greenish white flowers and the female rather cone-like fruit clusters, covered in rusty-red fur. These often hold on throughout winter and provide valuable food for birds. But it is the long, pinnate leaves that make the most effect, starting a show of brilliance—red, yellow and purple —in late August that goes on for a couple of months.

Stag's-horn sumach has a splendid variant with almost fern-like leaves, *R. t.* 'Dissecta'—it is a female and therefore adds furry fruits to the effect. Sadly, it seldom reaches even half the height of the type, but it is admirable as an architectural focal point in a small garden, perhaps planted in a raised bed.

A rather similar species, also from eastern North America, is the shining sumach (*R. copallina*), with a wide natural range. Plants from the south—it is happy into zone 9—are more likely to reach 20 feet (6 m) or so.

Oriental sumachs include *R. chinensis*, one of the best. In North America, it revels in summer heat and full sun. It reaches the usual sumach height of 20 feet (6 m) or so, and the pinnate leaves set off showers of white flower spikes in late summer. 'September Beauty' is especially good.

The varnish tree (*R. verniciflua*) is another highly ornamental tree with handsome leaves and strings of bead-like fruit. Descriptions typically add, almost as an afterthought, that the sap can cause a severe skin rash. That this should give pause for thought is emphasized now that, along with its cousins the North American poison ivies and poison oaks, it has been moved into a separate genus, *Toxicodendron*. This is suitably self-descriptive.

Robinia pseudoacacia
Black locust, false acacia

This is one of those potentially highly desirable plants that, because of a certain ebullience when it finds conditions to its satisfaction, gets the unfortunate

Showering golden foliage of Robinia pseudoacacia *'Frisia', a small tree happy in city gardens.*

description of weed tree. But not in Britain, where a cooler climate doesn't encourage excess. Here its virtues predominate: an elegant and, when old, picturesquely rugged tree with deeply fissured bark. Its flowers hang in chains, laburnum-like, which against the feathery leaves give a cool Regency green-and-white effect. Mature trees can be 70 to 80 feet (20–25 m) high.

Growth is rapid when the tree is young and always remains rather brittle, so trees must be watched for potentially unsafe branches. 'Appalachia' is one of the so-called shipmast locusts selected in Virginia and introduced to Long Island in 1707 for strong straight trunks; recommended in North America for street planting, it seems not to have crossed the ocean.

Black locust is able to accept the poorest soil, which is why it has so happily colonized railway sidings and motorway banks in its home and in Europe. A couple of selections get a better press: *Robinia pseudoacacia* 'Frisia' is agreed to be one of the best golden-foliaged trees throughout the season, and 'Umbraculifera' keeps a mop-headed habit when top-grafted onto a stem of the type. This can be useful in formal situations, lining a walk or in pairs pointing to a view. Worth searching out is *R.* x *ambigua* 'Decaisneana'. Even more than the basic black locust, it needs more summer heat than Britain can provide and therefore doesn't flower well. But in the Great Lakes area, for instance, its soft pink flowers, lovely against a June sky, make a good show. It is probably of hybrid origin, appearing first in France in 1863, and its putative other parent *R. viscosa* passes on not only the flower color but a more restrained habit of growth.

Salix
Willow

There is no certainty that the trees by the waters of Babylon on which the captive Israelites hung up their harps and under which they wept, as described in Psalm 138, were willows—some translations merely refer to "the trees that were therein." But Linnaeus, naming a pendulous willow *Salix babylonica* and thereby attaching the epithet weeping to this and all other trees of similar habit

The Peking willow (Salix babylonica *var.* pekinensis) *is an elegant conical tree.*

seems to have thrown his weight behind the attribution.

Weeping willows may conjure up the above story; in Britain, they certainly evoke idylls of golden summers past as the punt drifts gently on placid waters through curtains of pale green foliage. Weeping willows spell water, to the point of their being planted close to innumerable little garden pools that in no time they will hide with their branches and fracture with their roots; the vision soon pales.

Where space is available, however, preferably with sufficient expanse of water to double the effect, no landscape picture can be better and more easily contrived. Cliché or not, it is beauty exemplified. But *S. babylonica* is no longer *the* weeping willow; the role is fulfilled much more effectively by its hybrid with the white willow, *S. alba*, the lovely *S. sepucralis* var. *chrysocoma*. It grows quickly and soon develops the expected form, with long, golden-yellow branchlets cascading to the ground. Eventually, in 50 or so years, it is a 50-foot-high (15 m) wide-spreading tree. Catkins appear with the unfolding leaves in early spring, and this effusion of palest green is one of the most encouraging moments of the year. Summer beauty concentrates on shape and movement, and autumn comes late as the leaves turn clear yellow. When they have gone, the branch effect etched with hoar frost is magical.

White willow (*S. alba*) itself is a tall, conical tree with distinctive narrow blue-gray leaves; again it is lovely by water, though this is not essential, as are the well-known yellow- and red-stemmed forms. These, *S. a.* var. *vitellina* and *S. a.* var. *v.* 'Britzensis' (syn. *S. a.* 'Chermesina'), are commonly pruned hard, rather as is done with dogwoods, to encourage quantities of

Clustered by a lake, white willows (Salix alba) *form billowing heaps of blue-gray foliage .*

the brilliant-barked young growth at a low level, but they are in fact most lovely when permitted to attain their narrow 40-foot (12.25 m) potential; they are best seen against an ice-blue winter sky with snow at their feet.

Distinctive texture is also the reason for growing the dragon's claw willow (*S. babylonica* var. *pekinensis* 'Tortuosa', syn. *S. matsudana* 'Tortuosa'). Twisted stems and twisted leaves build up an unmistakable picture; foliage is sparse enough for the branch pattern to be apparent even in midsummer. In North America (where all these willows are happy within the 4–8 zone range), two intriguing variants are offered called *S.* 'Erythroflexuosa' (syn. *S.* 'Golden Curls' and 'Scarlet Curls', and these are worth searching for.

S. caprea is a common European willow fully deserving a place in country gardens for its early spring show: in Britain, good forms can often be seen in high hedgerows, looking as bright as florists' mimosa. Before the male catkins burst to show their yellow stamens, they are like small, silky, gray rabbit tails: at this stage it is the "palm" traditionally gathered for church decoration for the Sunday before Easter. In our more secular age, the name "florists' willow" becomes commoner.

Sambucus
Elder

Most elders remain shrubby and are grown for their flowers and fruit as well as for their golden or variegated foliage. A couple, however, attain small-tree status

The creamy white flowers of the common elder (Sambucus nigra).

Strangely inconsistent leaves of Sassafras albidum.

and are worth encouraging. In Britain, the common elder (*S. nigra*) is often regarded as a weed—hardly surprising when if it is not pulled up as soon as seen, it is likely to be cruelly chopped back; it then responds by pushing out long, soft water shoots that just provoke further mutilations. A self-perpetuating muddle. But while accepting that elder is not a plant for sophisticated gardens, in the country, a small 20-foot (6 m) tree is an arresting sight. The pale, rugged trunk supports a fine head of pinnate leaves; in June the creamy scented flower heads can be close to 12 inches (30 cm) across (in Britain, these traditionally flavor gooseberry fool and make delicious elderflower "champagne"). Then in September, the purple berries are ornamental for a month unless harvested for wine or added to apple pies. In Britain, few rare exotics offer as much; in North America, it *is* an exotic and is therefore more highly regarded in zones 5–7.

The variegated-leaved forms are unlikely to make trees and in any case are pruned hard to encourage the foliage. The relatively new pink-flowered and purple-leaved 'Guincho Purple', however, has that potential.

The blue elderberry (*S. nigra* subsp. *caerulea*, syn. *S. caerulea*) of western North America can reach 50 feet (15 m) in the wild and with its black fruits covered with a grape-like bloom can look striking. It is also available in Britain (just), where it should be tried more often.

Sassafras albidum

This is a classic tree of North America's Carolinian forest flora, which extends from the Carolinas up the Niagara escarpment into southern Ontario, an area packed with good plants both woody and herbaceous. Anyone there with a bit of zone 4–8 woodland will want to add sassafras to its edge, especially for the brilliant fall colors—almost up to tupelo standard. But it is quietly noteworthy earlier in the year with its strange green and gray leaves of mixed shape, some oval, some lobed—often on one side only, some almost fig-leaved. They are also most agreeably aromatic, and it is no surprise that both the native peoples and later the Shakers used sassafras leaves in their medicinal remedies.

Moist acid soil is preferred, but deep woodland leaf mold above limestone suits too, as long as young plants are used. It doesn't transplant easily.

Sophora japonica
Scholar tree

This is really a sort of upmarket black locust from China (in spite of its specific epithet) and were it as common might well be less regarded. The common name also helps, referring to its traditional Chinese use for marking scholars' graves.

Sophora makes a tidy, rounded tree, ultimately over 50 feet (15 m) high, with typical leguminous pinnate leaves and sprays of creamy white pea-flowers. Their advantage over robinia is the late flowering—August in hot-summer America and September in Britain—which gives a feeling of freshness when most other things seem to be winding down. Masses of fallen flowers then whiten the ground like prunus petals in spring.

It is planted more frequently in North America in zones 3/4–7 and also used as a street tree, for which the slightly narrower 'Regent' has been selected. It is tolerant of poor soils and hot conditions. A weeping form S.j. 'Pendula' is also available, usually having been top-grafted on to a stem of the type: this makes a charming arbor.

Sorbus
Rowan (mountain ash)
and whitebeam

The almost 200 species of *Sorbus* continue to exercise taxonomic botanists, who agonize over their relationships and nomenclature. Sorbus seem in Britain to encourage an almost stamp-collecting frenzy among those who have the space to add the new cultivars and species being introduced. In North America, they are grown less often, since many species resent the hot summers; even where *Sorbus aucuparia*, for example, grows well it seems to tire in September and drop its leaves with obvious relief. It is also susceptible to fire blight and sawfly larvae.

Nonetheless, there are in this genus some lovely small trees offering especially fine autumn effects of fruit and foliage on both sides of the Atlantic.

There are two apparently distinct groups: the whitebeams, with entire rounded leaves, and the rowans, with pinnate foliage—but then they interbreed, and all is confusion. (Promiscuity also extends to the sorbus hybridizing with other genera such as *Aronia*, *Pyrus* and *Cotoneaster*.)

S. aria is the classic whitebeam and a well-known plant of the lime-rich chalklands of southern England and France, the whiteness of its foliage seeming to reflect the soil from which it springs. Especially in the cultivars 'Lutescens' and 'Majestica', *S. aria* provides superb silvery foliage and splendid red-fruit displays on balanced 40-to-50-foot-high trees (9–15 m). *S. x thuringiaca* 'Fastigiata', a small upright whitebeam hybrid, is commonly available in North America, even to zone 4, but is less silver in its oak-like leaves and duller red in fruit. Also in this group is *S. thibetica* 'John Mitchell' with particularly fine foliage, the biggest of any.

European sorbus find many parallels in the Orient and a valuable Japanese whitebeam is *S. alnifolia*. The bark becomes gray, veined with buff; and the fruit display, especially in North America (zones 3–7), is outstanding.

S. aucuparia is the wild or common rowan seen throughout Britain, but most usually on the acid soils of heathlands and upland burnsides in Scotland: hence, of course, mountain ash. It's a plant for country gardens, giving late interest to plantings of azaleas and rhododendrons. The natural ferny foliage is accentuated in cultivars such as 'Aspleniifolia'. Its fruits are among the first to color: a flash of orange can give an unwonted frisson of autumn even in July; by August, they are ripe and immediate prey to blackbirds in

Sophora japonica *is a hardy September-flowering tree with elegant leaves.*

The mountain ashes (or rowans) are almost all grown for their fruit and autmn leaf color. Here are Sorbus aucuparia *and* S. cashmiriana.

Britain and cedar waxwings in North America, a flock of which can clear a big rowan in a day. Such elegant birds are easily forgiven; they almost justify the tree.

Other fine forms of common rowan include 'Beissneri', with its yellow-green foliage and distinctive coral-red shoots that darken to coppery-orange on branches and trunk. 'Sheerwater Seedling' is the best of the vertical growers, and *S. a.* var. *xanthocarpa* with yellow fruits discourages the birds for a bit as they hang around waiting for conventional ripening. These are 3–6 zoners in North America.

Oriental rowans, their hybrids and forms, continue to proliferate. Red-fruited trees include *S. commixta* 'Embley', renowned also for its superb autumn color, as is *S. sargentiana*. Here the flower heads and fruit clusters can grow to 12 inches (30 cm) across; distinctive, too, are the big, crimson winter buds, almost the size of those of horse chestnut. *S. scalaris* is a fine "Chinese" Wilson introduction with fern-like leaves, dark above, pale below; again, with huge heads of small fruit among the red and purple autumn leaf tints.

It is to the Orient that we turn for other fruit colors. 'Joseph Rock' is deservedly famous. A tidy, upright small tree (these are all in the 20-to-30-foot/6–9 m range), quietly elegant throughout summer, it casts all restraint aside to become a column of red and orange and purple further enlivened by bunches of bright yellow berries. *S. cashmiriana* is an unusual Himalayan: a small tree with heads of soft pink flowers in May followed by bunches of shining-white, marble-sized fruit that can hang on almost till spring. (The floral effect of rowans and whitebeams has not been mentioned; almost always hawthorn-white, it is apt to be rather passed over in anticipation of the autumn display.) Another fine Wilson plant is *S. hupehensis*. This is a robust small tree with bluish green pinnate leaves that turn a fine red as

Stewartia pseudocamellia, *perhaps the most reliable of an exquisite genus.*

the heads of small white fruit take on a faint pink tinge. Often they last well into winter, depending upon the sophistication of the local bird population.

Finally, the ideal rowan for small gardens: this is *S. vilmorinii* from western China. It seldom grows above 20 feet (6 m) in height, even after many years, and the fern-like leaves are joined by dangling clusters of rose-red fruits, which gradually pale through every shade of pink and end up white as the leaves turn crimson. Conventional standard trees, often grafted upon common rowan stocks, have a tendency to look too contrived. Three seedlings planted together offer the possibility of a charming multi-stemmed effect; well fed and watered, they grow quickly.

Most sorbus are perfectly easy to grow—frost-hardiness is no problem—but they resent summer drought, which is why the best specimens are to be found in our Western gardens, both in Britain and North America. It explains, too, their relative infrequency on our east coasts.

Stewartia (Stuartia)
The alternative spellings of the genus name here indicate an 18th-century nomenclatural confusion still not fully resolved (John Stuart, Earl of Bute, being the dedicatee: he was momentarily prime minister but better at helping Princess Augusta with her new botanic garden at Kew).

There are fewer than a dozen species in this camellia-related genus, all beautiful. They have elegant foliage, which often colors magnificently in autumn, cream,

orange and gray flaking bark and a warm white flower display for weeks in July and August, usefully late. The two Americans *Stewartia malacodendron* and *S. ovata*, from the moist, summer-sultry woodlands of Georgia, were the first species to be brought into cultivation. But they remain rare, both at home in North America and in Britain, where they seldom attain tree status.

So it is necessary to turn east for hardier and much more garden-friendly species. Being naturally woodlanders, all require moist lime-free soil—rhododendron country—and, in North America, a bit of summer shade, in zones 5–7.

The Japanese *S. pseudocamellia* is probably most generally available, but *S. sinensis* and *S. pseudocamellia* Koreana Group are catching up; the latter,

Styrax japonicus 'Roseus' is a pink-flushed form of the more usual white-flowered snowbell, both charming little trees.

especially, seems to be proving the most satisfactory of the stewartias for general garden use. All three species are highly recommended. Size depends so much on conditions offered, but it is unlikely that any planter will see the 50 feet (15 m) plus attained in their homelands.

Styrax
Storax, snowbell

For what is apt to be considered a rather esoteric genus, it is noteworthy that of the mere half-dozen species grown, three have been given the AGM; this is a clear signal that they should be grown more. Use of the descriptive North American name snowbell should encourage this.

Gum storax is an aromatic resin obtained from the only European species, *Styrax officinalis*. This grows well enough in warm English gardens, but it never puts on much of the show of milky white bells that is such a joy of plants which grow in Cretan river flats in May. It needs more heat. Once again, therefore, for garden-worthy trees, we turn east to that incredible Japanese flora, much of which spreads up into Korea and parts of China.

S. japonicus is most generally available, and provided its need for good drainage in a leafy lime-free soil is met, it is an ideal small-garden tree. It's even used as a suburban street tree in Seattle. While it is often trained to have a single trunk, a three- to five-stemmed specimen is more graceful. Starting it small provides the choice. Elegant foliage is joined in June by masses of fragrant snowdrop-like flowers (rather like a later halesia), with yellow stamens. Ideally, it

is sited to afford views from underneath. 'Pink Chimes' is a pale pink cultivar from Japan; 'Emerald Pagoda' is bigger in all its parts and grows commendably vigorously when young. This is a splendid plant that is rare, expensive but worth the search: zone 5, just.

Very different with its pale, downy, almost circular leaves, is *S. obassia*, eventually a small round-headed tree of 20 feet (6 m) or so. Its season is slightly later; the white scented bells hang in sprays that, though rather lost among the foliage from a distance, have great charm at close quarters and from beneath. This is a marginal zone 5 plant in North America—a wicked winter can knock it to the ground, but it will grow again with huge soft foliage as if to compensate.

The brilliant turquoise-blue fruit of Symplocos paniculatus *gives it the evocative name sapphire berry. The gem-like effect is not easy to achieve.*

S. *hemsleyanus* is a similar Chinese species with smaller leaves that compete less with its also more obvious flower spikes: when picked off the tree, these could be taken for the flower spikes of a particularly fine deutzia.

Symplocos paniculatus
Sapphire berry

From Japan and China, this is a small twiggy zone 4+ tree, desirable for its May–June fuzz of white flower clusters; indeed, it received an AGM for this back in 1938. But there are a lot of other things flowering white at that time. What makes this so desirable a plant turns symplocus

into sapphire berry. In late September as the leaves begin to thin, the full splendor of the masses of little round fruits, brilliant turquoise-blue, become evident. Often they hold on well into winter, blue food not being expected by birds (or humans).

This is not a difficult plant to grow, as long as it gets sufficient summer heat. It is not particular about soil. However, not only is it not self-pollinating, but there need to be several plants of different clones close enough to do the job. Thus sapphire berry is for big gardens or a neighborhood combined operation; what a plan that would be, for Acacia Avenue, read Sapphireberry Street.

Syringa
Lilac

Everyone knows lilac, at least the common lilac-colored (of course) type species. It must have been one of the favorite plants of early settlers to the northeastern United States and Canada because even though their hard-won holdings may have long since reverted to bush, their beloved lilacs continue to flower bravely by the ruins of old farmsteads today. This is the European plant that has spawned hundreds of forms; don't just "go down to Kew in lilac-time," as the poem has it, but visit the Royal Botanical Gardens in Ontario where the world's definitive collection amazes

Late-flowering Japanese tree lilac (Syringa reticulata).

Showering pink sprays of Tamarix tetrandra.

every year. There it will be seen that for profusion of bloom it is necessary to prune regularly; left alone, hard, rugged trunks will grow to 20 feet (6 m) or so, but the flowers are then out of nose range and its fortnight of splendor is half wasted. Out of flower it is nothing much, so *Syringa vulgaris* becomes pretty pointless as a tree.

Not so the Japanese tree lilac (*S. reticulata*). This reaches 30 feet (9 m) in height and is covered in huge heads of creamy white flowers in June and July—at least it is in North America, where it demonstrates amazing versatility. Happy in virtually any soil in zones 3–9, it may be grown as a multi-stemmed specimen or as

a formal standard and is always available as large semi-mature stock for instant effect. The well-named cultivar 'Ivory Silk' has been more recently joined by 'Regent' and 'Summer Snow'.

In Britain, there is certainly scope for these lovely plants in the relatively more continental climate of East Anglia, where a small midsummer-flowering avenue tree is required.

Tamarix
Tamarisk

Wherever it is seen, an old tamarisk tree is immediately evocative of Mediterranean holidays in little fishing villages. There,

growing out of the sand, the rugged old trees gave a bit of welcome shade to a modest bar or two: in such a spot, nothing much else would grow. This southern European plant was probably *Tamarix tetrandra*, with wispy branches lined by the tiny scale-like leaves shared by the whole genus. In gardens, it is a May-flowering plant and makes a wide-spreading tangle of branches that becomes a mass of soft pink flowers, often weeping to the ground. If the bigger branches are propped, it makes a perfect arbor for alfresco meals.

T. ramosissima is a later-flowering plant and the fine plumes of little pink flowers are particularly valuable in August and September; 'Pink Cascade' and 'Rubra', both self-descriptive names, are admirable cultivars. Once a trunk and framework of branches gets to the desired height (20 feet/6 m) is likely to be the ultimate), it is usual, though not obligatory, to prune it back hard to encourage a flush of growth for next season's flower display. This Asiatic is a much tougher plant than the spring-flowering European and even takes zone 2 winters in North America. Tamarisks are naturally adapted to the salt-laden soils which spell death to most plants, but that does not mean such conditions are essential. Inland gardens can still use these lovely plants, but there does seem to be a suitability to their being in sight of the sea. Then they are at home.

A mature weeping lime tree, or silver linden (Tilia *'Petiolaris'*).

Tilia
Linden

Avenues leading to great houses, fine parkland specimens with perfectly level browse lines like the underside of a table, regular street trees enhancing buildings on either side, lindens are among the most noble of deciduous trees. They epitomize summer, with the drowsy buzz of bees feeding on the nectar, and on warm nights, especially in continental Europe and North America, the scent is positively intoxicating.

There are a number of interesting lindens from China and Japan, such as *Tilia oliveri* with huge leaves and *T. mongolica*, which appear in arboretum collections. North America has a half-dozen native species, often known as basswoods, but those usually grown are clustered round a couple of Europeans, their hybrids and selected cultivars. Central to the European group is the small-leaved linden (*T. cordata*), known in North America as the nicely alliterative littleleaf linden. Ancient trees of 100 feet (30 m) in height are known, but it is for the regular habit and growth of recent selections that *T. cordata* has become such an important amenity tree, especially in North America. 'Greenspire' and 'Chancellor' make upright narrow trees; the quick-growing 'Glenleven' is rather wider, while 'Handsworth' and 'Winter Orange' are grown for their noticeably colored twigs, so striking after leaf fall. These are all zone 3–7 plants. In some years, aphid infestation causes showers of honeydew; a sticky layer on cars parked beneath and messy sooty mold on the leaves are the result. In North America leaves of young trees are also prey to voracious Japanese beetles. Yet this is still a most valuable and beautiful tree.

Its hybrid *T. × euchlora* seems to avoid the aphids but doesn't offer the range of the littleleafs and seems unlikely to rival *T. cordata* itself when old.

For the biggest spaces, there are three splendid lindens with a somewhat southeast Europe emphasis; they are all 100-footers (30 m) given the chance. *T.* 'Petiolaris' is the weeping or pendent white lime. This hasn't the complete weeping-willow effect, so pendent is the better adjective for the graceful downward-sweeping branches. White-backed leaves flash in the wind. It is late-flowering, in July or even August, and the scent is heavily pervasive—and so highly attractive that bees have been observed to drop drunk or dead from this and other linden trees.

It has been suggested that this is just a particularly fine form of the European white linden (*T. tomentosa*)—known as silver linden in North America—and certainly in the wild, the latter exhibits varying amounts of the showering habit. All have the attractive white-backed leaves, and this attribute is accentuated in the American cultivar 'Sterling Silver'. 'Brabant' is a Dutch cultivar of less spreading habit. These are zones 4/5–7 trees.

For colder areas, even to zone 2, the broad-leaved lime—not a helpful name as the leaves are no bigger than those of common lime (*T. × europaea*), avoided nowadays because of its suckers—

is native even into Sweden. This is *T. platyphyllos*, which exists in a wide range of cultivars. The red-twigged linden (*T.p.* 'Rubra'), glowing splendidly in winter sun, is the usual big tree, but for smaller spaces, the distinctive cut-leaf linden (*T. p.* 'Laciniata') is about half-sized. It flowers prodigiously in late June.

Trochodendron aralioides

The fingers of two hands are hardly needed to list broad-leaved evergreen tree genera that are generally hardy in British gardens. Perhaps we are unduly cautious; olives are not unknown in London, griselinia is looking well, though still a shrub, at the RHS's Hyde Hall in winter-

A branch of Tilia *'Petiolaris'. The leaves flash white in the wind.*

Trochodendron aralioides *is a remarkably hardy broad-leaved evergreen tree with a layered branch pattern and heads of sharp green flowers.*

chilly Essex and, of course, famously mild west coast sites offer further living suggestions that might be more often tried. So it is odd that trochodendron, which is recorded as having performed well in especially cold winters, is not seen more often.

In its Japanese forest home, *Trochodendron aralioides* reaches 80 feet (25 m) or so; in Britain to see one a third of that is, in Michelin parlance, worth a detour. Its specific epithet, *aralioides*, "aralia-like," is only descriptive after

making a further botanical link, that of ivy being in the aralia family (*Araliaceae*). The wavy, bright green trochodendron foliage is extremely like that of ivy when it has got to the top of its support and changes to its arborescent form. The May flower heads, too, are ivy-like and vividly green.

Shade or sun in any decent soil seems to suit. The elegantly layered branch pattern is slow to develop and apt to be hampered further by the depredations of keen indoor flower arrangers. Some wind shelter is also desirable.

Zelkova

Until a few years ago, in any alphabetical review of hardy trees, the final entry would have been *Ulmus*. But no more. It is fortuitous that these fine elm relations, which seem to be immune to the plague, follow on. But being uncommon and expensive, they are unlikely ever to fill the gap in the wider countryside. These are big garden trees.

Zelkova carpinifolia is from the Caucasus and therefore prefers the closest Britain can offer to a continental climate

Following the devastating loss of most elms on both sides of the Atlantic, zelkovas are worth seeking out as replacements.

in the southeast, where 100-foot-high (30 m) plants exist. But it grows slowly, gradually building up a dense head of upright sky-reaching branches, and clearly has the ability to be extremely long-lived.

Rather smaller is its Japanese cousin *Z. serrata*, which therefore has more potential for general use. Elegant narrow leaves are held in a rank on each side of the twigs; autumn color can be good— dusky red and orange.

Both zelkovas are zone 4+ plants in North America, where the Japanese species has received much acclaim (and grows better), succeeding from New Brunswick to Florida. Selections continue to appear; 'Green Vase' and 'Village Green' are both narrower in outline than the species (in fact leaning toward the shape of the Caucasian) and are relatively fast-growing in the deep, rich soil they prefer. There is need to encourage a good leader in the early years by suitable pruning and staking, after which fine trees should result.

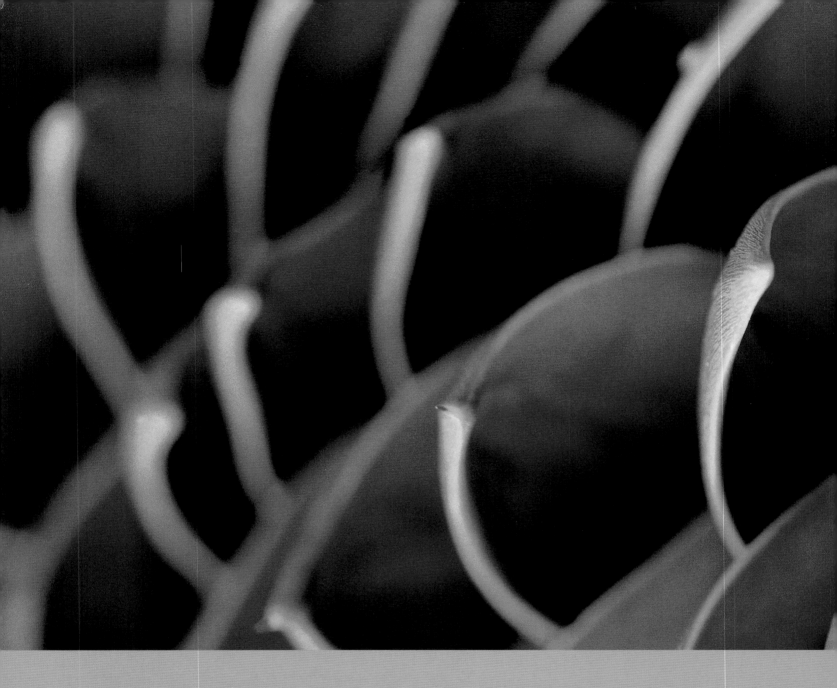

directory of conifers

The pendulous cones of the Norway spruce (Picea abies).

Abies
Fir

There is always confusion between firs and spruces, but identification is easy to remember: while firs (*Abies*) have cones that sit vertically upon the branches, those of spruce (*Picea*) are pendulous. Note the triad of p's and accept without concern that Norway spruce is confusingly named *Picea abies*—we should just blame some long-dead-botanist and not fuss. Non-fruiting specimens can be distinguished by the fact that the needles of firs are shed (or pulled off) leaving a clean scar; those of spruce leave rather prickly pegs. More p's.

For big spaces in high rainfall areas, the giant fir and noble fir (*Abies grandis* and *A. procera* respectively) fully live up to their names. Both are David Douglas introductions of 1830 from Oregon. The Californian red fir (*A. magnifica*) is comparable, with a rather narrower habit. Given the conditions they relish, all grow quickly—at least a couple of feet a year—and make elegant gray-green Christmas tree shapes to begin with and thus, so long as one can be strong-minded, may have to be removed before they outgrow their spaces. Better is to buy a sheltered glen in western Scotland and plant prodigiously.

The white fir (*A. concolor*) is an upland plant from Colorado and Arizona and is much less dependent upon the soft conditions of the coast. As a result it is welcomed on the other side of the continent in zones 3–7 and is the best fir for general use. Eventually huge, it is beautiful in youth with blue-green leaves (dramatically silver-blue in the Violacea Group) that are almost round in section. In Britain, it succeeds well in the drier south though grows more slowly and will probably not make monster size.

A. balsamea is rather an enigma in cultivation: it is easy in northeastern North America with its native distribution from Labrador down to Pennsylvania—zones 3–5 or so—but in Britain, it often doesn't last long. This may not be a problem, especially in small spaces where an elegant narrow pyramid, its leaves banded silver beneath, can give 20 years of pleasure before going over the top. This is the plant that provides the resin called Canada balsam or balm of Gilead. It makes a marvelous Christmas tree, exquisitely scented, and holds on to its needles even if a bit is kept for months.

European mountain firs (*A. cephalonica* and *A. pinsapo*, from Greece and Spain respectively) are much better adapted to summer heat and limy soils. The blue-gray leaf pattern of the latter is highly distinct, the leaves being held all around the branchlets like a flue brush. The Caucasian fir (*A. nordmanniana*) is widely grown throughout Britain and in zones 4–6 in North America. It has lustrous black-green foliage on sweeping tiered branches, which carry big 8-to-10-inch (20–25 cm) cones. Like most other firs, it will get huge, but it looks good when young. Gardeners with space wishing to extend pinetum planting will also look into the range of oriental firs. There are some beautiful plants—*A. fargesii* from western China and the Japanese *A. homolepis* do well. Others are susceptible to late frosts on unfurling spring growth.

Only one is at all commonly seen and available; this is the Korean fir (*A. koreana*). Although it exceeds 50 feet (15 m) in height in its home, a height of half that in cultivation is a success. Its claims to fame are a profusion of striking purple-blue cones sitting on the horizontal branches and the fact that it fruits when very young: a 4-foot (1.25 m) specimen, like a stubby blue-green Christmas tree, may carry a couple of dozen cones, and they remain attractive for many months. Korean fir accepts zone 5 conditions; good soil will keep it slowly moving, tier on tier.

Araucaria araucana
Monkey puzzle, Chile pine

Monkey puzzles are loved or loathed. Certainly the anti brigade gains lots of ammunition from those scrubby old trees languishing in front gardens of decaying Victorian villas in once-prosperous

The unmistakable silhouette of the monkey puzzle (Araucaria araucana).

industrial towns. One can only be surprised that they live at all; it just indicates that this extraordinary South American plant will take almost any conditions in a zone 7+-ish climate.

Good trees in moist soil make a great dome 50 feet (15 m) high or so, clothed to the ground with spreading branches of dark, prickly leaves: a wonderful sight. The cones are the size and shape of half-pint beer mugs. Obviously, a mature monkey puzzle needs broad acres—even avenues—to be in scale. But so distinct is the branch pattern in youth that they have an architectural role, if only for 20 years or so, in smaller spaces. The vertical trunk-to-be, wreathed with leaves for years, puts out perfectly regular whorls of branches at 18-inch (45 cm) intervals, building up a symmetrical silhouette unlike anything else we can grow.

It is as a lawn specimen—but not plonk in the middle—that a monkey puzzle grows conventionally well; but when it is grown with other exotic forms such as cordyline and phormium in a rocky (natural or contrived) setting, a remarkable association can be built up that will always catch the eye—to the point that traffic roundabouts in Leeds, so planted, are a positive danger to gardening motorists.

Calocedrus decurrens
Incense cedar

Coming from mountainous areas of Oregon down to lower California, this is the Lombardy poplar of conifers, a dark finger pointing skyward. A well-grown single plant is remarkable, but a group, where space permits, is dramatic. This desirable habit is not constant, neither in cultivation nor in the wild; it seems to be not a genetic trait but an inexplicable response to climate. The similar conditions of West Coast Washington state and eastern England produce the narrowest trees, 100 feet (30 m) in height and only a few feet wide; elsewhere they widen. Perhaps this is the only occasion when the mildness of western Britain and the extremes of eastern North America have the same effect—a noticeable portliness in incense cedars. Acceptance of zones 5–8 does not commit the plant to any particular form. But anywhere, it is a lovely tree. Not a true cedar, it has sprays of cypress-like leaves and marble-sized cones within which, unlike most conifers, the seeds ripen in one season.

Cedrus
Cedar

Cedar of Lebanon (*Cedrus libani*) is the classic tree of grand British country-house landscapes, chosen for its great horizontal layers of dark evergreen foliage that so contrast with other plants. Left behind when an estate is broken up and the area turned into suburban housing, often an old cedar still presides over the scene as a memory of golden times past.

In the wild, cedars of Lebanon extend far beyond that small country into the Taurus mountains of Turkey and westward almost to the Aegean Sea. Then a smaller variant turns up in Cyprus, known as *C. brevifolia*. Farther west and across the Mediterranean, the Atlas

Calocedrus decurrens *is one of the narrowest of all hardy conifers.*

mountains of Algeria and Morocco are the home of *C. atlantica*, now considered a further geographical variant of the Lebanon species. Certainly at comparable ages they look very similar, but the branches of Mount Atlas cedar often exhibit a slightly upward lift like an airplane's wing; eventually, they are as flat-topped as the Lebanon tree.

C. deodara is from the western Himalayas, where it grows in huge stands, the close-packed trunks rearing up to a dark canopy 200 feet (60 m) above. Coming from the northern reaches of the Raj, it became a very popular tree in Britain; tea was taken under it on innumerable vicarage lawns, and it even became the subject of a drawing-room ballad: "Under the deodar/Dumdy dumdy dum afar" etc. This is the most elegant cedar in youth—the others begin rather gawkily—with a clear leader and pendulous branchlets, rather grayish in general effect. Leaves of all cedars are grouped like little brushes on short stubby shoots; smooth barrel-shaped cones line the branches.

A number of variants have been selected and propagated. By far the most significant is the blue Atlantic cedar (*C. atlantica* Glauca Group); in the best cultivars it is pale blue-white, offering a color and form—superb as a foil to other plants—that are unique.

Cedars are big trees, eventually reaching above 100 feet (30 m) in height and almost that across, and they obviously need space as the dominant specimen tree in the scene. With good, deep soil, growth can be 3 feet (90 cm) a year and, unlike the North American West Coast conifers, they have no objection to limy soil. It is vital that cedars are planted young. All make fine plants throughout Britain; in North America, they prefer the zone 6–8 range. The deodar succeeds up to Boston; the Arnold Arboretum has selected a fine bluish cultivar and called it 'Shalimar', evoking of course yet another Edwardian ballad, "Pale hands I love, beside the Shalimar." Few conifers can compete.

Chamaecyparis
False cypress

From a type species native to Oregon and north California, *Chamaecyparis lawsoniana* (Lawson cypress, Oregon cedar, etc.) has produced in 150 years of cultivation hundreds of different cultivars. Almost any gardener's requirement (other than full East Coast hardiness—these are

The typical horizontal branch pattern of the cedar of Lebanon (Cedrus libani).

more 5–7 zoners for the moist West) can be found. They range from fine forest trees towering close to 200 feet (60 m) to tiny dwarf cultivars the size of garden gnomes; foliage tints vary from the typical mid-green to gold, gray, near blue, variegated white or yellow. You pays your money and takes your pick.

Typically, foliage is in elegant sprays of tiny, overlapping scale-like leaves, and the full tree-sized forms build up to huge pyramids, clothed to the ground, before rather opening out in maturity. Maintaining a single leader in youth will obviously develop a more regular plant, but the natural tendency is for a number of trunks to develop, which when old and buttressed can look superb. This is anathema to the tidy minds of economic foresters. There is always visual confusion between Lawson and other cypress/cedar (in America) lookalikes. Here in addition to spherical pea-sized cones—thuja's are somewhat elongated—the tip of the leader is invariably bent and blowing in the wind, as if backbone has not yet caught up with speed of growth. Which is probably the case.

Lawson will succeed in any decent soil. Irrigation may be necessary in serious summer drought; this is certainly worthwhile with garden specimens. Because there are so many cultivars, with new ones appearing all the time, it makes huge sense for potential planters to visit gardens where they grow and make a list of what seems most desirable. Reliable, well-tried cultivars include 'Alumii', 'Triomf van Boskoop', 'Fletcheri', and 'Pembury Blue' in the gray/blue range; yellows are 'Stewartii' and 'Lutea'; 'Green Hedger' is self-descriptive. Hardy alternatives to narrow Italian cypress are

The small characteristic leaves of a Lawson cypress (Chamaecyparis lawsoniana *'Pottenii'*).

'Columnaris', 'Green Pillar' and 'Kilmacurragh'. So, too, is the wonderful 'Wisselii': narrow, blue-gray with crowded tufts of foliage alight in spring with tiny red male "cones."

A common mistake is to buy dear little plants from the local garden center without realizing their potential. Not only do we plant *de novo*; we also inherit: often we

find youngish trees 15 to 20 feet (4.5–6 m) high that obviously have pretensions and will get above themselves. Lawson cypress responds to clipping well and while it is annoying to be committed to giving an annual haircut, for which scaffolding may be required, it is possible to maintain an obelisk or cone of foliage at the optimum height. Felling the tree or living with ever-

An old tree of Cryptomeria japonica.

A couple of Japanese species offer a huge range of dwarf varieties as well as some useful small trees. The Hinoki cypress (*C. obtusa*) has brilliant green foliage sprays, even brighter in the golden cultivar 'Crippsii'. This is a most elegant little tree (at least in the lifetime of most planters) and looks good at any age. Full sun, moist soil.

The Sawara cypress (*C. pisifera*) has also proliferated into a great number of garden variants. Many are dwarfs. *C.p.* 'Filifera' is extraordinary in its trailing showers of whip-like branches, slowly getting close to 40 feet (12.25 m) in height, while 'Squarrosa' has contrasting billowing heaps of soft foliage. A blue-gray variant is the ubiquitous 'Boulevard', seen throughout zones 4–8 in North America. It becomes attractively purplish in cold weather. This needs to be used as a part of a considered foliage association: plonking it in concrete pots each side of a front door, where it freezes in winter and dries out in summer, is not kind. No wonder it can look resentful.

Cryptomeria japonica
Japanese cedar

This is the most important native lumber tree in Japan, and there were hopes that it would prove equally valuable in Britain, but other things have done better. This doesn't detract from its useful ornamental role here and in zones 6–8 North America; it likes a life that is both mild and moist.

Eventually a tree of 100 feet (30 m) in height, this is a relation of the redwoods. Long shoots carry forward-pointing, incurved triangular leaves. They are tightly packed, so you can, as with a cat's tail, happily stroke it only with the grain. Mature trees have a distinctive red peeling bark, like its *Sequoiadendron*

Cunninghamia lanceolata.

cousin but not so soft and spongy.

Cryptomeria has produced a lot of bush-sized garden cultivars in various colors. *C. j.* Elegans Group starts thus but eventually becomes tree-sized. The foliage remains in a juvenile state, soft and feathery and carried in cumulus-cloud-like heaps. There is a feeling of smoke bush as its pale green in summer turns bronzy red with the onset of winter. Unfortunately, the weight of the foliage is apt to break branches and can be damaged by wet snow. Preventative pruning can help and is well worth the trouble.

Cunninghamia lanceolata
Chinese fir

This is an unusual redwood relation from central and southern China that looks more like an aberrant monkey puzzle. It is a plant that enjoys a moist climate, both at the root and in the air, and succeeds best in the west of Britain and North America, zone 7-ish; it does well in Vancouver, British Columbia.

increasing shade are worse alternatives and may ruin the garden picture.

From farther north in North America, right up to the base of Alaskan glaciers, comes *C. nootkatensis*, which has zone 4 acceptance, happy in the Great Lakes area. In its 'Pendula' form it makes a striking column with curtains of hanging leaf sprays—quickly.

Few conifers make good multi-stemmed specimens, but here several trunks, with warm red-brown bark, build up to an attractive whole. Sharp-tipped leaves are up to 3 inches (7 cm) long with two conspicuous silver stripes on the underside. The lovely cultivar *Cunninghamia lanceolata* 'Glauca' has noticeably blue-green foliage.

Leaves turn bronzy in winter, and as some old foliage is retained, the plant avoids the predominant green darkness of so many conifers. Cunninghamia makes a fine lawn specimen—enjoying a bit of wind shelter. Trees well over 50 feet (15 m) can be eventually expected, but its distinctive irregular outline starts building up from the earliest years.

One of the fastest-growing conifers, x Cupressocyparis leylandii '*Castlewellan*'.

x *Cupressocyparis leylandii*
Leyland cypress

It is sad that such a splendid plant, one of the few hybrid conifers to exist, has had such a bad press. This is hardly surprising when a dense evergreen tree that can grow taller than a house in 10 years is planted in all directions; no wonder there are problems. But this should not lead to complete avoidance, as if it is like some dire incursion of triffids or ents. The virtues must be lauded, the reservations taken into account.

The original chance hybrid occurred in Wales in 1888. Two others appeared within the next half-century, all crosses between *Chamaecyparis nootkatensis* and *Cupressus macrocarpa*. They combined some of the hardiness of the nootka (putting the hybrid in the zone 6–9 range) with the ebullience of the southern Monterey cypress. Ease of propagation by cuttings and the huge potential trade for quick, simple-to-grow hedges and screens have made it ubiquitous in recent years.

Leyland cypress naturally makes a dense, cone-shaped tree, clothed to the ground. Single specimens well sited with plenty of space or short avenues can look splendid. Extensive screens—the plant takes exposure even at the seaside—are highly effective, but the effect is somber. This can be mitigated by using the range of colored-leaved cultivars and adding deciduous trees to the mix.

'Leighton Green' and 'Greenspire' are bright green; 'Castlewellan' and the more recent 'Robinson's Gold' are yellow; 'Haggerston Gray', 'Naylor's Blue' and 'Silver Dust' proclaim their alternatives. A group of these where there is plenty of space makes a marvelous effect—but for built-up city areas, not the countryside.

The inevitable shade cast by such solid growth must also be taken into account. So must the fact that planting too close together fails to filter wind and dangerous eddies whirl round as from buildings.

Politically correct planters now expunge Leyland cypress from housing developments, but the fact that owners have let their hedges get out of hand should not demean the plant itself. It can be kept to 5 to 6 feet (less than 2 m) easily enough if clipped three or four times a year, to make a perfect gray or golden wall; only when it is neglected do the problems arise.

Two other Nootka hybrids are just beginning to become available; these are crosses with the Arizona and Mexican cypresses and seem likely to be less aggressive than Leyland. They are worth looking out for.

Cupressus
True cypress

The dark, pointing fingers of the Italian cypress (*Cupressus sempervirens* Stricta Group) are a vital part of the Mediterranean scene from Spain to Turkey, just as they are in paintings idealizing those classical landscapes, from the Italian Primitives through Claude and Poussin to today. This is the world that more northern gardeners so often attempt to evoke by planting narrow fastigiate trees of all types. As a zone 7 plant, it should be safe throughout much of Britain and North America, but it seems so to long for the light and ambience of its home that it never quite belongs elsewhere. Obviously it finds other Mediterranean climatic areas entirely acceptable; in more northern climes, though, it works better in town courtyards

Showering blue-gray curtains of Cupressus cashmeriana, *one of the most beautiful conifers.*

in association with buildings, preferably against a Corinthian column or two, which it soon rivals in height.

Other true cypresses are more useful generally. They are distinguished from *Chamaecyparis* by 3-D foliage sprays and much bigger spherical cones that often stay on the tree for years after the seeds are shed. They are also likely to be less hardy.

The Monterey cypress (*Cupressus*

macrocarpa)—one of Leyland's parents—has a tiny natural distribution in California, where splendidly architectural old trees fight it out with the elements on the rocks at the very edge of the ocean on Monterey Bay. Not surprisingly, it was hailed as the ultimate tree for wind shelter. And so it is in mild western Britain, making a quick cone of bright green leaves (even brighter yellow in 'Lutea', 'Donard Gold' and 'Goldcrest') and then flattening out into an almost Lebanon cedar silhouette. No true cypresses transplant well, and it is vital that trees for shelter are planted small; they must get their roots down before offering wind resistance or they will never do their job.

Of more general garden use is the smooth Arizona cypress (*C. arizonica* var. *glabra* syn. *C. glabra*. This makes a fine conical tree of 50 feet (15 m) or so, which keeps its shape and looks good as it is getting there. Gray-blue foliage, red bark peeling to show flashes of purple and yellow and acceptance in zone 7 on any soil from lime to acid make it one of the most desirable of conifers. Excellent as a hedge—it is used a lot in Provence and doesn't turn a hair, or leaf, in that climate of wicked extremes —it can be trimmed or left to grow as a tall screen. Cultivars offer varying amounts of blueness or narrowness of form, and all can be expected to be 15 feet (4.5 m) in height within 10 years. This is a much better bet than cowering behind a row of out-of-control Leylands.

C. cashmeriana is one of the most beautiful trees in cultivation, anywhere. A conical 50-footer (15 m) draped in curtains of palest blue-gray that blow in the breeze, it is, at best, only for zone 8. But anyone with a sheltered dell in Cornwall should reach for their *RHS Plant Finder*.

Ginkgo biloba
Maidenhair tree

Plants that are grown because they are "living fossils" or because they are rare and endangered or even extinct in the wild are apt to be what the catalogues describe as "of botanical interest only." In other words, dull. Ginkgo is all those things except the last, for, with its clean shining

fan-shaped leaves that turn bright yellow in autumn, it is one of the most beautiful garden trees. The fact that it is a relict conifer whose only relations died with the dinosaurs is obviously fascinating but in no way detracts from its virtues.

Maidenhair tree has been in Britain since the mid-18th century, and the famous old tree at Kew planted in 1762 still flourishes, the typical upright form now with elegantly showering upper branches. In North America, where it accepts zone 4–9 conditions, it is clearly unfazed by heat and cold. The narrow habit makes it ideal for

The fan-like deciduous leaves and fleshy fruit of the unusual conifer Ginkgo biloba.

street planting; atmospheric pollution is no problem, and it is seen happily growing in the skyscraper canyons of New York and Pittsburg and looking particularly fine against the elegant red-brick 18th-century façades in Washington's Georgetown area.

Especially narrow cultivars have been selected. These range from the long-established 'Fastigiata' to more recent, especially North American, introductions such as 'Princeton Sentry'. 'Autumn Gold' and 'Saratoga' are more cone-shaped and all are noted as being male plants. A lot of fuss is made of the spherical yellow, plum-like fruits being "malodorous" and having "a strong offensive odor"; it is more constructive to note that within the soft casing is a thin-skinned nut, the flesh of which is delicious fried in oil or butter. Prospective gastronomes therefore should search out female clones such as 'Ohazuki' and the improbably named 'King of Dongting'. The Chinese know more about these things.

Ginkgo grows in any well-drained soil, but it is especially necessary to give it a good, rich diet to begin with; starved trees sit sullenly for years without putting out extension growth.

Juniperus
Juniper

That there are five full columns of junipers in *Andersen's Source List* indicates not only the range of this important genus but also how much of it is used in gardens. In the wild, they spread around the northern hemisphere from the subtropics to the arctic, and they even have an outpost in east Africa. Many are invaluable ground-hugging forms, but there is also a number of good small to medium-sized trees which often provide a Mediterranean-cypress feel

to areas where that would normally be no more than a dream. Most shrug off adverse conditions without a thought and care little about soil: in Britain, common juniper (*Juniperus communis*) grows wild on the chalk of Salisbury Plain, as well as on acid hillsides in Scotland.

Like others of the cypress family, junipers have two distinct foliage forms, the prickly juvenile leaves usually giving way to the soft sprays of overlapping scale-like leaves as maturity develops. With junipers the prickliness may be retained.

The Chinese juniper (*J. chinensis*) has a huge native range and has given rise to numbers of garden forms. The wild plant is a broadly upright tree to 50 feet (15 m) or so, usually exhibiting both gray foliage forms on the same plant. Narrower cultivars include the gray-green 'Mountbatten' and the golden-leaved 'Aurea', which, also known as Young's golden juniper, is apt to burn in full sun. 'Kaizuka', the Hollywood juniper, is a splendidly statuesque form with an erratic branch pattern and bright-green clustered foliage. Commonly used in small rock gardens, it soon outgrows its space; much better is to use it where the architectural effect is emphasized. These are 3–8 zoners in North America.

European common juniper (*J. communis*), whose aromatic fruits flavor gin and are used as a kitchen spice, seldom makes much of a tree, but the narrow cultivar *J. c.* 'Hibernica' is admirable for formal planting even in small spaces as it seldom gets much above 10 feet (3 m) in height. Less tight in habit but quicker to make an effect are forms of the Rocky Mountain juniper (*J. scopulorum*), which is just as hardy. 'Skyrocket' is bright gray-green and when 20 feet (6 m) high is still only a

Juniperus chinensis *'Mountbatten'*.

couple of feet across. 'Blue Heaven' is wider; 'Tolleson's Blue Weeping' makes a silvery-blue shower of foliage.

The weeping effect is maintained for zone 7 gardens by the lovely *J. recurva* var. *coxii*. This Himalayan makes an admirable small specimen tree and associates particularly well with rhododendrons and azaleas.

J. virginiana is the pencil cedar or eastern red cedar of the Atlantic states and the Great Lakes forest region. Again accepting poor soils, it is one of the earliest woody colonizers of abandoned farmland, standing up sharply among the asters and goldenrod and eventually reaching 50 feet (15 m) or so. Of the many cultivars, 'Blue Arrow' is self-descriptive; 'Burkii' is also blue in summer but darkens to purplish bronze with the onset of winter.

A number of other, mainly oriental, junipers are seen in specialist collections, such as *J. drupacea*, a fine large-coned tree from Asia Minor, and the Himalayan *J. wallichiana*; these may move more commonly into the garden scene as availability increases.

Larix
Larch

Of the dozen larches native to the mainly mountainous regions of the northern hemisphere, only three species and their variants are commonly grown. European larch has been in Britain since the early 17th century, and famous old trees planted in 1738 still flourish at Dunkeld in Perthshire. These and other magnificent 100-foot-high (30 m) veterans have become almost cedar-like in outline, with branches hanging from the high crown. But for the first decades, larches are typically cone-shaped. Becoming more beautiful by the year, they are ideal both as garden trees and in the broader landscape.

Larches are, of course, deciduous conifers. They leaf out in early spring like the faintest watercolor wash, sometimes with a soft pink overlay from the young cones. Summer shade is light, and the season ends in a cloud of warm yellow late in November. While the typical *Larix decidua* is a lovely plant in its own right, variants are available that offer narrower or more pendulous habits; the dwarf forms are, of course, not *trees*.

European larch accepts most conditions except the thinnest limestone soils and the most acidic wet soils. In North America, it accepts the colder zones 2–6. There, too, the native larch or tamarack (*L. laricina*) grows in the most inhospitable swamps as far north as trees occur. With horizontal branches and drooping branchlets, it is less elegant than the European larch but invaluable for cold wet conditions in its own country. When ripe, the cones look like lines of unfolding wooden rosebuds.

The Japanese larch (*L. kaempferi*) is used more for commercial forestry; with its heavier branch pattern and denser shade, it is less useful as a garden tree. However, 'Diane' is an interesting contorted cultivar, as is the weeping 'Pendula'.

The hybrid *L.* × *marschlinsii* (syn. *L.* × *eurolepi*s brings Europe and the Orient together. It has all the qualities of the European species with greater vigor and perhaps an ability to take even more difficult conditions.

Larches share with true cedars a distinctive leaf and branch pattern. Extension shoots have leaves singly set around the twig, while most foliage is held, brush-like, on stubby little spurs.

The autumn gold display of the deciduous Larix europaea.

This occurs also with the uncommon *Pseudolarix amabilis* from eastern China. Now more available and carrying an AGM seal of approval, the golden larch makes a good specimen tree wider than true larches. The leaves are longer and the autumn color more spectacular—hence its common name. In Britain, this is usually a mild west coast tree, but it accepts zone 6 New York winters. Summer wood ripening and avoidance of late spring frosts seem to be the key to real success.

Though the choicer forms of larch are almost always sold as potted specimens, wherever possible larches should be planted small and young, bare root, with protection from rodents, rabbits and deer until they are well established.

Metasequoia glyptostroboides
Dawn redwood

Here is a tree, known to science, like ginkgo, from 200-million-year-old fossil records, that was suddenly "discovered" by a Chinese botanist in 1941. Of course, like North America before Columbus, it was always there and known perfectly well to the residents, in this case, those living on the Hubei/Sichuan borders. Seeds were collected, sent to the Arnold Arboretum and distributed to major gardens in Europe and America in 1948. Translated, the botanical name is suitably descriptive, but the coining of the romantic English name was an inspired thought, suggesting a plant from the dawn of knowledge and hinting at the colors of a shepherd's-warning morning in its pink-buff autumn tints.

For this is, like its swamp cypress relations, a deciduous conifer. Like taxodium, it accepts, though doesn't insist upon, wet sites and, as with larch,

it leafs early and colors late. Similarly, therefore, dawn redwood is a valuable large garden tree. It is fast growing—specimens have already reached 100 feet (30 m) in height in 50 years of cultivation—and so far, it seems to maintain its youthful conical shape; the

reddish trunk becomes noticeably rugged and buttressed.

In North America, zones 5–8 seem about right where, as in Britain (for the best trees are in the southeast), summer wood-ripening warmth is welcomed. Any but dry, sandy soils are accepted. Dawn

The dawn redwood (Metasequoia glyptostroboides).

Stiff silvery blue needle leaves of Picea pungens *'Koster'.*

Christmas tree. Time was when they were always sold with their roots on and, potted up, they often survived in pre-centrally heated houses to be planted out year after year until they ultimately gave up or became too big to bring inside in Britain. Trees in various states of health strewn around suburbia pay witness to that period of innocence. This is Norway spruce, not a garden tree of much virtue, but there are other spruces that really do earn their keep.

Identificational differences between firs (*Abies*) and spruces have already been mentioned (see page 174). In cultivational terms, the latter accept more extreme conditions.

A first meeting with a good plant of *P. breweriana* at Westonbirt Arboretum in Gloucestershire or another great garden produces instant conversion to the genus, though it is a state to which few can really aspire. Brewer's weeping spruce is the most elegant of conifers, with its curving branches upturned toward the ends, like Chinese eaves, from which hang curtains of dark branchlets. The whole thing sways in the breeze. This is a rare native tree of northern California, eventually reaching 100 feet (30 m) or so in the wild. Half that is a triumph in cultivation and that only after many years; a dozen or so must elapse before the typical beauty begins to take shape, and this from seedlings. Grafted plants should be avoided; though early growth is quicker, they fail to make good specimens.

Those of us with less patience, less time left or in doubt of posterity would do well to settle for the Serbian spruce (*P. omorika*). With the same Chinese eaves but shorter curtains, this is a wonderfully elegant tree, having a narrow head of

redwood should be planted young to encourage early quick growth; bigger "specimens" are apt to stand still and look ratty for years and are, as usual, a trick to achieve instant results. Reasonable wind shelter and full sun combine to encourage well-furnished plants.

Already a number of cultivars have been named: 'National' is narrower in form than the species and the new 'Gold Rush'—a selection from Japan—is highly

recommended for summer-long foliage effect. Metasequoia is typically planted as a single specimen, but where there is space for three or five or the opportunity for a whole grove is grasped, the effect is stunning.

Picea
Spruce

Everyone knows *Picea abies*, if not as a growing plant, then as the commonest rich green foliage with white-banded undersides. It takes high pH as happily as peaty soils and succeeds in zones 4–7, though there are reports of windburn in exposed places. Reaching 100 feet (30 m) in height in the wild, it seems not to be long-lived in cultivation. But it makes its effect quickly, even in urban gardens, where its narrow spires cast little shade. A third species with pendulous sub-branches is the west Himalayan *P. smithiana*. In North America, this is a zone 7+ tree and, needing moisture and high humidity to do well, is a west coast plant on both continents. In suitable spots, it eventually looks like a large Brewer, growing more quickly and soon making a fine effect.

The name of *P. orientalis* refers to the Near, not the Far, East, and it would help if it were known more often as Caucasian spruce. It is one of the most elegant of spruces, like a very upmarket Christmas tree: regular tiers of branches, tidy, short needles, a dense deep-green in general effect. In contrast is the cultivar 'Aurea,' whose May flush of new needles makes a brilliant show. Naturally this is slower and eventually smaller than the 100 feet (30 m) that may be expected from the type. Again, from zone 4 up.

Seen everywhere throughout North America in zones 2–7 is the Colorado spruce (*P. pungens*), especially in one of the blue forms. There is no doubt that when young, this is a striking little tree, making regular pyramids of eye-catching silvery blue—'Hoopsii' and 'Koster' (the latter is apt to be somewhat variable) are those generally promoted. Indeed, it could be said that they are *too* generally available, having become an inevitable constituent of new "landscaping" (a concept that is also somewhat variable).

Marbled trunks of Mediterranean stone pine (Pinus pinea).

Small trees sitting alone look strange and should be resisted, but in a combination with other evergreens and deciduous species a fine picture can be contrived; then if the spruce becomes ratty, as is quite likely, it can be taken out without much loss.

Pinus
Pine

More than 100 species of pines circumscribe the northern hemisphere, and almost every habitat is used. There are pines as far north and at altitudes as trees succeed; others flourish in the subtropics of Central America and the Philippines. There are pines of the seashore and of deep forests. There are pines for almost all landscapes and soils.

At an early age, most pines share the typical conical form of conifers, spreading out and often becoming flat-topped in maturity. Some, such as the stone pine

(*Pinus pinea*), develop utterly characteristic silhouettes: this is the open umbrella of every Mediterranean vista, contrasting with the cypress's furled-umbrella effect. Stone pine, by the way, is the source of pine "nuts," essential ingredients of many Mediterranean recipes. Pine's foliage pattern is also distinctive. When pines are young, the leaves are carried around the shoots and then a system develops that groups leaves—invariably long and needle-like—into bundles that are pretty constant species by species. Two-, three- and five-needled pines are the rule; *P. monophylla*, one of the Pinyon pines with single bluish needles and edible pine-nut seeds from southwest North America, breaks it. This is a lovely, slow-growing garden tree for zone 6 and above. It just gets into Mexico where, farther south, several highly distinctive five-needled pines grow, such as the evocatively named *P. montezumae*. These have mops of soft needles, up to 12 inches (30 cm) long, arranged like chimney sweeps' brushes. In cultivation,

The Scots pine (Pinus sylvestris).

they are for Britain's milder counties and are beautiful from youth into old age.

Returning up the West Coast of North America, there are species that offer further extremes. *P. coulteri* has the heaviest cones of any—up to 7 pounds (3.25 kg) in weight; *P. lambertiana* the longest—up to 36 inches (90 cm) in length. These are really pinetum curiosities, but other West Coasters relate more to normal life. Just as restricted to that wonderful bit of coast up from Carmel as the Monterey cypress is *P. radiata*, the Monterey pine. There, fighting the elements, this three-needled pine is seldom seen above 50 feet (15 m) in height, splendidly contorted and picturesque. In cultivation in better soil, it can reach that size in less than 10 years. It has become a traditional part of Britain's coastal scenery since David Douglas introduced it in 1833. Obviously it does better on the moister, milder west side. It's a three-needled pine with 6-inch (15 cm) cones that hold tightly in rings on the branches, counting back several years of fruiting.

David Douglas sent back seeds of several more fine pines: specimens of his *P. ponderosa* planted in 1829 still survive at over 100 feet (30 m) high, but sadly, those of the even finer sugar pine (*P. lambertiana*) have not, having fallen (literally) victim to the dread blister rust. This disease also affects the most beautiful of eastern North American species, *P. strobus*. Known at home as white pine and in Britain confusingly as Weymouth pine—nothing to do with the town, but referring to an 18th-century Lord W., who planted it extensively. Across the Channel, it is called *le pin du lord*.

White pine's huge natural range, from Newfoundland into the Great Lakes area

and down the Appalachians, accounts for a zone 3–8 tolerance. It is a splendid garden tree, growing fast with bright green shoots, smooth bark and brushes of soft blue-green needles in fives. In Britain, blister rust will probably carry it off in adolescence, but it will have well earned its keep; in North America, trees up to 200 feet (60 m) are recorded, but having been aggressively logged—not least for ships' masts—in the 19th century, such great trees are now seldom seen. Early 20th-century paintings by Canada's Group of Seven give the flavor of their majesty. 'Fastigiata', 'Pendula' and others vary the form and, surprisingly, white pine also makes a lovely hedge, soft as silk to the touch.

Several European pines are valuable in the zone 4–7 band. Austrian pine (*P. nigra*) has little elegance but will accept exposure on the coast and even on bare limestone hillsides where few other evergreens will grow; Corsican pine (*P. n.* subsp. *paricio*) is a variant with a little more finesse, useful in big spaces on poor soils and as a nurse plant. In North America, Austrians are badly affected by diplodia disease, and shelter belts should be sequentially replaced before it is too late. For smaller areas, again as happy on peat as on chalk, the Arolla pine (*P. cembra*) makes a dense columnar tree with a blue-green cast. That this is a plant which reaches the snow line in the Alps proclaims its hardiness.

Britons have a deep attachment to the Scots pine (*P. sylvestris*); after all, it's one of our only three native conifers. Probably only in a few remote glens in Scotland is it truly wild, but it has been widely planted for centuries. Old, gnarled specimens with sparse branches coming from a red-barked upper trunk look wonderfully romantic, but these are a long-awaited inheritance. Nonetheless, it is attractive from youth with blue-green paired needles and a regular outline; more striking in leaf color is the bluer 'Argentea' and yellow Aurea Group. The latter is much slower-growing, the gold foliage becoming brightest in winter.

Any glance at Chinese silk paintings or Japanese screens immediately notices the oriental interest in the picturesque effects afforded by pine trees. These stylized silhouettes are a joint product of the painter's eye and the gardener's craft and led, almost inevitably it seems, to the intensely oriental art of bonsai. There may be no space for a landscape or a proper tree, but their essence can be distilled and literally potted.

It is not surprising that those plants on which so much care was lavished have innate garden value. The Japanese red pine (*P. densiflora*) is a favorite bonsai tree; in the garden, it becomes rather like a green Scots pine, though with a wider spreading head of upward-thrusting limbs. The Chinese lace-bark pine (*P. bungeana*) was introduced by Robert Fortune with ecstatic descriptions of its milk-white bark that peeled, he said, like arbutus. This seems not to have quite occurred in 150 years of cultivation. Nonetheless, as this small, low-branching tree eventually develops, it has, unique in pines, a green-gray flaking trunk marbled with patches of purple, brown and yellow. The shining leaves are in threes. These are 5–7 zoners in North America, as is the five-needled Korean pine (*P. koraensis*), which makes a fine open gray-green tree, preferring the more extreme continental climate there.

The Himalayan pine (*P. wallichiana*), although native to parts of Assam and getting into Afghanistan, is relatively

hardy, certainly zone 6 in eastern North America. It provides an immediate feeling of lush growth quickly building up into a high cone, branched to the ground if not hemmed in. The banana-shaped cones are also quick to appear, hanging among the soft five-needled foliage. It takes any soil, except the thinnest limestone, and is one of those plants that, though capable of reaching for the sky at 100 feet (30 m) or so, is perfectly suited to relatively small spaces so long as a clear sequence of succession is planned and maintained.

Specialist collections and nurseries can offer many more species as well as horticultural forms, especially dwarfs. They need to be seen. As this is perhaps the most important coniferous genus with huge garden and parkland potential, it should be emphasized that unlike some of the others, they prefer high light concentrations and grow unevenly even in partial shade. Planting when small is important, especially for shelter: when a big stake is required for a specimen that has blown over, it is probably too late.

Sciadopitys verticillata
Japanese umbrella pine

Unlike the Mediterranean umbrella pine, with this tree, the word "umbrella" refers not to the tree's silhouette but to the way the needles are carried on the shoots. Growing in whorls, they create an effect like that of the ribs of a blown-out umbrella and also, it might be said, of that first whorl of leaves that a pine seedling grows. But, in fact, this lovely Japanese plant is a redwood relation, as its nearly round cones suggest.

This is an unusual but immediately recognizable little tree, taking many

The Japanese umbrella pine (Sciadopitys verticillata).

years in cultivation to reach 20 to 30 feet (6–9 m), with its yellow-backed dark green leaves. There is little indication it could reach more than the 100 feet (30 m) it does in its native home. Though it will take zone 5 cold, it prefers a moist, more temperate climate with summer warmth to encourage growth. Then a single leader must be encouraged so that it really shows its quality. A spot should be chosen with protection from the north and east. A leafy woodland soil is also a help; on thin, limy soil the plant becomes chlorotic and looks sick.

Sequoia sempervirens
Coast redwood
Sequoiadendron giganteum
Sierra redwood, wellingtonia, big tree

It makes sense to consider this pair of amazing trees together. They are closely related and indeed were at first included in the same genus. As is well known, they are the mammoths of the plant world, but in spite of terrible depredations through thoughtless forestry in the past, they are, unlike the animal, nowhere near extinct. Specimens of the coast redwood have been recorded at heights of 350 feet (106 m) with 25-foot-diameter (7.5 m) trunks; they are probably 2,000 years old. Wellingtonias, though up to twice as old, are less lofty, a mere 300 feet (90 m), but with even more impressive trunks of a size to provoke man's dottiest insults— driving a road through one monster, setting up a dance floor on the stump of another. To name it "big tree" is the ultimate understatement.

Seeds reached Europe in 1840s and 1850s, and young trees were soon growing in great gardens around Britain; everybody had to have them, and in no time they were showing satisfaction with the climate. Original trees are now over 150 feet (46 m) in height and still growing. Not surprisingly, towering as they do above any other vegetation, they are apt to be the focus of lightning strikes. Single specimens may be seen in, for example, village vicarage gardens, competing for dominance with the adjacent church spire and dating from a time when vicars were still allowed to show off a bit. These are obviously trees for the grandest landscapes.

Sequoia sempervirens and *Sequoiadendron* are easily distinguished both in foliage and in fruit. *Sequoia sempervirens* has sprays of hemlock-like leaves and little near-round cones; those of *Sequoiadendron* are more like small smooth pine cones and the foliage more resembles that of cypresses. There is wonderful red bark on both trees, that of wellingtonia being soft and spongy.

Specimens in public parks invariably have an area on which small boys show off their strength: bruised knuckles identify the coast redwood.

Both trees flourish in Britain, the coast redwood preferring the moister west. Wellingtonia succeeds anywhere except

on the thinnest lime soils and is an ideal plant, space permitting, for commemorative planting singly, in a grove or even as an avenue. It looks good from an early age.

Generally considered zone 7–8 trees in North America, these Californians are not plants for the extremes of the East Coast states.

The barrel-shaped cones of Sequoiadendron giganteum, *trees for the grandest landscapes.*

Taxodium distichum
Swamp cypress

If the redwoods are the pride of North America's West Coast flora, the swamp, or bald, cypress lays fair claim to that title in the East, if only because of its frequency in the wetlands of South Carolina and Georgia and down into Florida's Everglades. Here is a deciduous conifer up to 150 feet (46 m) in height that is able to exploit an apparently under-used habitat and make it its own. Its origin and its common name make it an almost inevitable choice for waterside planting.

The peculiar vertical roots of the swamp cypress (Taxodium distichum).

Sprays of pale foliage, much like that of the dawn redwood, unfold in April and maintain that spring freshness until turning a warm yellow-brown in autumn. In Britain, growth is initially slow—*Metasequoia*, with which in youth it can be easily confused, gets on with it much more quickly—but gradually builds up into a fine, narrow tree. If space permits, a small group looks best; those planted by water eventually develop strange knobbly vertical roots known as pneumatophores, which emerge from the water surface like snorkels (often in their native home with a turtle or two balanced on top) or from the ground as a hazard to lawn mowers. It is presumed these assist in the plant's gaseous exchange system in waterlogged soil because they are not produced when taxodium is grown in normal conditions, where surprisingly it is equally happy. Where taxodium is intended to grow— actually in shallow water—it is necessary to plant it on a small island, perhaps surrounded by vertical logs. These can be removed or left to rot and the soil will gradually subside, leaving the developing tree emerging from the water.

A narrower, smaller and possibly less hardy tree is the pond cypress (*Taxodium distichum* var. *imbricatum*, syn. *T. ascendens*). In Britain, both trees do better in the south and east, obviously relishing as much summer heat as can be provided. In North America, though *T. d.* var. *imbricatum* is generally considered a zone 6 plant, examples exist in sheltered areas designated a couple of notches down the scale, where summer heat helps to compensate. *T. distichum* 'Shawnee Brave' is a recommended selection available in North America, while in

Britain, the pond cypress has a charming cultivar known as 'Nutans', in which the deciduous summer shoots stand up along the supporting branches before bending over and becoming pendulous. This carries the AGM accolade.

Taxus
Yew

In Britain, yew is yew (*Taxus baccata*) and no other designation is needed, not least because the other few species that exist are seldom grown and not nearly as good. In North America, *T. baccata* is generally called English yew to distinguish it, more from a winter hardiness than a visual point of view, from Japanese yew (*T. cuspidata*) and *T.* × *media*, the hybrid between them. The latter pair are zone 5 plants, the English yew a zone 6.

Specimens of *T. baccata* are the oldest European trees, with ages that compare to the great redwoods. Yet this is not demonstrated by size. Venerable trees increase infinitesimally slowly; 50 feet (15 m) in height with a similar spread is enormous. But it must be emphasized that early growth with encouraging cultivation is quite quick: 12 inches (30 cm) or so a year can be expected. A 10-year-old hedge can give a new garden a feeling of real maturity.

Aged trees in English churchyards frequently long pre-date the church they appear to protect and indicate, as in the appropriation of pagan rites as festivals of the Christian Church, the continued use of sites and seasons celebrated as holy for thousands of years. Yew will grow almost anywhere. There are pure wild stands on the dry chalk (limy) downs of southern England, while in Scotland, it grows as wet acid woodland understory.

This Irish yew (Taxus baccata *'Fastigiata') is used to frame an important garden vista.*

Success in the shade of mature beech trees is a major feat for any plant. This, in addition to its ability to accept endless clipping (the famous topiary trees at Levens Hall in Cumbria were planted in 1692), make it a valuable garden plant.

The black-green foliage is maintained year round, only varied for a short time in spring by prodigious quantities of little yellow male cones and the red fleshy "berries" on female trees in autumn. The juicy exterior is pleasant-tasting, the seed very poisonous; it is always fun to show off by eating some, but don't cough by mistake. The foliage, too, is highly toxic, though erratically so, to browsing animals, and seems to be worse when cut and wilted. Thus external hedges bordering fields containing livestock must be wired off. Interestingly, the poisonous alkaloid taxine concerned has been identified as a remedy for several forms of human cancers, and there is now a market for hedge clippings when available in large quantities.

Yew, then, is admirable for evergreen shelter among deciduous trees and shrubs with the desirable attribute of relatively rapid early growth. It is the best of all evergreens for topiary, and hedges are always able to regenerate from old wood. Hedges that have become too wide can be brought back to manageable size over two years by taking one side back to the trunks at a time, feeding and watering to encourage new growth.

Columns or obelisks can be contrived with common yew, but the effect is achieved sooner with Irish yew (*T. b.* 'Fastigiata'). This is one of the best formal trees available; it is a female clone with typical red fruit. 'Fastigiata Lutea' has yellow fruit that can make quite a good show. There are also a number of golden-leaved variants of both the Irish and English yew.

In North America, English yew is seen mainly on the West Coast; on the East its roles are taken up just as effectively by *T. x media* and its cultivars. The vertical 'Hicksii', for example, might be considered a transatlantic Irish yew, ideal for planting around a pool whose water is dyed green for St Patrick's Day—even if the clever allusion is wasted on everyone but the planter.

Thuja
The arborvitaes

On both sides of the Atlantic, this is a small but valuable garden genus. Thujas are closely related to and can be confused with the false cypresses: they have the same sort of flattened sprays of scale-like leaves, but they are rather thicker and more resinous, deliciously fragrant when crushed; there are the same little cones, but they are elongated and sit upright on the branches. Viewing the whole tree, one notices that the terminal shoot is not bent over and waving in the wind as with Lawson cypress.

The architectural effect of an old Western red cedar (Thuja plicata).

Western hemlock (Tsuga heterophylla) *is valuable in shade or as a quick-growing hedge.*

weeks after snow-melt, and this across Canada from the coast, north to James Bay and all around the Great Lakes, as well as farther south. As a result, it is a zone 2 plant for shelter for hedging and mixed planting.

The wild plant is seldom above 50 feet (15 m) in height. It is narrow and dense and often turns yellow-bronze in winter. Old trees with several stems and shredding bark look splendidly architectural. In cultivation, better conditions give more regular plants and numbers of cultivars have been selected. 'Brandon' and 'Fastigiata' are columnar, 'Smaragd' ('Emerald') is broader and maintains bright green foliage throughout the year, and 'Sunburst' lives up to its name.

T. occidentalis is not a good plant in Britain. As so often happens, plants adapted for extreme conditions are less happy when the living is easier, so it was convenient when Pacific North America subsequently offered western red cedar (*T. plicata*), which needs at least zone 5 conditions. This is yet another magnificent species from that amazing evergreen flora. Up to 200 feet (60 m) tall in the wild, it has reached more than half that from 19th-century plantings in Britain. Open-ground trees are clothed to the ground with a buttressed trunk and an almost wellingtonia profile. Virtually any soil is tolerated, but it does best in the wetter west. It makes a splendid hedge and the scent is such that clipping becomes a pleasure.

Again, cultivars extend the range in shape, size (as always, there are rock garden dwarfs), texture and foliage color. 'Fastigiata' makes a narrow column of green; 'Zebrina' with striped foliage is one of the best of all gold-leaved conifers;

In eastern North America, the native *Thuja occidentalis* is known simply as cedar and is an essential part of the scene (the now confusing *occidentalis* "from the west" is a Linnaean name coined before Europeans knew that there was a west coast of America, let alone another

thuja). Brought to France by Jacques Cartier, a tree planted at Fontainebleau in the mid-1530s was probably the first North American tree to cross the Atlantic. It grows wild, often in the most uncomfortable swampy sites, frozen solid in winter, in standing water for

'Aurea' is even brighter.

China, Japan and Korea each have a native thuja, but they cannot compare in garden value to the North Americans. Well worth consideration, however, is a close arborvitae relation, *Thujopsis dolabrata* from Japan. The waxy foliage is heavier than that of true thujas, dark, shining green above and white beneath. It slowly builds up to a wide, often multi-stemmed tree of 50 feet (15 m) or so. This is a west coast tree for gardens in both North America and Europe; high humidity and wind shelter are necessary.

Tsuga
Hemlock

Another small group of valuable conifers with an occidental/oriental distribution range that is very similar to that of thujas. Again, the eastern North American species is native to Newfoundland, inland around the Great Lakes and then southward, gradually taking to the mountains as it goes. This is the eastern hemlock (*Tsuga canadensis*). (Hemlock here is nothing to do with the fennel relation used to put Socrates to death. They are supposed to smell similarly.) When young it is elegant and graceful, its foliage held in flat sprays with 1-inch-long (2.5 cm) cones carried at the ends like little plumb bobs. The leading shoot droops away from the prevailing wind. As it ages, the tree becomes somewhat gnarled and rugged, leading to a timber that is full of knots. In youth, therefore, it is an excellent garden evergreen: tolerating shade, clipping well as a hedge and happy in zone 4.

All these virtues, however, relate only to its homeland; in Britain, it is dark and dreary and cannot compete for a moment with its West Coast cousin,

T. heterophylla. Growing wild from south Alaska down into California, in cultivation, it is a zone 6 needing plenty of moisture and thus admirably adapted to most of Britain. It has all the virtues of the eastern plant with more of its own: it grows very quickly and seems likely to attain the 200 feet (60 m) or so as in its favorite areas at home. Again, it makes a beautiful hedge. As parkland specimens, 'Greenmantle' and 'Laursen's Column' are both narrow with downward- and upward-growing branches respectively.

Obviously, the mature western hemlock is not a tree for small spaces, but as a part of a planned sequence it is admirable, to be taken out as necessary. The mountain hemlock (*T. mertensiana*) is a smaller, slower-growing plant with blue-gray foliage arranged all around the branchlets rather than the customary flat hemlock sprays and with cones at least twice the length. Again, it needs plenty of moisture and a lime-free soil. Some botanists suggest it should join another native of those amazing West Coast forest regions in a genus that we might, if we merely translated the Latin, call false hemlock. This is *Pseudotsuga*. The Douglas fir (now *P. menziesii*) suitably commemorates both David Douglas's contribution to gardening and forestry and that of his predecessor Archibald Menzies. Menzies found the plant—and lots of others—when acting as surgeon on Captain Vancouver's ship in the 1790s. Douglas collected seed and introduced it to Britain a couple of decades later.

Douglas fir is a tree of the largest size in its native woodlands, almost reaching redwood heights, and 19th-century specimens are the tallest trees in Britain; not a plant for small spaces. Foliage can

be confused with that of spruces, but the terminal buds are distinctive—long and pointed and almost as sharp as those of beech. Though not developing great size in eastern North America, Douglas fir will accept zone 5 winters there, and it adds another coniferous effect to the large garden scene.

trees with special attributes

What follows is by way of an *aide-mémoire*; trees listed generically (and occasionally specifically) according to particular roles and attributes. Those marked with an * are especially suited to small gardens.

Trees accepting potentially difficult types of soil

Heavy clay
Acer
Aesculus
Alnus
*Betula
Carpinus
Carya
*Cercidophyllum
*Crataegus
Corylus
*Eucalyptus
Fraxinus
*Ilex
*Laburnum
Liquidambar
*Magnolia
*Malus
Populus
*Prunus
Pterocarya
Quercus
Salix
*Sorbus
Tilia
Zelkova

Conifers
Abies
*Chamaecyparis

Ginkgo
*Juniperus
Larix
Pinus
Taxodium
*Taxus
Thuja

Acid soils
Ailanthus
*Betula
Castanea
*Cercis
*Elaeagnus
Gleditsia
*Ilex
Nyssa
Quercus
Robinia
*Sorbus aucuparia

Conifers
*Cupressus
Pinus
Sequoiadendron
Tsuga

**Thin soils over
chalk or limestone**
Acer campestre,
  A. platanoides,
  A. pseudoplatanus
Aesculus
Carpinus
*Cercis siliquastrum
Fagus
Fraxinus
*Malus
*Morus
*Sorbus aria

Conifers
*Juniperus communis
Pinus nigra
*Taxus
Thuja
Thujopsis

Trees for quick height

*Acer
Ailanthus
Alnus
*Betula
*Eucalyptus
Paulownia
Populus
Salix

Conifers
x Cupressocyparis
*Cupressus
Larix
Metasequoia
Pinus
Pseudotsuga
Sequoia

Sequoiadendron
Tsuga

Trees for towns

*Acer
Aesculus
Ailanthus
*Albizia
Alnus
Catalpa
*Crataegus

Gleditsia
*Ilex
*Ligustrum
*Magnolia
Platanus
Populus
*Prunus

*Pyrus
Robinia

Conifers
Ginkgo
Pinus nigra

Trees for wind shelter in maritime exposure

Those typical contorted trees, leaning away from the prevailing wind, show the effects of a hundred gales. Their shape is usually caused not by plants being blown by the wind but by the wind damaging the young growth as it tries to grow upward; however, on the lea side, the tree's own body is protective, and therefore extension growth occurs only on that side. The effect is exacerbated by salt winds off the sea, which can burn exposed leaves on plants growing several miles inland.

Acer pseudoplatanus
Castanea
Eucalyptus
Fraxinus
*Ilex
*Phillyrea

Populus alba, P. x
  canescens,
  P. tremula
Quercus
*Sorbus aria,
  S. aucuparia

Conifers
Chamaecyparis
x Cupressocyparis
*Cupressus
Pinus

Gardeners needing wind shelter in mild west coast Britain should also consider a number of New Zealand plants well adapted to such conditions but generally not frost-tolerant enough to grow well elsewhere. These trees, not individually described here, include species of Senecio, Olearia, Pittosporum and Griselinia.

Trees with weeping forms

*Betula
Fagus
Fraxinus
Populus
*Prunus

*Pyrus
Salix
Tilia

Conifers
*Chamaecyparis
Larix
Picea
Taxodium

Trees of naturally upright habit or having fastigiate forms

*Acer	Quercus	Ginkgo
Carpinus	*Sorbus	*Juniperus
Fagus		Picea omorika
Liriodendron	**Conifers**	Taxodium
*Malus	Calocedrus	Thuja
Populus	*Chamaecyparis	
*Prunus	*Cupressus	
*Pyrus	x Cupressocyparis	

Trees for reliable autumn color

*Acer	*Malus	**Conifers**
*Betula	Nyssa	Cryptomeria
Carpinus	*Oxydendrum	Ginkgo
Carya	Parrotia	Larix
*Cercidiphyllum	Populus	Metasequoia
*Cornus	*Prunus	Pseudolarix
*Crataegus	Quercus	Taxodium
Fagus	*Rhus	
Fraxinus	*Sorbus	
Gymnocladus	*Stewartia	
Liquidambar		

Trees with purple leaves

*Acer	*Prunus
*Betula	Quercus
Catalpa	
Fagus	
*Malus	

Trees with gray or silver leaves

*Elaeagnus	**Conifers**
*Eucalyptus	*Abies
Populus	Cedrus
*Pyrus	*Cupressus
Salix	*Juniperus
	Picea

Trees with noteworthy bark (trunk or twigs)

*Acer	Parottia	**Conifers**
*Arbutus	Platanus	Cryptomeria
*Betula	*Prunus	Pinus
Carya	*Stewartia	Sequoiadendron
*Eucalyptus	Tilia	
Fraxinus		
*Luma		

Trees with bold foliage

*Acer	*Magnolia
Ailanthus	Paulownia
*Aralia	Platanus
Catalpa	Pterocarya
Gymnocladus	*Rhododendron
Idesia	*Sorbus
Kalopanax	

Trees with golden or variegated leaves

*Acer	Liriodendron	*Juniperus
Alnus	Populus	*Taxus
Catalpa	Quercus	*Thuja
Castanea	*Robinia	
*Cornus		
Fagus	**Conifers**	
*Gleditsia	*Chamaecyparis	
*Ilex	x Cupressocyparis	
*Ligustrum	Cupressus	

Trees with ornamental fruit

Ailanthus	*Malus	Picea
*Arbutus	*Prunus	Pinus
Catalpa	Pterocarya	*Taxus
Fraxinus	*Sorbus	
*Ilex		
Koelreuteria	**Conifers**	
*Magnolia	*Abies	

zone maps

Zone	Celsius°	Farenheit°	
1	below -45	below -50	
2	-45 to -40	-50 to -40	
3	-40 to -35	-40 to -30	
4	-35 to -29	-30 to -20	
5	-29 to -23	-20 to -10	
6	-23 to -18	-10 to 0	
7	-18 to -12	0 to 10	
8	-12 to -6	10 to 20	
9	-6 to -1	20 to 30	
10	-1 to 5	30 to 40	

Hardiness zones

The hardiness zone ratings allocated to plants are based on the zones of average annual minimum temperature devised by the United States Department of Agriculture, and suggest the approximate minimum temperature the plant will tolerate in winter. However, this can only be a rough guide, as hardiness depends on many factors, including the depth of a plant's roots, the duration of cold weather, the force of wind and the temperatures encountered during the preceding summer. Good or bad soil drainage is also important.

As British gardeners will testify, such broad-brush indication of climatic zones here is no more than the vaguest of guides. Knowledge of local conditions and the realization that every garden has microclimatic possibilities are far more important.

where to see and buy trees

Throughout this book, we've emphasized the importance of trees to people and indeed to the planet Earth's very well-being. But much more specific is the book's aim to help those who want to plant trees where they are living, whether that is in the city, the suburbs or the country. But books can only advise. Ultimately, the selection is made by the readers, and it will inevitably be related to those readers experiences "in the field" and to their esthetic ambitions. So the best advice any book can offer is the exhortation that would-be tree planters be conscious of trees in their daily lives.

Looking at trees from the bus or the train on the way to work or anywhere else is an education in itself; buses expose commuters to trees along the street and in front yards, while trains look onto the much more individual back gardens (and often give surprisingly personal glimpses of other lives) as well as providing views of country houses framed by long-established plantings. Even when one is driving a car and giving one's full attention to the road, one cannot fail to be affected by the variations of light and shade caused by the size and texture of the passing trees.

Such observations can only be relatively general if the plants concerned are no more than "trees." They must be identified. They need names, so that we are able to look and compare. As a result, it becomes essential to visit places that have good examples of trees and tree collections and that these are labelled. Such a search naturally takes us to botanic gardens. The role of their plant collections is threefold: scientific inquiry, education and public amenity. Often such gardens were established by universities' botany departments almost exclusively for their students' education and as a resource for research. Today, they are available to the wider public and are often supported by "Friends" and volunteer groups, which in turn creates a rewarding "town and gown" amalgam. It is heartening that those wonderful botanic gardens and parks and arboreta set up in industrial towns by 19th-century philanthropists and city fathers are today being returned to their rightful place within the culture of their communities.

We are also fortunate that many great private gardens are available to the public. In Britain, there are particular concentrations of tree-rich gardens in Sussex—High Beeches, Leonardslee, Sheffield Park and Nymans, for instance—where the first plantings from the famous early 20th-century plant collectors have reached maturity. In Cornwall, Wales and right up the West Coast of Scotland, tenderer exotic species have demonstrated their potential. Wherever one lives, there are gardens which support that most successful of charities, the National Gardens Scheme (or Scotland's Gardens Scheme, north of the border), which show trees flourishing in just the same sort of conditions as our own—something the beginner gardener may have thought impossible. The owner is often present and only too happy to discuss the advantages of this or that plant; there are occasionally plants for sale.

The scale of North America makes such concentrations of gardens less likely, but the pattern is repeated across Canada and the United States. A visit to a nearby university or municipal botanic garden can make for a pleasant afternoon. Garden clubs and horticultural societies often organize tours of members' gardens. The increasingly significant Garden Conservancy does this on a major scale. Its annual Open Days Directory lists close to 500 fine private gardens otherwise unavailable to the visitor. Garden Conservancy membership thus becomes essential.

The important thing is to be able to see what is possible where, to build up one's knowledge of trees and to develop one's own esthetic. What follows is a small selection of good places to see trees within the climatic zone areas relevant to the book's A–Z tree list.

Where to see trees: USA

Colorado
Denver Botanic Gardens
909 York Street, Denver
CO 80206
303-331-4000

Delaware
Mount Cuba Centre
P.O. Box 3570, Greenville, DE19807
302-239-4244

The Henry DuPont Museum
Route 54, Winterthur, DE19735
308-888-4880

District of Columbia
Dumbarton Oaks
1703 32nd Street NW,
Washington DC 20007
202-342-3290

US National Arboretum
3501 New York Avenue NE,
Washington DC 20002
202-245-3875

Georgia
Atlanta Botanical Garden
1345 Auburn Avenue NE,
P.O. Box 77426, Atlanta GA 30357
404-876-5859

Callaway Gardens
US Highway 27, P.O. Box 2000,
Pine Mountain, GA 31822
706-663-5150

The State Botanical Garden
University of Georgia, 24505
Milledge Avenue, Athens, GA 30605
706-542-1244

Illinois
Chicago Botanic Garden
1000 Lake Cook Road,
P.O. Box 400, Glencoe, IL 60022
847-835-4484

The Morton Arboretum
Route 53, Lisle, IL 60532
708-986-0074

Maine
Pine Tree State Arboretum
P.O. Box 344, Augusta, ME 04332
207 621 0013

Maryland
Brookside Gardens
1500 Glenallan Avenue, Wheaton,
MD 20902
301-929-6509

Massachusetts
Arnold Arboretum
Harvard University, 125 Arborway,
Jamaica Plain, MA 02130
617-524-1718

Michigan
Matthaei Botanical Gardens
University of Michigan,
1800 N. Dixboro Road, Ann Arbor,
MI 48105
313-998-7061

New York
Brooklyn Botanic Garden
100 Washington Avenue, Brooklyn,
NY 11225
718-622-4433

Cornell Plantations
One Plantations Road,
Cornell University, Ithaca, NY 14850
607-255-3020

New York Botanical Garden
200th Street, Bronx, NY 10458
718-817-8700

Planting Fields Arboretum
Planting Fields Road, P.O. Box 58,
Oyster Bay, NY 11771
516-922-9200

Wave Hill
675 West 252nd Street, Bronx,
NY 10471
718-549-3200

Old Westbury Gardens
71 Old Westbury Road,
P.O. Box 430, Old Westbury,
NY 11568
516-333-0048

North Carolina
North Carolina Arboretum
P.O. Box 6617, Asheville, NC 2816
704-665-2492

North Carolina Botanical Garden
C.B. Box 3375, Tolten Center,
University of North Carolina,
Chapel Hill, NC 27599
919-962-0522

North Carolina State University
Arboretum
P.O. Box 7609, Raleigh, NC 27695

Ohio
Cleveland Botanical Garden
11030 East Boulevard, Cleveland,
OH 44106
216-721-1600

Holden Arboretum
6500 Sperry Road, Kirtland,
OH 44094
216-256-1110

Pennsylvania
The Barnes Arboretum
300 North Latches Lane,
P.O. Box 128, Merion Station,
PA 19066
610-667-0290

Chanticleer
786 Church Road, Wayne,
PA 19087
610-687-6894

Morris Arboretum
100 Northwestern Avenue,
Philadelphia, PA 19118
215-247-5777

Longwood Gardens
Route 1, P.O. Box 501,
Kennett Square, PA 19348
610-388-6741

South Carolina
Brook Green Gardens,
1931 Brook Green, Gardens Drive,
Murrills Inlet, SC 29576
803-237-4218

Magnolia Plantation
Route 4, Charlston, SC 29414
803-571-1266

Virginia
Monticello
Route 58, P.O. Box 316,
Charlottesville, VA 22901
804-984-9808

Colonial Williamsburg
134 North Henry Street,
Williamsburg, VA 23187
804-229-1000

Washington
The Bloedel Reserve
7571 NE Dolphin Drive, Bambridge,
WA 98110
206-842-7631

Washington Park Arboretum
2300 Arboretum Drive East,
P.O. Box 358010, Seattle,
WA 98195
206-543-8800

Where to see trees: Canada

Alberta
Calgary Zoo Botanical Gardens
P.O. Box 3036, Station B, Calgary,
AB T2M 4R8
403-232-9372

University of Alberta Botanic Gardens
Highway 60, Edmonton,
AB T5J 2RZ
403-497-3054

British Columbia
The Buchart Gardens
800 Benvento Avenue,
P.O. Box 4010, Brentwood Bay,
Victoria, BC V8M 1J8

The University of British Columbia
Botanical Garden
6804 SW Marine Drive, Vancouver,
BC V6M 4H1
604-878-9274

Van Dusen Botanical Gardens
5251 Oak Street, Vancouver,
BC V6M 4H1
604-878-9274

New Brunswick
The New Brunswick Botanical
Garden
CP/Po Box 599, Saint Jacques,
NB E0L 1K0
506-739-6335

Newfoundland
Memorial University Botanical Garden
Pippy Park, 306 Mount Scio Road,
St. Johns, NF A1C 5S1
709-532-4681

Ontario
Mount Pleasant Cemetery
375 Mount Pleasant Road, Toronto,
ON M4T 2V8
416-485-9129

Dominion Arboretum
Central Experimental Farm, Ottawa,
ON K1A 0C6
613-995-3700

The Arboretum
The University of Guelph, Guelph,
ON N1G 2W1
519-842-4120

Niagara Botanical Gardens
P.O. Box 150, Niagara Falls,
ON L2E 6T2
905-354-1721

Lakehead University Arboretum
School of Forestry, Lakehead
University, Thunder Bay,
ON P1B 5E1
807-345-2121

Laurentian University Arboretum
Ramsey Lake Road, Sudbury,
ON P3E 2C6
705-675-1151

Royal Botanical Gardens
680 Plains Road West,
P.O. Box 399, Hamilton,
ON L8N 348
416-527-458

Quebec
Les Jardins de Metis, Grand-Metis
PQ, CP 242, Mont-Joli,
PQ G5H 3L1
418-775-2221

Montreal Botanical Garden
4101 East Sherbrooke Street,
Montréal, PQ H1X 2B2
514-872-1400

Mount Royal Cemetery
1297 chemin de la Forêt,
Outremont, QC H2V 2P9
514-279-7358

Where to see trees:
England and Wales

Abbotsbury
Bullers Way, Abbotsbury,
Dorset DT3 4LA
Tel 01305 871387

Alton Towers
Alton, Staffordshire CT10 4DB
0870 520 4060

Antony House
Torpoint, Plymouth PL11 2QA
01752 812191

Audley End
Saffron Walden, Essex CB11 4JF
01799 522842

Bath Botanical Gardens
Royal Victoria Park, Bath BA1 2NQ
01225 482624

Bedgebury National Pinetum
Park Lane, Goudhurst, Kent
TN1 2SL
01580 211044

Bicton Park Gardens,
East Buddleigh, Nr. Exeter, Devon
EX9 7DJ
01395 568465

Birmingham Botanical Gardens
Westbourne Road, Edgbaston,
Birmingham B15 3TR
0121 454 1860

Bodnant Garden
Tal-y-Cafn, Colwyn Bay, Wales
LL28 5RE
01492 650460

Borde Hill
Balcombe Road, Haywards Heath,
Sussex RH16 1XP
01444 450 326

Bramham Park
Wetherby, West Yorkshire LS23 6BD
01937 846000

University of Bristol Botanic Garden
Bracken Hill, North Road,
Leigh Woods, Bristol BS8 3PF
0117 9733682

Caerhays Castle
Gorran, St Austell, Cornwall
PL26 6LY
01872 501870

Castle Howard
York, Yorkshire YO60 7DA
01653 648444

Clyne Gardens
Blackpill, Swansea
01792 298637

Colby Woodland Garden
Amroth, Narberth, Pembrokeshire
SA67 8PP
01834 811885

Deene Park
Corby, Northamptonshire
NN17 3EW
01780 450278

Exbury Gardens
Exbury, Hampshire SO45 1AZ
023 8089 1203

Forde Abbey
Chard, Somerset TA20 4LU
01460 220231

Glansevern Hall Gardens
Glansevern, Welshpool, Powys
SY21 8AH
01686 640200

Harcourt Arboretum
Nuneham Courtenay, Oxfordshire
OX44 0PX
01865 343501

Harlow Carr Botanical Gardens
Crag Lane, Harrogate,
North Yorkshire HG3 1QB
01423 565418

Hergest Croft Gardens
Kington, Herefordshire HR5 3EG
01544 230160

Hillier Gardens and Arboretum
Jermyns Lane, Ampfield, Romsey,
Hampshire SO51 0QA
01794 368787

Holehird Gardens
Patterdale Road, Windermere,
Cumbria LA23 1NP
01539 446008

Holker Hall
Cark-in-Cartmel,
Grange-over-Sands,
Cumbria LA11 7PL
01539 558328

Hyde Hall
Rettendon, Chelmsford, Essex
CM3 8ET
01245 400256

Royal Botanic Gardens, Kew
Richmond, Surrey TW9 3AB
020 8332 5655

Kingston Maurward Gardens
Dorchester, Dorset DT2 8PY
01305 215003

Muncaster Castle
Ravenglass, Cumbria CA18 1RQ
01229 717614

National Botanic Garden of Wales
Llanarthne, Carmarthenshire
SA32 8HG
01558 668768

Ness Botanic Gardens
Ness, Neston, South Wirral
CH64 4AY
01513 530123

Newby Hall and Gardens
Ripon, North Yorkshire NG4 5AE
01423 322583

Newstead Abbey Park
Ravenshead, Nottinghamshire
NG15 8NA
01623 455900

Nymans
Handcross, Nr. Haywards Heath,
W. Sussex RH17 6EB
01444 400321

Oxford University Botanic Garden
High Street, Oxford OX1 4AZ
01865 286690

Plas Newydd
Llanfairpwll, Anglesey LL61 6DQ
01248 714795

Portmeirion Botanic Garden
Penrhyndeudraeth LL48 6ET
01766 770228

Rosemoor Garden
Rosemoor, Great Torrington,
North Devon EX38 8PH
01805 624067

Savill Garden
The Great Park, Windsor, Berkshire
SL4 2HT
01753 847518

Sheffield Botanic Garden
Clarkehouse Road, Sheffield
S10 2LN
0114 2676496

Sheffield Park Gardens
Sheffield Park, Uckfield, E. Sussex
TN22 3QX
01825 790231

Stourhead
Stourton, Warminster, Wiltshire
BA12 6QD
01747 841152

Thorp Perrow Arboretum
Bedale, North Yorkshire DL8 2PR
01677 425323

Trebah Garden
Mawnan Smith, Cornwall TR11 5JZ
01326 250448

Trelissick Garden
Foeck, Nr. Truro, Cornwall TR3 6QL
01872 862090

Wakehurst Place
Ardingly, Nr. Haywards Heath,
West Sussex RH17 6TN
01444 894066

Wartnaby Gardens
Wartnaby, Melton Mowbray,
Leicestershire LE14 3HY
01664 822296

Westonbirt Arboretum
Tetbury, Gloucestershire GL8 8QS
01666 880220

Winkworth Arboretum
Hascombe Road, Godalming, Surrey
GU8 4AD
01483 208477

Wisley Gardens
Woking, Surrey GU23 6QB
01483 224234

Where to see trees: Scotland

Ardkinglas Arboretum
Adkinglas Estate Office, Cairndow,
Argyll PA26 8BH
01499 600261

Arduaine Garden
Oban, Argyll PA34 4XQ
01852 200366

Blair Castle
Blair Atholl, Pitlochry, Perthshire
PH18 5TL
01796 481207

Blairquhan
Straiton, Maybole, Ayrshire
KA19 7LZ
01655 770239

Brodick Castle
Isle of Arran KA27 8HY
01770 302202

Crarae Garden
Inveraray, Argyll PA32 8YA
01546 886614

Crathes Castle
Banchory, Aberdeenshire AB31 5QJ
01330 844525

Dawyck Botanic Garden
Stobo, Peeblesshire EH45 9JU
01721 760254

University of Dundee Botanic Garden
Riverside Drive, Dundee DD2 1QH
01382 566939

Edinburgh Royal Botanic Garden
20A Inverleith Row, Edinburgh
EH3 5LR
0131 552 7171

Glasgow Botanic Gardens
730 Great Western Road,
Queen Margaret Drive, Glasgow
G12 0UE
0141 334 2422

Inverewe Garden
Poolewe, Rosshire IV22 2LG
01445 781200

Logan Botanic Garden
Port Logan, Stranraer, Wigtonshire
DG9 9ND
01776 860231

Scone Palace
The Woodlands Manager, Perth
PH2 6BD
01738 552308

St. Andrews Botanic Garden
St. Andrews, Fife KY16 8RT
01334 476452

Threave Gardens
Castle Douglas,
Dumfries & Galloway DG7 1RX
01556 502575

Younger Botanic Garden
Cowall Peninsula, Benmore, Dunoon
PA23 8QU
01369 706261

Almost all the above-listed gardens have plants for sale. Having enjoyed visiting the place, one is suitably softened up for the sales table, but in many places it must be realized that what is on sale has little connection with the garden; it is bought-in stuff perhaps of good quality but not dissimilar from that at one's nearest garden centre. At some properties, however, plants have been propagated on the spot from plants one has just admired. Sometimes these are particularly good forms that have been selected at the property and there is always pleasure in growing at home something that recalls an especially fine garden.

There is increasing reciprocity to this: specialist nurseries that exist to propagate and sell plants and which may be visited on specific days or by appointment. Often it can be arranged that plants ordered from the catalogue can be collected for immediate planting in previously prepared sites at home. This is obviously very good for the plants concerned: they may hardly notice the move.

Where to buy trees: USA

Arbor Village
15606 County Road CC
P.O. Box 227
Holt, MO 64048
Telephone 816-264-3911
Fax 816-264-3760

Broken Arrow Nursery
13 Broken Arrow Road
Hamden, CT 06518
Telephone 203-288-1026
Fax 203-287-1035
brokenarrow@snet.net
http://www.brokenarrownursery.com

Camellia Forest Nursery
125 Carrie Road
Chapel Hill, NC 27516
Telephone 919-968-0504
Fax: 919-960-7690
camforest@aol.com

Carlson's Gardens
P.O. Box 305
26 Salem Hill Road
South Salem, NY 10590
Telephone 914-763-5958
bob@carlsonsgardens.com
http://www.carlsonsgardens.com

Cold Stream Farm
2030 Free Soil Road
Free Soil, MI 49411-9752
Telephone 231-464-5809
csf@jackpine.com
http://www.jackpine.com/~csf

Collector's Nursery
16804 NE 102nd Avenue
Battle Ground, WA USA 98604
Telephone 360-574-3832
Fax 360-571-8540
dianar@collectorsnursery.com
http://www.collectorsnursery.com

Colvos Creek Nursery
P.O. Box 1512
Vashon Island, WA 98070
Telephone 206-749-9508
Fax 206-749-0446
mlla@mindspring.com

Fairweather Gardens
P.O. Box 330
Greenwich, NJ 08323
Telephone 856-451-6261
Fax 856-451-0303
http://www.fairweathergardens.com

Forestfarm
990 Tetherow Road
Williams, UR 97544-9599
Telephone 541-846-7269
Fax 541-846-6963
forestfarm@rvi.net
http://www.forestfarm.com

Heronswood Nursery
7530 NE 288th Street
Kinston, WA 98346-9502
Telephone 360-297-4172
Fax 360-297-8321
heronswood@silverlink.net
http://www.heronswood.com

Niche Gardens
1111 Dawson Road
Chapel Hill, NC 27516
Telephone 919-967-0078
Fax 919-967-4026
mail@nichegardens.com
http://www.nichegardens.com

Raintree Nursery
391 Butts Road
Morton, WA 98356
Telephone 340-496-6400
Fax 888-770-8358
order@raintreenursery.com
http://www.raintreenursery.com

RareFind Nursery Inc.
957 Patterson Road
Jackson, NJ 908527
Telephone 732-833-0613
Fax 732-833-1965
info@rarefindnursery.com
http://www.rarefindnursery.com

Roslyn Nursery
211 Burrs Lane
Dix Hills, NY 11746
Telephone 631-643-9347
Fax 631-427-0894
roslyn@roslynnursery.com
http://www.roslynnursery.com

St. Lawrence Nurseries
325 State Hwy 345
Potsdam, NY 13676
Telephone 315-265-6739
trees@sln.potsdam.ny.us
http://www.sln.potsdam.ny.us

Twombly Nursery Inc.
163 Barn Hill Road
Monroe, CT 06468
Telephone 203-261-2133
Fax 203-261-9230
info@twomblynursery.com
http://www.twomblynursery.com

Where to buy trees: Canada

Connon Nurseries
P.O. Box 200, Waterdown, Ontario
L0R 2H0
905-628-4144

Cannor Nurseries Ltd
48291 Chilliwack Central Road,
Chilliwack BC V2P 6H3
604-795-5993

Mori Nurseries
RR2 Niagara-on-the-Lake, Ontario
L05 1JO
905-468-3217

V.K. Kraus Nurseries Ltd
P.O. Box 180, Carlisle, Ontario
L0R 1HO
905-689-4022

Canadale Nurseries
269 Sunset Drive, St. Thomas,
Ontario N5R 3C4
519-631-7264

Sheridan Nurseries Ltd
RR4 Georgetown, Ontario L7G 457
416-798-7970

PAO Horticulture
5312 Trafalgar Road, Hornby, Ontario
L0P 1E0
905-875-0055

Where to buy trees: United Kingdom

Aberconwy Nursery
Graig, Glan Conwy, Conwy, Wales
LL28 5TL
01492 580875

Ardkinglass Tree Shop
Cairndow, Argyll PA26 8BH
01499 600263

Barnsdale Gardens
Exton Avenue, Exton, Oakham,
Rutland LE15 8AH
01572 913200

Bowood Garden Centre
Bowood Estate, Calne, Wiltshire
SN11 0LZ
01249 816 818

Bridgemere Nurseries
Bridgemere, Nr. Nantwich, Cheshire
CW5 7QB
01270 521100

Burncoose and South Down
Nurseries
Gwennap, Redruth, Cornwall
TR16 6BJ
01209 860316

Clapton Court Gardens
Crewkerne, Somerset TA18 8PT
01460 73220

Duchy of Cornwall
Cott Road, Lostwithiel, Cornwall
PL22 0HW
01208 872668

Hartshall Nursery Stock
Walsham le Willows,
Bury St. Edmunds, Suffolk IP31 3BY
01359 259238

Kenwith Nursery (Gordon Haddow)
Blinsham, Nr. Torrington, Beaford,
Winkleigh, Devon EX18 8NT
01805 603274

Landford Trees
Landford, Salisbury, Wiltshire
SP5 2EH
01794 390808

Langthorns Plantery
High Cross Lane West,
Little Canfield, Dunmow, Essex
CM6 1TD
01371 872611

Madrona Nursery
Pluckley Road, Bethersden, Kent
TN26 3DD
01233 820100

Mallett Court Nursery
Curry Mallett, Taunton, Somerset
TA3 6SY
01823 480748

Merrist Wood Plant Shop
Merrist Wood College, Worplesdon,
Guildford, Surrey GU3 3PE
01483 884000

Nettletons Nursery
Ivy Mill Lane, Godstone, Surrey
RH9 8NF
01883 742426

Norfields Llangwm Arboretum
Usk, Monmouthshire NP15 1NQ
01291 650306

Otter Nurseries Ltd
Gosford Road, Ottery St. Mary,
Devon EX11 1LZ
01404 815815

Perrie Hale Forest Nursery, Northcote
Hill, Honiton, Devon EX14 8TH
01404 43344

Perryhill Nurseries Ltd
Hartfield, East Sussex TN7 4JP
01892 770377

R.V. Roger Ltd
The Nurseries, Pickering, Yorkshire
YO18 7HG
01754 472226

Scotts Nurseries
Merriot, Somerset TA16 5PL
01460 72306

Smallscape Nursery, Stradishall,
Suffolk CB8 9YF
01440 820336

Starborough Nursery
Starborough Road, Marsh Green,
Edenbridge, Kent TN8 5RB
01732 865614

Stone Lane Gardens
Chagford, Devon TQ13 8JU
01647 23311

Christie Elite
Forres, Morayshire IV36 3TW
01309 672633

The Bluebell Nursery
Blackford by Swadlincote, Derbyshire
DE11 8AJ
01283 222091

Trees Please
Corbridge, Northumberland
NE45 5QY
01434 633049

Waterwheel Nursery
Usk Road, Shirenewton, Chepstow,
Gwent NP6 6SA
01291 641577

index